D1195592

A BIBLIOGRAPHY
OF CALIFORNIA INDIANS

GARLAND REFERENCE LIBRARY
OF SOCIAL SCIENCE
(VOL. 48)

A BIBLIOGRAPHY
OF CALIFORNIA INDIANS
*Archaeology, Ethnography,
Indian History*

Robert F. Heizer
Albert B. Elsasser

with the collaboration of
James C. Bard, Edward D. Castillo
and Karen M. Nissen

GARLAND PUBLISHING, INC. • NEW YORK & LONDON
1977

Library of Congress Cataloging in Publication Data

Heizer, Robert Fleming, 1915-
  A bibliography of California Indians.

  (Garland reference library of social science ; v. 48)

  Includes indexes.

  1. Indians of North America—California—Bibliography.
I. Elsasser, Albert B., joint author. II. Title.
Z1209.U52C228   [E78.C15]   016.9794'004'97   76-52687
ISBN 0-8240-9866-8

PRINTED IN THE UNITED STATES OF AMERICA

CONTENTS

PART II: INDIAN HISTORY

MAPS

PREFACE

This bibliography is in two parts; the first treats ancient California Indian history or, perhaps better, prehistory—that is, archaeology—and the second deals with Indian history after the European discovery of California by Cabrillo in 1542. The entries are numbered consecutively and are indexed at the end by author and tribe. While some ethnography is listed in the second half, this represents only a sampling. For the fullest bibliography prepared to date on California Indian ethnography, the reader is referred to Volumes 1 and 3 of G. P. Murdock and T. J. O'Leary, *Ethnographic Bibliography of North America* (New Haven, 1976).

We have attempted to list works that are available in large libraries or which can be secured on interlibrary loan. Archival collections, such as that in The Bancroft Library at the University of California, Berkeley, or the National Archives in Washington, may contain tens of thousands of documents, but these are available for consultation only under special conditions; for this reason individual items are not cited here. We have cited a limited number of unpublished M.A. and Ph.D. dissertations which can usually be secured on interlibrary loan or in Xerox form from University Microfilms, Ann Arbor, Michigan.

Where we thought that the content or nature of a publication could not be determined from its title, we added a brief parenthetical annotation in the hope of informing the reader whether the publication contained information of interest.

A few words about the two indexes to be found at the end may be helpful. The first lists authors, with their publications indicated by number. This index refers to both parts of the bibliography. The second index is to tribes of California. Works referring to all California Indians, both contemporary and aboriginal, are listed under "General California Indians." Then come two groups of references listed under "Central and Northern California Tribes" and "Southern California Tribes," in which a series of native groups are treated in individual works. The so-called Mission Indians, comprising reservationized groups south of Santa Barbara, are included in the Southern California Tribes index. Works treating one or two tribes are listed under the tribal names, but additional information on individual tribes will also be found in the General, Central and Northern, and Southern tribes entries. Contemporary Indian matters are indexed in the last-mentioned entries.

Both of the bibliographies contained in this volume were preceded by shorter published versions, now out of print. The favorable response to these earlier attempts has encouraged us to offer a much fuller and more up-to-date listing. For assistance in assembling, ordering and checking the several thousand references, we gratefully acknowledge C. William Clewlow, Jr., James C. Bard, Karen M. Nissen, Edward D. Castillo and Frances Fischer.

ABBREVIATIONS

AA American Anthropologist
AAA-M American Anthropological Association—
  Memoirs
A. Ant. American Antiquity
AJA American Journal of Archaeology
AJPA American Journal of Physical Anthropology
AMNH-AP American Museum of Natural History—
  Anthropological Papers
  -B —Bulletin
  -M —Memoirs
ARA-CCA Archaeological Research Associates—
  Contributions to California Archaeology
ASASC-N Archaeological Survey Association of
  Southern California—Newsletter
  -P —Papers
BAE-AR Bureau of American Ethnology—Annual
  Report
  -B —Bulletin
BP-PA Ballena Press—Publications in Anthropology
  -PAEH —Publications in Archaeology, Ethnology,
  and History
CARD Center for Anthropological Research, Davis
  (University of California)
CAS-OP California Academy of Sciences, San Francisco
  —Occasional Papers
  -P —Proceedings
  -PD —Pacific Discovery
CDPR-AR California (State) Division of Parks and
  Recreation—Archaeological Report
CDRMP-AR California (State) Division of Resource
  Management and Protection—Archaeological
  Report

GP-MP	Gila Pueblo—Medallion Papers
GPO	Government Printing Office
GSA-B	Geological Society of America—Bulletin
ICA	International Congress of Americanists (Proceedings)
JAFL	Journal of American Folk Lore
JCA	Journal of California Anthropology
JRAI	Journal of the Royal Anthropological Institute
KASP	Kroeber Anthropological Society Papers
MAIHF-C	Museum of the American Indian, Heye Foundation—Contributions
-IN	—Indian Notes (a separate series, often not clearly distinguished from INM)
-INM	—Indian Notes and Monographs (separately numbered series with same title, sometimes noted as "MS," i.e., *Miscellaneous*)
MAPOM	Miwok Archaeological Preserve of Marin
NGS-RR	National Geographic Society—Research Reports
NSS-MRSG	National Speleological Society—Monthly Report of the Stanford Grotto
PCAS-OP	Pacific Coast Archaeological Society— Occasional Papers
-Q	—Quarterly
-S	—Newsletter—"Smoke Signals"
PM-P	Peabody Museum (Harvard University)— Papers
-AR	—Annual Report
-R	—Reports
SAA-N	Society for American Archaeology—Notebook
SBCMA-Q	San Bernardino County Museum Association —Quarterly
-SS	—Scientific Series
SBMNH-AR	Santa Barbara Museum of Natural History— Annual Report
-B	—Bulletin (Anthropology Department)
-L	—Leaflet

-OP	—Occasional Papers
SCA-N	Society for California Archaeology—Newsletter
SCAS-B	Southern California Academy of Sciences—Bulletin
-M	—Memoirs
SDM-B	San Diego Museum—Bulletin
-ETN	—Ethnic Technology Notes
-P	—Papers
SFSC-TAMP	San Francisco State College—Treganza Anthropology Museum Papers
SI-AR	Smithsonian Institution—Annual Report
-CK	—Contributions to Knowledge
-CNAE	—Contributions to North American Ethnology
-MC	—Miscellaneous Collections
-RBS	—River Basin Surveys
SLOCAS-OP	San Luis Obispo County Archaeological Society—Occasional Papers
SM-M	Southwest Museum—Masterkey
-P	Papers
SWJA	Southwestern Journal of Anthropology
UC-AR	University of California—Anthropological Records
-ARF	—Archaeological Research Facility
-AS-R	—Archaeological Survey—Reports
-C-ARF	—Contributions of the Archaeological Research Facility
-IA	—Ibero-Americana
-PA	—Publications in Anthropology
-PAAE	—Publications in American Archaeology and Ethnology
-PG	—Publications in Geography
-PGE	—Publications in Geology
-PL	—Publications in Linguistics
-PZ	—Publications in Zoology
UCLA-AS-AR	University of California, Los Angeles—Archaeological Survey—Annual Report

-JNWA	—Journal of New World Archaeology
USGS-AR	United States Geological Survey—Annual Report
-P	—Professional Papers
-WCM	—West of 100th Meridian
USNM-AR	United States National Museum—Annual Report
-P	—Proceedings
UU-AP	University of Utah—Anthropological Papers
-B	—Bulletin
-MP	—Miscellaneous Papers
YNN	Yosemite Nature Notes
ZE	Zeitschrift für Ethnologie

PART I: ARCHAEOLOGY

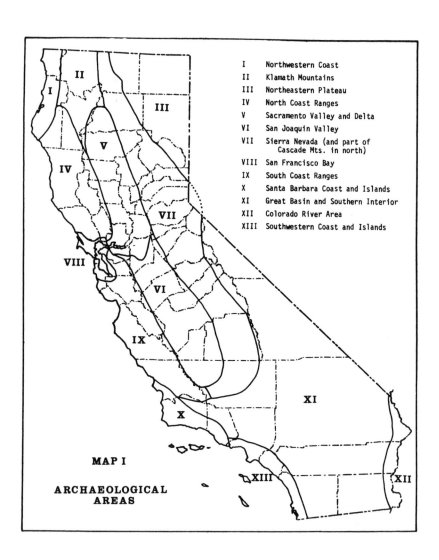

I	Northwestern Coast
II	Klamath Mountains
III	Northeastern Plateau
IV	North Coast Ranges
V	Sacramento Valley and Delta
VI	San Joaquin Valley
VII	Sierra Nevada (and part of Cascade Mts. in north)
VIII	San Francisco Bay
IX	South Coast Ranges
X	Santa Barbara Coast and Islands
XI	Great Basin and Southern Interior
XII	Colorado River Area
XIII	Southwestern Coast and Islands

MAP I

ARCHAEOLOGICAL AREAS

I. CALIFORNIA: PHYSICAL AND BIOLOGICAL BACKGROUND

1. Antevs, E. Precipitation and water supply in the Sierra Nevada. Bull. Amer. Meteorological Soc. 20:89-91, 1939.

2. _____ Climatic changes and prewhite man. In The Great Basin, with emphasis on glacial and postglacial times. UUB 38: 168-191, 1948.

3. Aschmann, H.H. Great Basin climates in relation to human occupance. UC-AS-R 42:23-40, 1958.

4. Ashkenazy, I. Cabrillo's lonely island. Westways 62(4):36,41, 58, 1970.
   [San Miguel Island-general history, geography]

5. Bailey, H.P. Climate, vegetation and land use in Southern California. State of California, Division of Mines, Bull. 170: 31-44. San Francisco, 1954.

6. Bailey, T.L. and R.H. Jahns. Geology of the Transverse Range Province, Southern California. State of California Division of Mines, Bull. 170:83-106. San Francisco, 1954.

7. Blackwelder, E. Pleistocene glaciation in the Sierra Nevada and Basin Ranges. GSA-B 42:865-922, 1931.

8. _____ The geological background. In The Great Basin, with emphasis on glacial and postglacial times. UUB 38: 3-16, 1948.

9. Blanc, R.P. and G.B. Cleveland. Pleistocene lakes of Southeastern California. State of Calif. Div. of Mines. Mineral Information Service 14(4):1-8; 14(5):1-8, 1961.

10. Bonnot, P. The abalones of California. Bulletin Calif. Fish and Game Comm. 34:141-169, 1948.

11. Bryan, K. Geology and ground water resources of the Sacramento Valley, Calif. USGS Water Supply Paper 495, 1923.

12. Campbell, D.H. and I.L. Wiggins. Origins of the flora of California. Stanford Univ. Publ. Sci., 10, no. 1, 1947.

13. Cannon, W.A. Tree distribution in Central California. Popular Science Monthly 85:417-424, 1914.

14. Casteel, R.W. Areal distribution of native freshwater fish fauna of California. In Papers on California and Great Basin prehistory. CARD Pub. No. 2, 1970.

15. Cooper, W.S. The broad-sclerophyll vegetation of California: An ecological study of the chaparral and its related communities. Carnegie Inst. Wash. Pub. 319, 1922.

16. Davis, W.M. The Lakes of California. Calif. Journal Mines and Geology 29:175-236, 1933.

17. Douglass, A.E. Survey of Sequoia studies. Tree Ring Bulletin 11:26-32, 1945; 12:10-16, 1945; 13:5-8, 1946.

18. Drake, N.F. The topography of California. Journal of Geology 5:563-578, 1897.

19. Eaton, J.E. Tie-ins between the marine and continental records in California. Am. Jour. Science 237:899-919, 1939.

20. _____ The Pleistocene in California. Calif. State Div. Mines, Bull. 118, Pt. 2:203-206, 1941.

21. Evermann, B.W. and H.W. Clark. A distributional list of the species of fresh water fishes known to occur in California. Bull. Calif. Fish and Game Comm. 35, 1931.

22. Gale, H.S. Geology of Southern California. Internat. Geol. Congr., 16th sess., Guidebook 15:1-68, 1932.

23. Grant, U.S. and H.R. Gale. Catalogue of the marine Pliocene and Pleistocene mollusca of California and adjacent regions. Mem. San Diego Soc. Nat. Hist. 1:19-77, 1931.

24. Grinnell, J. Distributional list of the mammals of California. CAS-P 3:265-390, 1913.

25. _____ The burrowing rodents of California as agents in soil formation. SI-AR 1923:339-350, 1923.

26. _____ A systematic list of the mammals of California. UC-PZ 21:313-324, 1923.

27. _____ A revised life-zone map of California. UC-PZ 40: 328-330, 1935.

28. Grinnell, J., S. Dixon and J.M. Linsdale. The fur-bearing mammals of California. U.C. Press, Berkeley, 1937.

29. Hall, H.M. and J. Grinnell. Life-Zone indicators in California. CAS-P 9(2):37-67, 1919.

30. Hay, O.P. The Pleistocene of the western region of North America and its vertebrated animals. Carnegie Inst., Washington, Publ. 322, 1927.

31. Hoover, R.L. Industrial plants of the California Indians. CAS-PD 25(5):25-31, 1972.

32. Hubbs, C.L. and Miller, R.R. The zoölogical evidence. In The Great Basin, with emphasis on glacial and postglacial times. UU-B 38:17-166, 1948.

33. Ingles, L.C. Mammals of California. Stanford Univ. Press, 1947.

34. Jenkins, O.P. Geologic map of California, Calif. State Div. Mines, 1938.

35. _____ Geomorphic provinces of California. _In_ Geologic formations and economic development of the oil and gas fields of California. Calif. State Div. of Mines, Bull. 118, Pt. 2:83-88, 1941.

36. Jenny, H. Exploring the soils of California. In California Agriculture: 317-394. U.C. Press, Berkeley, 1946.

37. Jensen, H.A. A system for classifying vegetation in California. Bull. Calif. Fish and Game Comm., Vol. 33, No. 4, San Francisco, 1947.

38. Jepson, W.L. The silva of California. U.C. Press, Berkeley, 1910.

39. _____ A flora of California. U.C. Press, Berkeley, 1936.

40. _____ A manual of the flowering plants of California. U.C. Press, Berkeley, 1951.

41. Kawahara, S. A survey of the physical setting of the Point Reyes Peninsula Area, Marin County, California. SFSC-TAMP 6: 1-64, 1972 (1970).

42. Keen, A.M. An abridged check list and bibliography of West North American marine mollusca. Stanford Univ. Press, 1937.

43. Keep, J. West Coast shells. Stanford Univ. Press, 1937.

44. McAdie, A.G. The rainfall of California. UC-PG 1:127-240, 1914.

45. Matson, R.G. The pollen evidence for a recent aboreal transgression into grasslands in Central California. In Papers on California and Great Basin Prehistory. CARD Pub. No. 2, 1970.

46. Merriam, C.H. The buffalo in Northeastern California. Journal of Mammalogy 7:211-214, 1926.

47. Morriss, P.A. A field guide to shells of the Pacific Coast and Hawaii. Houghton Mifflin Co., Boston, 1952.

48. Munz, P.A. and D.D. Keck. A California flora. U.C. Press, Berkeley, 1959.

49. Murdock, J. and R.W. Webb. Minerals of California. Calif. State Div. Mines, Bull. 173, 1956.

50. Murphy, G.I. A key to the fishes of the Sacramento-San Joaquin basin. Bull. Calif. Fish and Game Comm., 27:165-171, 1941.

51. Packard, E.L. A quantitative analysis of the molluscan fauna of San Francisco Bay. UC-PZ 18:299-336, 1918.

52. Philbrick, R.N. Proceedings of the symposium on the biology of the California Islands. Santa Barbara, 1967.

53. Reed, R.D. The geology of California. Tulsa, Okla., 1933.

54. _____California's record in the geologic history of the world. Calif. State Div. Mines, Bull. 118:99-118, 1941.

55. Reed, C.F., C.E. Grunsky, and J.J. Crawford. Report of the examining commission on rivers and harbors to the governor of California. Sacramento, 1890.

56. Russell, R.J. Climates of California. UC-PG 2:73-84, 1926.

57. _____Instability of sea level. Amer. Scientist 45: 414-430, 1957.
    [San Francisco Bay shore line, pp. 415,418]

58. Sedelmeyer, H.A. Preparation of a new relief map of California. Calif. State Div. Mines, Bull. 27:73-77, 1931.

59. Shedd, S. Bibliography of the geology and mineral resources of California. Calif. State Div. Mines, Bull. 104, 1931.

60. Shinn, C.H. Let's know some trees: brief descriptions of the principal California trees. U.S. Dept. Agric., Misc. Circular no. 31, 1931.

61. Smith, A.F. and F. Curtis. Snails and other invertebrates from Indian village sites, principally Contra Costa County, California. The Veliger 6:227-229, 1964.

62. Sperisen, F.J. Gem minerals of California. Calif. Jour. Mines and Geol. 34:34-74, 1938.

63. Storie, R.E. and W.W. Weir. Key to soil series of California. Berkeley, 1941.

64. Stuster, J. The California grizzly and the origin of a maritime economy. SM-M 44:144-157, 1970.

65. Sudworth, G.B. Forest trees of the Pacific slope. U.S. Dept. Agric., Forest Service, 1908.

66. Treganza, A.E. An evaluation of the pre-Caucasian human resources of Northwestern California. In Natural resources of Northwestern California: 67-90. U.S. National Park Service, 1958.

67. Weide, D.L. Earth science and archaeology. SCA-N 6:3, 1972; 7:6, 1973; 7:8, 1973.

68. Weide, M.L. Seasonality of Pismo clam collecting at Ora-82. UCLA-AS-AR 11:127-141, 1967.

69. Weir, W.W. Subsidence of peat lands of the Sacramento-San Joaquin Delta, California. Hilgardia 20(3):37-56, 1950.

70. Werner, S.B., et al. An epidemic of coccidioidomycosis among archaeology students in Northern California. The New England Journal of Medicine 286(10):507-512, 1972.

71. Werner, S.B. Coccidioidomycosis among archaeology students. A. Ant. 39:367-370, 1974.

72. Wilmarth, G.M. Names and definitions of the geologic units in California. USGS Bull. 826, 1931.

73. Yates, L.G. The Mollusca of the Channel Islands of California. 9th Annual Report of the State Mineralogist, pp. 175-178, Calif. State Mining Bureau, 1890.

74. _____Stray notes on the geology of the Channel Islands. 9th Annual Report of the State Mineralogist, pp. 178-188, 1890. Calif. State Mining Bureau, 1890. [P. 173, fresh water in Anacapa caves]

II. ETHNOGRAPHIC BACKGROUND

75. Ames, J.G. Report on Mission Indians of California. Washington: GPO, 1873.

76. Bancroft, H.H. The Native races of the Pacific Coast. 1. Wild tribes. San Francisco, 1882.

77. Bard, C.L. Medicine and surgery among the first Californians. Touring Topics 22:20-30, 1930.

78. Baumhoff, M.A. Ecological determinants of aboriginal California populations. UC-PAAE 49:155-236, 1963.

79. Bean, L.J. and T.C. Blackburn. Native Californians: A theoretical retrospective. Ballena Press, Ramona, 1976.

80. Bean, L.J. and K.S. Saubel. Cahuilla ethnobotanical notes: The aboriginal uses of the mesquite and screwbean. UCLA-AS-AR 5:51-78, 1963.

81. Beattie, G.W. California's unbuilt missions: Spanish plans for an inland chain. Los Angeles, 1930.

82. Beattie, G.W. and H.P. Beattie. Heritage of the Valley. San Pasqual Press, Pasadena, 1939.

[Meticulously researched history of San Bernardino Valley
& Southern California]

83. Blackburn, T. Ethnohistoric descriptions of Gabrielino material
culture. UCLA-AS-AR 5:1-50, 1963.

84. _____A manuscript account of the Ventureño Chumash.
UCLA-AS-AR 5:155-160, 1963.

85. Browne, J.R. The Indian reservations of California. In W.W.
Beach, Indian Miscellany. Pp. 303-322. Albany, 1877.

86. Caughey, J.W. The Indians of California in 1852. San Marino:
Huntington Library. 1952.

87. Chace, P.G. Ethnographic approach to the archeology of the
Luiseño Indians. SBCMA-Q 12(2), 1964.

88. Cowan, R.E. Alexander S. Taylor, 1817-1876 - first bibliographer
of California. Calif. Hist. Soc. Quarterly 12:18-24, 1933.

89. Davis, E.L. An ethnography of the Kuzedika Paiute of Mono Lake,
Mono County, California. UU-MP 8, 1965.

90. Dietz, S.A. Echataunal: a study in Coast Miwok acculturation.
SCA-N 8:8, 1974.

91. Du Bois, C. The 1870 Ghost Dance. UC-AR 3(1), 1939.

92. Du Bois, C.G. Religion of the Luiseño Indians. UC-PAEE 8(3),
1908.

93. Ellison, W.H. The Federal Indian policy in California, 1846-
1860. Mississippi Historical Rev. 9:37-67, 1922.

94. Engelhardt, Z. The Franciscans in California. Harbor Springs,
Michigan, 1897.

95. _____The Missions and Missionaries of California. San
Francisco, 1908-1916.

96. Gardner, L. The surviving Chumash. UCLA-AS-AR 7:277-302, 1965.

97. Geary, (Rev.) G.J. The secularization of the California Missions
(1810-1846). Catholic Univ. of America, Studies in
American Church History, 1934.

98. Gould, R. Aboriginal California burial and cremation practices.
UC-AS-R 60:149-168, 1963.

99. Grinnell, E. Making acorn bread. UCAS-R 41:42-45, 1957.
[Reprint of an 1893 account from Yosemite Valley]

100. Heizer, R.F. The Indians of Los Angeles County: Hugo Reid's
letters of 1852. SM-P 21, 1968.

101. Heizer, R.F., and Elsasser, A.B. Original accounts of the lone woman of San Nicolas Island. UC-AS-R 55, 1961.

102. Heizer, R.F., Nissen, K.M. and E.D. Castillo. California Indian History: A classified and annotated guide to source materials. BP-PAEH 4, 1975.

103. Heizer, R.F., and M.A. Whipple. The California Indians: A source book. U.C. Press, Berkeley, 1951. [2nd, revised edition 1971]

104. Hewes, G.W. California flicker-quill headbands in the light of an ancient Colorado cave specimen. A. Ant. 18:147-154, 1952.

105. Hodge, F.W. Hupa rod armor. SM-M 24:167, 1950.

106. Hoffman, W.J. Miscellaneous ethnographic observations on Indians inhabiting Nevada, California, and Arizona. USGS-AR 10, 1878.

107. Hoopes, A.W. Indian affairs and their administration, with special reference to the Far West 1849-1860. Philadelphia, 1932.

108. James, G.W. Basket makers of California at work. The Basket 1(3):3-18, Pasadena, 1903.

109. Jones, N. Indian caches explained by raids of menfolk on food stored by squaws. San Diego, Calif. Tribune December 14, 1935.

110. Klimek, S. Culture element distributions: I The structure of California Indian culture. UC-PAEE 37:1-70, 1935.

111. Krause, F. Die Kultur der Kalifornischen Indianer. Leipzig, 1921.

112. Kroeber, A.L. The dialectic divisions of the Moquelumnan family. AA 8:483-494, 1906.

113. _____Ethnography of the Cahuilla Indians. UC-PAAE 8: 29-68, 1908.

114. _____The anthropology of California. Science 27:281-290, 1908.

115. _____The tribes of the Pacific Coast. ICA, 19th Sess., pp. 385-401, 1917.

116. _____Games of the California Indians. AA 22:272-277, 1920.

117. _____Handbook of the Indians of California. BAE-B 78, 1925.

118. Kroeber, A.L. Culture element distributions: III Area and climax. UC-PAAE 37:101-116, 1936.

119. _____ Cultural and natural areas of native North America. UC-PAAE 38, 1939.

120. _____ Two papers on the aboriginal ethnography of California. UC-AS-R 56, 1962.

121. Mason, J.A. The ethnology of the Salinan Indians. UC-PAAE 10: 97-240, 1912.

122. Mason, O.T. The Ray collection from Hupa Reservation. Smithsonian Inst. Report 666:205-239, 1886.

123. Merriam, C.H. Totemism in California. AA 10:558-562, 1908.

124. _____ Studies of California Indians. Univ. of California Press, 1955.
     [Publication of E.H. Harriman Fund]

125. _____ The Hang-e or ceremonial house of the Northern Miwok of Hachana village near Railroad Fist, Calaveras County, Calif. UC-AS-R 38:34-35, 1957.

126. _____ Ethnographic notes on California Indian Tribes. UC-AS-R 68 Part I, pp. 1-166, 1966.

127. _____ Ethnological notes on Northern and Southern California Indian tribes. UC-AS-R 68 Part II, pp. 167-256, 1967.

128. _____ Ethnological notes on Central California Indian tribes. UC-AS-R Part III, pp. 257-448, 1967.

129. _____ Village names in twelve California mission records. UC-AS-R 74:1-175, 1968.

130. Moriarty, J.R. Pre-Spanish marine transport and boat building techniques on the Upper and Lower California Coast. The Brand Book 1 part 2, San Diego Corral, Westerners 1: 19-27, 1968.

131. Pastron, A.G., et al. Aboriginal warfare in Northern California. SM-M 47:136-142, 1973.

132. Pilling, A.R. The archaeological implications of an annual coastal visit for certain Yokut groups. AA 52:438-440, 1950.

133. Powers, S. Tribes of California. SI-CNAE 3, 1877. [Reprinted University of California Press, 1976]

134. Putnam, G.R. A Yuma cremation. AA 8:264-267, 1895.

135. Read, C.H. An account of a collection of ethnographic specimens formed during Vancouver's voyage in the Pacific Ocean. JRAI 21:99-108, 1891.

136. Reid, H. Letters on the Los Angeles County Indians to the Los Angeles Star in the 1850's.
[Reprinted various places: Dakin, S.B., A Scotch Paisano, UC Press, 1939; Johnson, B.E., California's Gabrielino Indians, Southwest Museum, 1962; Hoffman, W.J., in Bull. of the Essex Inst., 17:1-33, 1885; Taylor, A.S., Indianology of Calif., 1860's; Heizer, R.F. SM-P 21, 1968. Not all of these print exactly the same letters]

137. Riddell, F.A. Ethnogeography of two Maidu groups. I. The Silom Ma'a Maidu. SM-M 42:45-52, 1968.

138. _____ Ethnogeography of two Maidu groups. II. The Tasaidum Maidu. SM-M 42:85-93, 1968.

139. Roberts, B.L. Descendants of the Numu. SM-M 39:13-22, 66-76, 1965.

140. Robinson, E. Vancouver's Californian bows. UC-AS-R 28:1-5, 1955.

141. Rostlund, E. Freshwater fish and fishing in native North America. UC-PG 9:1-313, 1952.

142. Sanchez, N. Spanish and Indian place names in California. San Francisco, 1922.

143. Schenck, W.E. Historic aboriginal groups of the California delta region. UC-PAEE 23:123-146, 1926.

144. Sherwin, J. Face and body painting practices among California Indians. UC-AS-R 60:81-147, 1963.

145. Taylor, A.S. The Indianology of California.
[Published serially in the California Farmer and Journal of the Useful Sciences, vols. 13-18. Feb. 22, 1860-Oct. 30, 1863. 151 installments]

146. Twitchell, E.W. The California pandemic of 1833. California and Western Medicine 23:592-593, 1925.

147. Walker, E.F. Indians of Southern California. SM-M 17:201-216, 1943.

148. Waterman, T. Native musical instruments of California and some others. Out West, Vol. XXVIII no. 4, April, pp. 276-286. San Francisco, 1908.

149. Weber, F.J. Indian "ballgame" at Mission San Luis Rey. SM-M 41:116-117, 1967.

150. Weber, F.J. Toypurina the temptress. SM-M 43:75-76, 1969.

151. Wheeler, B.I. and F.W. Putnam. Ethnological and archaeological survey of California. AA 5:727-792, 1903.

152. Willoughby, N.C. Division of labor among the Indians of California. UC-AS-R 60:7-80, 1963.

153. Wilson, N. Notes on traditional foothill Nisenan food technology. In Papers on Nisenan environment and subsistence. CARD Pub. No. 3, 1972.

154. Yates, L.G. On recent ethnological explorations on the West Coast. Alameda County Independent, Vol. 1, No. 7, pp. 246-248, 1877.

III. TECHNIQUES OF STONE WORKING; OBSIDIAN SOURCE ANALYSIS

155. Anonymous. Primitive bows and arrows; their character and uses in North America and the wounds caused by them. Forest and Stream 69:808-810, 848-851, 1907.
[Flint chipping in the Clear Lake area]

156. Barbieri, J.A. Technique of the implements from Lake Mojave. SM-P 11:99-107, 1937.

157. Beckwith, E.G. Report of explorations for a route for the Pacific railroad on the line of the forty-first parallel. In Repts. of explor. and survey for a railroad from the Mississippi River to the Pacific Ocean, 1853-1854, 2:1-66, 1855.

158. Belcher, E. On the manufacture of works of art by the Esquimaux. Trans. Ethnol. Soc. of London 1:129-146, 1861.
[Mentions flint chipping by Indians at Monterey]

159. Bixby, L.B. Flint chipping. A. Ant. 10:353-361, 1945.

160. _____ How to chip flint arrowheads. Archery, p. 48, Jan. 1965.
[Popular article, by author of listed article in A. Ant. (1945), giving details of materials, tools, method, & difficulties]

161. Bowman, H.R., F. Asaro, and I. Perlman. Composition variations in obsidian sources and the archaeological implications. Archaeometry 15:123-127, 1973.

162. Brott, C. How stone tools became tools and weapons. In Ancient hunters of the Far West (R.F. Pourade, ed.). Part V; pp. 141-193. Union Tribune Publ. Co., San Diego, 1966.

163. Bryan, B. The manufacture of stone mortars. SM-M 35:134-139, 1961.

164. Carter, G.F. Artifacts and naturifacts: Some parallels be-
     tween Japanese and American stonework. Anthropological
     Journal of Canada 5(1), 1967.

165. Chever, E.E. The Indians of California. Amer. Naturalist 4:
     129-148, 1870.

166. Coyer, R.J. and J.R. Moriarty. A San Dieguito sawing tool.
     SM-M 49:65-69, 1975.

167. Dills, C.E. Mortars and their measurement. In Papers on the
     Chumash. SLOCAS-OP 7:170-195, 1975.

168. Dixon, R.B. The Northern Maidu. AMNH-B 17:119-346, 1905.

169. Eberhart, H. The cogged stones of Southern California. A. Ant.
     26:361-369, 1961.

170. _____The Milling Stone Complex, genuine or spurious?
     A. Ant. 30:352-353, 1965.

171. Farmer, M.F. Lightning spalling. A. Ant. 4:346-348, 1939.
     [Summary of Laudermilk and Kennard, 1938]

172. _____Southern California discoidals. SM-M 27:177-183,
     1953.

173. Gebhard, P. Concerning grooved axes in California. A. Ant.
     12:54, 1946.

174. Goddard, P.E. Life and culture of the Hupa. UC-PAAE 1:1-88,
     1903.
     [P. 34]

175. Gould, R. A case of heat treatment of lithic materials in
     aboriginal Northwestern California. JCA 3(1):142-144,
     1976.

176. Harner, M.J. Thermo-facts vs. artifacts: An experimental study
     of the Malpais industry. UC-AS-R 33:39-43, 1956.

177. Harrington, M.R. There's no mystery about arrowheads. Desert
     Magazine 5(2):10-13, 1941.
     [How arrowheads are chipped - esp. Paiute]

178. Heizer, R.F. The occurrence and significance of Southwestern
     grooved axes in California. A. Ant. 11:187-193, 1946.

179. Heizer, R.F. and Kelley, H. Scraper plane burins. SM-M 35:
     146-150, 1961.

180. Henshaw, H.W. Perforated stones from California. BAE-B 2:1-37,
     1887.

181. Hester, T.R. Heat treating of siliceous stone among California Indians. SM-M 47:110-111, 1973.

182. _____On the function of "Stockton" points. SM-M 48: 153-156, 1974.

183. Hester, T.R. and Heizer, R.F. Arrow points or knives? Comments on the proposed function of "Stockton" points. A. Ant. 38:220-221, 1973.

184. Hoffman, W.J. The Menomini Indians. BAE-AR 14:266-268, 1896. [Details on drilling of shell beads by the Chumash. Includes reference to small flint bladelets - cf. Heizer and Kelley, 1961]

185. Holmes, W.H. Handbook of aboriginal American antiquities. BAE-B 60, 1919. [Pp. 296,299,311-316,318,320,326-329]

186. Jackson, T.L. and P.D. Schulz. Typology, trade and trade analysis: A test of local manufacture of Sacramento Valley obsidian tools. UCLA-JNWA 1(2):1-8, 1975.

187. Johnson, E.N. The serrated points of Central California. A. Ant. 6:167-170, 1940. [Description of the Stockton-type points from the Delta country]

188. Kowalski, B.R. Classification of archaeological artifacts by applying pattern recognition to trace element data. Analytical Chemistry 44:2176-2179, 1972. [California obsidians]

189. Latta, F.F. Handbook of Yokuts Indians. Oildale, Calif., 1949. [Pp. 139-141]

190. Laudermilk, J.D. and Kennard, T.G. Concerning lightning spalling. Am. J. Sci., 25, 5th ser., 104-122, 1938.

191. Loeffelholz, K. von. Account of the Tsorei Indians of Trinidad Bay, 1850-1856. In R.F. Heizer and J.E. Mills, The four ages of Tsurai. U.C. Press, Berkeley, 1952.

192. Lyon, C. How the Indians made stone arrowheads. History Magazine 3:214, 1859.

193. Meredith, H.C. Aboriginal art in obsidian. Land of Sunshine 11:255-258, 1899.

194. Miller, D. The great Mendocino blade cache. SCA-N 7:6, 1973.

195. Miller, M.L. The so-called California "Diggers". Popular Science Monthly 50:201-214, 1896.

196. Nance, J.D. Lithic analysis: Implications for the prehistory of Central California. UCLA-AS-AR 12:62-103, 1970.

197. _____Functional interpretations from microscopic analysis. A. Ant. 36(3):361-366, 1971.
[Late Horizon-Central California, "Stockton" points]

198. Nelson, N.C. Flint working by Ishi. Holmes Anniversary Volume, pp. 397-401. Washington, 1916.
[Reprinted in A.L. Kroeber and T.T. Waterman, Source Book in Anthropology, pp. 244-249, N.Y., 1931]

199. Pitzer, J.M., T.R. Hester, and R.F. Heizer. Microblade technology of the Channel Islands. SM-M 48:124-135, 1974.

200. Pope, S.T. Making Indian arrow heads. Forest and Stream 81: 796, 1913.
[Description of flint chipping by Ishi]

201. _____Yahi archery. UC-PAEE 13:103-152, 1918.
[Pp. 116-118]

202. _____Bows and arrows. U.C. Press, Berkeley, 1962.

203. Powers, S. Tribes of California. SI-CNAE 3, 1877.
[P. 104: Wiyot flint chipping. This volume reprinted by U.C. Press, Berkeley, 1976]

204. Putnam, F.W. Perforated stones. USGS-WCM 7:135-189, 1879.

205. _____On a collection of perforated stones from California. Proc. Boston Society for Nat. Hist. 23:356, 1888.

206. Ray, P.H. Manufacture of bows and arrows among the Natano (Hupa) and Kenuck (Klamath) Indians. Amer. Naturalist 20:832-833, 1886.
[Reprinted in SI-AR 1886, pp. 228-229, 1889]

207. Redding, B.B. How our ancestors in the stone age made their implements. Amer. Naturalist 13:667-674, 1879.
[McCloud River Wintu flaking methods]

208. _____ Prehistoric treasures. Californian 1:125-128, 1880.
[Preparation and use of flint and obsidian by the Wintun and neighboring tribes]

209. Ritter, E.W. and R.G. Matson. Form categories, cluster analysis and multidimensional scaling: a case study of projectile points. Southwestern Lore 37:102-116, 1972.

210. Roberts, M.E. Microwave analysis and Franciscan chert lithics. In Papers on the Chumash, SLOCAS-OP 9:117-169, 1975.

211. Rogers, M.J. The stone art of the San Dieguito Plateau. AA
      31:454-467, 1929.

212. Rust, H.N. Tom, the arrow maker. Land of Sunshine 8:13-15,
      1897.
      [Washo chipping techniques with illustration of obsidian
      points and flaking implements]

213. _____The obsidian blades of California. AA 7:688-695,
      1905.

214. Sapir, E. Yana texts. UC-PAEE 9:1-235, 1910.
      [P. 43, note 62]

215. Sapir, E. and L. Spier. Notes on the culture of the Yana. UC-
      AR 3:239-298, 1943.
      [Spier's comments on Sapir's notes on Yana flint chipping.
      P. 268]

216. Schumacher, P. Remarks on the kjökken möddings on the North-
      west coast of America. SI-AR 1873:354-362, 1874.
      [Pp. 355-356, Yurok flint chipping]

217. _____The method of manufacture of several articles by
      former Indians of Southern California. PM-R 11:258-268,
      1878.
      [Pp. 265-268, "weights for digging sticks", - - Reprinted
      in UC-AS-R 59:77-82, 1963]

218. _____L'age de pierre chez les Indiens Klamaths. Revue
      d'Ethnographie 1:500-504, 1882.
      [Also printed in Bull. U.S. Geol. and Geog. Surveys of
      the Territories 3:547-549, 1877]

219. Snyder, J.F. The method of making stone arrow points. The
      Antiquarian 1:231-234. Columbus, Ohio, 1897.
      [Eldorado County Maidu]

220. Spanne, L.W. Preform or finished artifact? In Papers on the
      Chumash, SLOCAS-OP 9:47-59, 1975.

221. Squier, R.J. The Manufacture of flint implements by the
      Indians of Northern and Central California. UC-AS-R 19:
      15-33, 1953.

222. Swartz, B.K., Jr. Blade manufacture in Southern California.
      A. Ant. 25:405-407, 1960.

223. Treganza, A.E. and L.L. Valdivia. The manufacture of pecked
      and ground stone artifacts: a controlled study. UC-AS-R
      32:19-29, 1955.

224. Waite, E.G. Letter to the Editor on flint chipping in Central and Northern California. Overland Monthly 12:185-186, 1874.

IV. TYPES, MANUFACTURE AND USES OF SHELLS AND BONES

225. Bennyhoff, J.A. and R.F. Heizer. Cross-dating Great Basin sites by Californian shell beads. UC-AS-R 42:60-92, 1958.

226. Bowers, S. Relics from an Indian grave. Science 7:35-36, 1886. [Village site, Conejo plateau, Ventura County]

227. Chagnon, N. Ecological and adaptive aspects of California shell money. UCLA-AS-AR 12:1-25, 1970.

228. Curtis, F. Microdrills in the manufacture of shell beads in Southern California. SM-M 38:98-105, 1964.

229. Gibson, R.O. The beads of Humaliwo. JCA 2:110-119, 1975. [Malibu, California]

230. Gifford, D.S. and E.W. Californian Olivellas. The Nautilus, Vol. 57:73-80, 1944.

231. Gifford, E.W. Californian bone artifacts. UC-AR 3:153-237, 1940.

232. _____Californian shell artifacts. UC-AR 9:1, 1947.

233. Heizer, R.F. Curved single-piece fishhooks of shell and bone in California. A. Ant. 15:89-97, 1949.

234. Holmes, W.H. Art in shell of the ancient Americans. BAE-AR 1880-81:179-305, 1883.

235. Hudson, J.W. Pomo wampum makers. Overland Monthly 30:101-108, 1897.

236. Ingersoll, E. Wampum and its history. Amer. Naturalist 17: 467-479, 1883. [Frequent mentions of California's shell beads]

237. King, C.D. Research results. SCA-N 6:4-5, 1972; SCA-N 7(1):8-10; SCA-N 7(2):10-12, 1973. [California shell beads]

238. _____The explanation of differences and similarities among shell beads in prehistoric and early historic California. In L. Bean and T.F. King (eds.), Antap: California political and economic organization. Ballena Press, Ramona, 1974.

239. Koloseike, A. On calculating the prehistoric food resource value of molluscs. UCLA-AS-AR 11:143-160, 1969.

17

240. Kroeber, A.L. Ethnography of the Cahuilla Indians. UC-PAEE 8: 29-68, 1908.
     [P. 63, pl. 13; shell beads of various types]

241. Orchard, W.C. Beads and beadwork of the American Indians. MAIHF-C 11, 1929.

242. Robinson, E. Shell fishhooks of the California coast. Occasional papers of the Bernice P. Bishop Museum 17:57-65, 1942.

243. Silsbee, J. Determining the general source of California _Olivella_ shells. UC-AS-R 41:10-11, 1957.

244. Stearns, R.E.C. Aboriginal shell money. Amer. Naturalist 11:344-350, 1877.

245. _____ Ethno-conchology - a study of primitive money. SI-AR 1887 2:297-334, 1889.

246. _____ Shell money. Amer. Naturalist 3:1-5, 1869.

247. Tower, D.B. The use of marine mollusca and their value in reconstructing prehistoric trade routes in the American Southwest. Papers of the Excavator's Club 2:3, 1945.

248. Treganza, A.E. and L.L. Valdivia. Painted shell artifacts from California. UC-AS-R 38:11-13, 1957.

249. Yates, L.G. Notes on the aboriginal money of California. Overland Monthly 27:337-342, 1877.

250. _____ Shell Money of California. SCAS-B 3:156-158; 4:16-17, 26-27, 1904-1905.

V. POTTERY, BAKED CLAY, CLAY AND CARVED STONE FIGURINES

251. Anonymous. More steatite objects. SM-M 21:104-105, 1947.
     [Four carved steatite objects said to be of aboriginal manufacture]

252. Anonymous. An unusual figurine. PCAS-S 14:5, 1975.

253. Baldwin, G.C. The pottery of the Southern Paiute. A. Ant. 16: 50-56, 1950.

254. Bryan, B. A clay figurine found in Southern California. SM-M 38:66-69, 1964.

255. Chace, P.G. Clay figurines, additional data. PCAS-Q 9:41-43, 1973.

256. Davis, J.T. Further notes on clay human figurines in the Western United States. UC-AS-R 48:16-31, 1959.

257. Douglas, F.H. and R. D'Harnoncourt. Indian art of the United States. New York, 1941.
[P. 37: steatite figurine and jar from Los Angeles Co.]

258. Drover, C.E. Three fired-clay figurines from 4-Ora-64, Orange County, California. PCAS-Q 7(4), 1971.

259. _____ Early ceramics from Southern California. JCA 2(1): 101-107, 1975.

260. Du Bois, C.G. Diegueño mortuary ollas. AA 9:484-486, 1907.

261. Elsasser, A.B. Two fired-clay figurines from Central California. A. Ant. 29:118-120, 1963.

262. Forbes, J.D. Pueblo pottery in the San Fernando Valley. SM-M 35:36-38, 1961.

263. Ford, J.A., et al. The Jaketown Site in West-Central Mississippi. AMNH-AP 45:53-55, 1955.
[A comparison of Poverty Point objects with baked clay "balls" of Central California]

264. Gayton, A.H. Yokuts and Western Mono pottery-making. UC-PAAE 24:230-255, 1929.

265. Gifford, E.W. Pottery making in the Southwest. UC-PAAE 23: 353-373, 1928.

266. Gladwin, H.S. The western range of the Red-on-Buff. GP-MP 5, 1930.

267. Goerke, E.B. and F.A. Davidson. Baked clay figurines of Marin County. UCLA-JNWA 1(2):9-24, 1975.

268. Greenwood, R.S. A Stone carving from the Browne Site. SM-M 36:4-7, 1962.

269. _____ Frogs, breasts, and primitive art: a reply to Jules Eisenbud. AA 67:1549-1555, 1965.

270. _____ A second stone sculpture from the Browne Site. SM-M 41:84-87, 1967.

271. Harner, M.J. Potsherds and the tentative dating of the San-Gorgonio-Big Maria Trail. UC-AS-R 37:35-37, 1957.

272. Harrington, M.R. Unique olla. SM-M 203, 1955.
[Diegueño incised decoration]

273. Hedges, K. Hakataya figurines from Southern California. PCAS-Q 9:5-40, 1973.

274. Heizer, R.F. Baked clay objects of the Lower Sacramento Valley, California. A. Ant. 3:34-50, 1937.

275. Heizer, R.F. and R.K. Beardsley. Fired clay figurines in Central and Northern California. A. Ant. 9:199-207, 1943.

276. Heizer, R.F. and D.M. Pendergast. Additional data on fired clay human figurines from California. A. Ant. 21:181-185, 1955.

277. Heye, G.G. Certain aboriginal pottery from Southern California. MAIH-INM 7:3-48, 1919.

278. Hoover, R.L. An unusual stone effigy from Southern California. SM-M 48:32-35, 1974.

279. _____ Some observations on Chumash prehistoric stone effigies. JCA 1(1):33-40, 1974.

280. King, T.F. Three clay figurines from Marin County. SM-M 41: 138-142, 1967.

281. Knight, L.C. A figurine from China Ranch (4-Iny-962). PCAS-Q 9:48-51, 1973.

282. Kroeber, A.L. and M. Harner. Mohave pottery. UC-AR 16:1, 1955. [Ethnographical analysis and a description for the archaeologist]

283. McKinney, A. and L. Knight. Baked clay figurines from Mason Valley, San Diego: Bowers Museum, Strandt Collection. PCAS-Q 9:44-47, 1973.

284. Meister, C.W., et al. Pottery from the New York and Providence Mountains survey sites. UCLA-AS-AR 8:275-278, 1966.

285. Morss, N. Clay figurines of the American Southwest. PM-P 49(1), 1954.

286. Nordenskiold, E. The American Indian as an inventor. JRAI 49: 273-310, 1929. [Sacramento Delta baked clay objects. Pp. 287-288]

287. Peck, S.L. Some pottery from the Sand Hills, Imperial County, California. ASASC Publ. no. 1, 1953.

288. _____ The diffusion of pottery in the Southwest. SM-M 29: 130, 1955.

289. Polk, M.R. Manufacture and uses of steatite objects by the Diegueño. PCAS-Q 8:1-26, 1972.

290. Rogers, M.J. Yuman pottery making. SDM-P 2, 1936.

291. Ruby, J. Southwestern pottery in Los Angeles County, California. A. Ant. 31:440, 1966.

292. Ruby, J. and T. Blackburn. Occurrence of Southwestern pottery
     in Los Angeles County, California. A. Ant. 30:209-210,
     1964.

293. Shipek, F.C. Diegueño pots. El Museo 1(2):5-116. Museum of
     Man, San Diego, 1951.

294. Steward, J.H. Pottery from Deep Springs Valley, Inyo County,
     California. AA 30:348, 1928.

295. _____ Ethnography of the Owens Valley Paiute. UC-PAAE
     33:334-335, 1933.

296. Treganza, A.E. An archaeological reconnaissance of Northeast-
     ern Baja California and Southeastern California. A. Ant.
     8:152-163, 1942.

297. True, D.L. Fired clay figurines from San Diego County, Calif-
     ornia. A. Ant. 22:291-296, 1957.

298. True, D.L. and C. Warren. A clay figurine from Santa Monica,
     California. SM-M 35:152-155, 1961.

299. Wallace, W.J. A clay figurine from Death Valley National Monu-
     ment. SM-M 31:131-134, 1957.

300. Wallace, W.J. and E.T. Palos Verdes carved stone figures. SM-M
     48:59-66, 1974.

VI.   BASKETRY AND TEXTILES

301. Anonymous. Two rare Chumash baskets. MAIHF-INM 5:266-267,
     1928.

302. Bailey, R.C. Collector's choice, the McLeod Basket Collection,
     Kern County Historical Society Annual Publication No. 13,
     1951.
     [Yokuts material - most of which is in Lowie Museum of
     Anthropology, University of California, Berkeley]

303. Barrett, S.A. Basket designs of the Pomo Indians. AA 7:648-
     653, 1905.

304. _____ The material culture of the Klamath Lake and Modoc
     Indians of Northeastern California and Southern Oregon.
     UC-PAAE 5:253-257, 1907.

305. _____ Pomo Indian basketry. UC-PAAE 7:134-308, 1908.

306. Baumhoff, M.A. Carbonized basketry from the Thomas Site. (Mrn-
     115). UC-AS-R 19:9-10, 1953.

307. _____ Catlow twine from Central California. UC-AS-R 38:
     1-5, 1957.

308. Baumhoff, M.A. and Heizer, R.F. Outland coiled basketry from the caves of West Central Nevada. UC-AS-R 42:49-59, 1958.

309. Cody, B.P. California Indian baby cradles. SM-M 14:89-96, 1940.

310. Craig, S. Ethnographic notes on the construction of Ventureño Chumash baskets: From the ethnographic and linguistic field notes of John P. Harrington. UCLA-AS-AR 8:197-214, 1966.

311. _____ The basketry of the Ventureño Chumash. UCLA-AS-AR 9: 78-149, 1967.

312. Davis, E.L. and W. Allan. Diegueño coiled baskets. SDM-ETN no. 1, 1967.

313. Dawson, L. and J. Deetz. A corpus of Chumash basketry. UCLA-AS-AR 7:193-276, Los Angeles, 1965.

314. Dixon, R.B. Basketry designs of the Maidu Indians of California. AA 2:266-276, 1900.

315. _____ Basketry designs of the Indians of Northern California. AMNH-B 17(1), 1902.

316. _____ The Shasta. AMNH-B 17:398-403, 1907.

317. Douglas, F.H. The main divisions of California Indian basketry. Indian Leaflet Series No. 83 and 84, Dept. of Indian Art, Denver Art Museum, 1937.

318. Du Bois, C. Wintu ethnography. UC-PAAE 36:131-139, 1939.

319. Elsasser, A.B. and R.F. Heizer. The archaeology of Bowers Cave, Los Angeles County, California. UC-AS-R 59:1-45, 1965.

320. Gifford, E.W. and W.E. Schenck. Archaeology of the Southern San Joaquin Valley, California. UC-PAEE 23:99-108, 1926.

321. Goddard, P.E. Life and culture of the Hupa. UC-PAAE 1:38-48, 1903.

322. Harrington, M.R. A remodeled basket. SM-M 16:141-142, 1942.

323. Heizer, R.F. One of the oldest known California Indian baskets. SM-M 42:70-74, 1968.

324. Heye, G.G. Chumash objects from a California cave. MAIHF-INM 3:193-198, 1926.

325. Holmes, W.H. Anthropological studies in California. USNM-AR 1900:155-187, 1902.

326. James, G.W. Basketmakers of California at work. Sunset Magazine, Vol. 8, San Francisco, 1901.
[Reprinted in The Basket, Vol. 1, no. 3, Pasadena, 1903]

327. _____ Indian basketry, New York, 1904.

328. Kelly, I.T. Yuki basketry. UC-PAAE 24:421-444, 1930.

329. Kirk, R.E. Panamint basketry - a dying art. SM-M 26:76-86, 1952.

330. Kroeber, A.L. Basket designs of the Indians of Northwestern California. UC-PAAE 2:105-164, 1904.

331. _____ Ethnography of the Cahuilla Indians. UC-PAEE 8: 41-51, 1908.

332. _____ California basketry and the Pomo. AA 11:233-249, 1909.

333. _____ Basket designs of the Mission Indians of California. AMNH-AP 20:149-183, 1922.

334. _____ Basketry designs of the Mission Indians. AMNH, Guide Leaflet No. 55, N.Y. 1922.

335. _____ Handbook of the Indians of California. BAE-B 78, 1925.

336. Mason, O.T. Aboriginal American basketry. USNM-AR 1902:171-548, 1904.
[California basketry included]

337. Merriam, C.H. Studies of California Indians. U.C. Press, Berkeley. (Pp. 106-130), 1955.

338. Merrill, R.E. Plants used in basketry by the California Indians. UC-PAAE 20(13), 1923.

339. Mohr, A. and L.L. Sample. Twined water bottles of the Cuyama area, Southern California. A. Ant. 20:345-354, 1955.

340. Moriarty, J.R. Evidence of mat weaving from an early La Jolla site. SM-M 40:44-53, 1966.

341. Nuttall, Z. Two remarkable California baskets. California Historical Society Quart. 2:341-343, San Francisco, 1924.
[Spanish coat of arms woven into basket: Mission Indians]

342. O'Neale, L.M. Yurok-Karok basket weavers. UC-PAAE 32:1-184, 1932.

343. Peck, S.L. A fragment of Northern California basketry from Southern California. A. Ant. 16:70, 1950.

344. Purdy, C. Pomo Indian baskets and their makers. Out West, Vol. 15 (6):438-449; Vol. 16(1):8-19; Vol. 16(2):151-158; and Vol. 16(3):262-273, 1901-1902.
[Reprinted Mendocino County Historical Society, 1971]

345. Putnam, F.W. Textile fabrics, basket-work, etc. (from Santa Barbara sites). USGS-WCM 7:239-250, 1879.

346. Schumacher, P. The method of manufacturing pottery and baskets among the Indians of Southern California. PM-AR 12:523-525, 1879.
[Cahuillas at Agua Caliente]

347. Smith, G.A. and R.D. Simpson. Basket makers of San Bernardino County. San Bernardino County Museum, 1964.

348. Spier, L. Klamath ethnography. UC-PAAE 30:177-193, 1930.

349. Steward, J.H. Two rare Chumash baskets. MAIHF-INM 5:266-267, 1928.

350. _____ Indian Tribes of Sequoia National Park Region. U.S. Department of Interior, National Park Service, pp. 12-15, 1935.

351. Walker, E.F. Finding an old Paiute mush basket. SM-M 15:10-12, 1941.

352. Wallace, W.J. A basket weaver's kit from Death Valley. SM-M 28:216-221, 1954.

353. Weltfish, G. Problems in the study of ancient and modern basket makers. AA 34:108-117, 1932.

354. Woodward, A. An immense Pomo basket. Indian. MAIHF-INM 5: 178-183, 1928.

VII. CHARMSTONES

355. Anonymous. Notice of a stone implement found near Woodbridge, California. CAS-P 4:18-19, 1873.

356. Anonymous. Stone plummets, Amer. Naturalist 20:85-86, 1886.

357. Blake, J. On some recently discovered aboriginal implements. CAS-P 4:221-222, 1873.

358. Elsasser, A.B. A charmstone site in Sonoma County, California. UC-AS-R 28:29-33, 1955.

359. Henderson, J.G. Notes on aboriginal relics known as "plummets". Amer. Naturalist 6:641-650, 1872.

360. Henshaw, H.W. The aboriginal relics called "sinkers" or "plum-
     mets". AJA 1:105-114, 1885.

361. Heye, G.G. Stone objects from San Joaquin Valley. MAIHF-INM
     3:107-111, 1926.

362. Holt, W.B. Charm stones (of the Santa Barbara region). SBMNH-L
     14:67-68, 1939.

363. Latta, F.F. Handbook of Yokuts Indians. Bear State Books,
     Oildale. Pp. 136,200-209, 1949.

364. Maguire, B. A stone pendant from Ora-82. PCAS-S 13:3, 1974.

365. McKinney, A. Cogged stones in private collections PCAS-Q 4:39-
     56, 1968.

366. Moorehead, W.K. Stone ornaments used by Indians in the United
     States and Canada. Andover. 1917.

367. Peabody, C. The so-called "plummets". Bull. of the Free
     Museum of Science and Art, Philadelphia 3:125-142, 1901.

368. Yates, L.G. Charm stones or "plummets" from California. USNM-
     AR 1886:296-305, 1889.

VIII. PETROGLYPHS AND PICTOGRAPHS

369. Anonymous. Giant etchings on California desert sands. Literary
     Digest. Nov. 12, 1932.
     [Blythe gravel figures]

370. _____Tule Lake petroglyphs believed not ancient. The March
     Of Pine 5:5; Klamath Falls, Oregon, 1948.

371. _____Tattooed rocks off U.S. 395. Sunset Magazine, Decem-
     ber 1953.

372. _____Pictograph site, Carrizo Plain. Sunset Magazine,
     December 3, 1955.

373. _____Educator studies carving on stone in Lassen Canyon.
     The Sacramento Bee, Dec. 25, 1957.
     [One photo. Headwaters of the Smoke Creek area]

374. _____Near Santa Barbara...pictographs inside a cave. Sunset
     Magazine, Nov. 1957.

375. _____Rock carvings in Bishop area lure visitors. Los
     Angeles Times. Vol. 77:1A:14, 1958.

376. _____Museum gets San Nicolas petroglyph. SM-M 36:36, 1962.

377. Anonymous. Petroglyph loop trip. Desert Magazine 26(8):8-9, 1963.

378. _____Unlocking the secrets graven on Mojave rock. Sunset Magazine, Oct. 1969.
[Renegade Canyon, Inyo County]

379. Apostolides, A. Swansea glyph site photo salvage operation. ASASC-N 8(2):11-12, 1961.

380. Armer, L.A. Ancient pictures on rocks pose questions. California Highways and Public Works 31:50-56, 1952.
[Walker Pass]

381. Arnold, H.H. Who drew these giants along the Colorado? Touring Topics, November:20-21, 1932.
[Reprinted in Westways 51:20-21, 1959]

382. Battye, C. Maize was always there. In Letter to Editor, Desert Magazine, Nov. 1941.
[Resident in the Needles area in 1880's, and a respected source of historical information]

383. Begole, R.S. The pictographs and figurine of Piedras Grandes. PCAS-Q 9:52-54, 1973.

384. Belden, L.B. Prehistoric man left his story carved in rock. San Bernardino Sun-Telegram, May 22, 1955.
[Black and Inscription Canyons, northwest of Barstow]

385. Blake, W.P. Railroad Reports 5:116-118, 1857.
[Trails and ground figures near Yuma]

386. Bloomquist, R.A. Trail to McCoy Spring. Desert Magazine, p. 8, December, 1969.

387. Bock, F.G. Visit to Big and Little Petroglyph Canyons. SBCMA-Q 16(3), 1969.
[China Lake area]

388. Bock, F. and A.J. The signs that man was here. SM-M 46:47-60, 1972.

389. _____ Eisen's enigma. SM-M 48:44-58, 1974.
[Mohave Desert]

390. Brandt, J.C., R.S. Harrington and M.M. Kennedy. A Northern California pictograph that may be another record of the Crab Nebula Supernova explosion. Bulletin American Astronomical Society 3:319, 1975.

391. Bruff, J.G. Indian engravings on the face of rocks along Green River Valley in the Sierra Nevada range of mountains. SI-AR 1872:409, 1873.
[N. of Honey Lake and La Fontanelle Cr., Lassen County]

392. Bruff, J.G. Gold rush. Columbia University Press, 1944.
     [Reprint of Bruff, 1873, with one additional illustration]

393. Chittenden, N.J. Prehistoric rock paintings, etchings and pic-
     tographs in California, Arizona, and New Mexico. Overland
     Monthly 42:106-110, 1903.

394. Clements, L. Pictographs discovered in Death Valley, California.
     SM-M 32:108-110, 1958.

395. Curtis, F. A preliminary report on Black Canyon material.
     ASASC-N 2(3):9-12, 1955.

396. Davis, E.L. The Mono Craters petroglyphs, California. A. Ant.
     27:236-239, 1961.

397. Davis, E.L. and S. Winslow. Giant round figures of the pre-
     historic deserts. Proceedings of the American Philosophi-
     cal Society 109:8-22, 1965.

398. Deetz, J. A datable Chumash pictograph from Santa Barbara
     County, California. A. Ant. 29:504-506, 1964.

399. Dunn, H.H. The prehistoric painter of Poway. Touring Topics,
     pp. 36-38,56, May 1930.
     [Petroglyph localities in San Diego County]

400. Eberhart, H. and A. Babcock. An archaeological survey of Matau
     Flat, Ventura County, California. ARA-CCA 5:1-17, 1963.
     [Excavation results and description of painted petro-
     glyphs]

401. Elsasser, A.B. A decorated stone implement from Mono County,
     California. UC-AS-R 38:7-9, 1957.

402. _____ Rock art on three continents. CAS-PD 29(2):15-20,
     1976.

403. Elsasser, A.B. and E. Contreras. Modern petrography in Central
     California and Western Nevada. UC-AS-R 41:12-18, 1957.

404. Engelhardt, Z. San Luis Rey Mission. Barry, San Francisco,
     1921.
     [Quotes selection from Diary of Fr. Sanchez, Sept. 1821,
     about pictographs along Pala Creek, possibly in the
     Pechanga Reservation]

405. Fenenga, F. Methods of recording and present status of know-
     ledge concerning petroglyphs in California. UC-AS-R 3,
     1949.

406. Finley, R.S. Note on the Orizaba Pictograph (Olson's) Cave,
     Santa Cruz Island, Santa Barbara, California. NSS-MRSG
     1:2-3, 1951.

407. Fleshman, G.L. Pit and groove rocks and cupules in San Luis Obispo County. In Papers on the Chumash, SLOCAS-OP 9:89-115, 1975.

408. Frederick, M.C. Some Indian paintings. Land of Sunshine 15: 223-227, Los Angeles, 1901.

409. Gallenkamp, C. Where ancients wrote in stone. Desert Magazine 18(5):16-18, 1955.

410. Gibson, R.O. and C.A. Singer. Ven-195: Treasure house of pre-historic cave art. UCLA-AS-AR 12:163-183, 1970.

411. Gorsline, E.P. Artist to the rescue. Desert Magazine 22(9): 23-24, 1959.

412. _____ Petroglyphs in peril. Natural History 48(2):110-112, 1959.

413. Grafton, L.O. A newly discovered petroglyph canyon. ASASC-N 2(1):2-6, 1954.

414. Grafton, H.W. and L.O. Some petroglyphs from a small site in the Coso Valley. ASASC-N 3(4):11, 1956.

415. Grant, C. Prehistoric painting of the Santa Barbara Region. SBMNH-MT 35:29-34, 1960.

416. _____ Ancient art in the wilderness. CAS-PD 14(4):12-19, 1961.

417. _____ Facsimile of Indian pictograph in Cuyama Area. SBMNH-AR, 1961.

418. _____ The cave paintings of the Chumash. Arts 36:38-40, New York, 1962.

419. _____ California's cave paintings. Desert Magazine 27(5): 16-20, 1964.

420. _____ Rock painting in California. IPEK (Jahrbuck für Prä-historische und Ethnographische Kunst) 21:84-90, 1964/65. Berlin.

421. _____ The rock paintings of the Chumash: prehistoric rock art of the Santa Barbara Region. Art Gallery, University of California, Santa Barbara, 1965.

422. _____ Rock art of the American Indians. Thomas Y. Crowell, N.Y. 1967. [Chap. 14]

423. _____ Rock art in California. In The California Indians, edited by R.F. Heizer and M.A. Whipple, 1971.

424. Grant, C., J.W. Baird, and J.K. Pringle. Rock drawings of the Coso Range. Maturango Museum, Publ. No. 4. China Lake, California, 1968.

425. Gruber, A. A Survey of petroglyphs in Black Canyon. SM-M 35: 108-115, 1961.

426. Haenszel, A. Keyhole Canyon. ASASC-N 17(2):22-39, 1970.

427. Haney, T. Treasure and art in Pinto Wash. Desert Magazine, p. 8, Feb. 1968.

428. Harnden, F.W. Indian pictographs in Pate Valley. Sierra Club Bulletin 6:258-259, 1908.

429. Harner, M.J. Gravel pictographs of the Lower Colorado River region. UC-AS-R 20:1-32, 1953.

430. Hedges, K. Rock art in Southern California. PCAS-Q 9:1-28, 1973.

431. Heizer, R.F. Sacred rain-rocks of Northern California. UC-AS-R 20:33-38, 1953.

432. Heizer, R.F. and M.A. Baumhoff. Prehistoric rock art of Nevada and Eastern California. U.C. Press, Berkeley, 1962. [Reprinted 1975]

433. Heizer, R.F. and C.W. Clewlow. Prehistoric rock art of California. Ballena Press, Ramona, 1973.

434. Henderson, R. Giant desert figures have been restored. Desert Magazine 20(11):5-8, 1957.

435. Hilton, J.W. Mystery of Jake Abram's lost wagon. Desert Magazine, p. 19, Dec. 1945. [Death Valley's Cottonwood Canyon, with photographs of petroglyphs]

436. Hintz, H.L. The records of a forgotten race: Hieroglyphics carved on Modoc stone bluff leave inscrutable Indian tales. The Fresno Bee. October 7, 1928.

437. Hoffman, W.J. Comparison of Eskimo pictographs with those of other American aborigines. Transactions of the Anthropological Society of Washington 2:128-146, 1883.

438. _____ Remarks on aboriginal art in California and Queen Charlotte's Island. Proceedings of the Davenport Academy of Natural Science 4:105-115, 1886.

439. Hoover, R. An unusual Chumash pictograph. UC-AS-R 71:117-119, 1968.

440. Hotz, V. and C.W. Clewlow. A Northern California petroglyph site. SM-M 48:148-152, 1974.

441. Irwin, M.C. Petroglyphs near Santa Barbara. SBMNH-MT 25:1-5, 1950.

442. Jackson, G.F. The China Lake petroglyphs. CAS-PD 22(3):23-27, 1969.

443. Johnston, P. Prehistoric pageantry in stone. Touring Topics 26:8-9,36, 1933.

444. Kamerling, B. The petroglyphs of Pinto Canyon. PCAS-Q 9:47-51, 1973.

445. Kelly, C. Murals painted by ancient tribesmen. Desert Magazine 13(8):11-12, 1950.

446. Kettl, J.W. Project petroglyph. SM-M 36:15-22, 1962.

447. Klette, W. Petroglyphs, pictographs and photography. Desert Magazine 34(6):16-19, 1971.

448. LaMonk, C.S. Pictograph Cave, Burro Flats. ASASC-N 1(2):8-9, 1953.

449. Lathrap, D.W. A distinctive pictograph from the Carrizo Plains, San Luis Obispo County. UC-AS-R 9:20-26, 1950.

450. Lawbaugh, A.L.V. Sacred mountain of the tribesmen. Desert Magazine 14(1):18-21, 1950.

451. Leadabrand, R. Day in Greenwater Canyon. Desert Magazine 18:16-18, 1955.
[Petroglyphs at "Indian Caves", Death Valley]

452. _____ Treasure canyon of the Coso ancients. Desert Magazine 19(2):26-28, 1956.
[Petroglyphs in China Lake(?) and Coso Range]

453. _____ Painted rock of Carrizo Plain. Westways, pp. 28-29, Sept. 1958.

454. _____ Let's explore a byway: Petroglyph country. Westways 63(3):9-12, 1971.
[Owens Valley and parts of Nevada along U.S. Hwy. 6]

455. _____ Rock art of the Coso Mountains. Desert Magazine 37(2):22-27, 1974.

456. Loew, O. Notes upon the ethnology of Southern California and adjacent regions. USGS-WCM 14:321-327, 1876.

457. Lyman, F. Indian signs (at site SBa-509). San Francisco _Examiner_, Sept. 1 and 4, 1930.

458. MacDougall, D.T. A decade of the Salton Sea. Geographical Review 3:457-473, 1917.
[Travertine Point petroglyph, Imperial County]

459. McDonald, P.M. Petroglyphs in the Lava Beds. Desert Magazine p. 12, Dec. 1967.

460. Mallery, G. Pictographs of North American Indians, 1882-1883. BAE-AR (1882-83):13-256, 1886.

461. _____Picture-writing of the American Indians. BAE-AR 1888-1889:52-72,638, 1893.

462. Marshall, G.C. Giant effigies of the Southwest. National Geographic Magazine, Vol. 102:389, 1952.

463. Mayer, D. Star patterns in Great Basin petroglyphs. In. A. Aveni, Archaeoastronomy in pre-Columbian America, pp. 109-130. Univ. of Texas Press, Austin, 1975.
[Cited here because it refers to seven California counties - not for its scientific value]

464. Mead, G.R. Rock art north of the Mexican-American border: An annotated bibliography. Colorado State College Museum of Anthropology Occasional Papers in Anthropology. Archaeology Series 5, Greeley, 1968.

465. Minor, R. Known origins of rock paintings of Southwestern California. PCAS-Q 9:29-36, 1973.

466. _____The pit and groove petroglyph style in Southern California. SDM-ETN 15, 1975.

467. Mitchell, R. Inside China Lake. Desert Magazine, p. 22, Feb. 1968.

468. Momyer, G.R. Indian picture writings in Southern California: Where to find them. San Bernardino, 1937.

469. Morrison, A.L. The painted rocks of the Carisa (Carrizo Plains). National Motorist, January 30, 1926.

470. Orcutt, C.R. Indian carvings. West American Scientist 5:9-10, 1888.

471. Painter, F. The Bear Mountain pictographs. The Chesopiean 10 (5):173-179, 1972.

472. Payen, L.A. Petroglyphs of Sacramento and adjoining counties, California. UC-AS-R 48:66-93, 1959.

473. Payen, L.A. A note on cupule sculptures in exogene caves from the Sierra Nevada, California. Caves and Karst 10:33-40, Castro Valley, 1968.

474. Payen, L.A. and D.S. Boloyan. "Tco'se" An archaeological study of the bedrock mortar-petroglyph at Ama-14, near Volcano, California. CDPR-AR 8, 1963.

475. Peck, S.L. An unusual petroglyph location. ASASC-N 1(2):6-7, 1953.

476. Pederson, C. Inscription Canyon: A report on the petroglyphs of Black Canyon. ASASC-N 3(2):9-27, 1956.

477. Pepper, C. Petroglyphs, mystery of the Southwest. Desert Magazine, p. 22, Nov. 1963.
[A discussion comparing designs from different parts of the Southwest including California sites]

478. Pepper, J. Mysterious cargo muchachos. Desert Magazine, p. 23, Jan. 1969.
[Photos of petroglyphs and trails in Indian Pass]

479. Pori, M. and Heizer, R.F. An attempt at computer analysis determination of California rock art styles. UC-C-ARF 20: 102-130, 1974.

480. Redtfeldt, G. Painted Rock site, Little Lake, California. ASASC-N 9(2):4-5, 1962.

481. Rozaire, C.E. Pictographs at Burro Flats. Ventura County Historical Society Quarterly 4(2):2-6, 1959.

482. Rozaire, C.E. and G. Kritzman. A petroglyph cave on San Nicolas Island. SM-M 34:147-151, 1960.

483. Sanburg, D.E. The Azusa Canyon pictograph site: LAn-164. California Anthropologist 1(1):73-83, 1971.

484. _____ A pictograph site near Los Angeles. SM-M 46:18-26, 1972.

485. Schoolcraft, H.R. A copy, by R.H. Kern, of an Indian drawing found on the trunk of a cottonwood tree in the valley of Kings River, California, which "evidently represents the manner of catching different wild animals with the lasso". Indian Tribes of the United States 4:252-253; plate 33, 1854.

486. Schumacher, G. Loop of the magic stone carvings. Westways, p. 26, Oct. 1961.
[The petroglyph "loop" north of Bishop: Photographs]

487. Schwacofer, L. Mystery of Black Canyon. The Grizzly Bear 78: 465, 1946.

488. Setzler, F.M. and Stewart, R.H. Seeking the secret of the giants. Nat. Geog. Magazine, vol. 102:390-404, 1952. [Giant effigies near Blyth]

489. Smith, G.A., et al. Indian picture writing of San Bernardino and Riverside Counties. SBCMA-Q 8(3):1-36, 1961.

490. Smith, V. Sheep hunting artist of Black Canyon walls. Desert Magazine, March 1944.

491. Speer, M.A. Western Trails. Huntington Beach, Calif., 1931. [P. 173, anthropomorphic figure in Topock "Maze"]

492. Steward, J.H. Rock writing. Touring Topics, May 1927.

493. _____ Petroglyphs of California and adjoining states. UC-PAAE 24:47-238, 1929.

494. _____ Petroglyphs of the United States. SI-AR 1936: 405-426, 1937.

495. Strong, W.D. Review of Petroglyphs of California and adjoining states, by J. Steward. AA 33:427-430, 1931.

496. Sullivan, E.Q. Prehistoric civilization along the Lower Colorado. Calif. Hwy's and Pub. Works, Feb.-Mar. 1928. [Topock "Maze" and Blyth ground figures]

497. Swift, R.H. Prehistoric paintings at Santa Barbara. SCAS-B 30:35-38, 1931.

498. Tatum, R.M. Distribution and bibliography of the petroglyphs of the United States. A. Ant. 12:122-125, 1946.

499. Taylor, F. Prehistoric pop at Coyote Hole. Desert Magazine, p. 31, Mar. 1967.

500. Thomas, D. Review of Rock drawings of the Coso Range, by Grant, Baird, and Pringle. AA 72:450-451, 1970.

501. Tripp, S. Rare picture writing found in Yosemite. YNN 13:26-27, 1934.

502. True, D.L. Pictographs of the San Luis Rey Basin, California. A. Ant. 20:68-72, 1954.

503. Turner, W., et al. Three essays on petroglyphology. SBCMA-Q 19(1), 1971.

504. Usher, F.A. Petroglyphs. Arts and Architecture 66:24-28, 1949.

505. Voegelin, C.F. Tübatulabal ethnography. UC-AR 2, 1938. [P. 58, pictographs]

506. Von Blon, J.C. Rock writings in Owen's Valley. Touring Topics 21:5:14-17, 1929.

507. von Werlhof, J.C. End of an Eon. CAS-PD 11(6):4-9, 1958.

508. _____ Petroglyph and pictograph sites in Eastern California and Southern Nevada. Yearbook of the American Philosophical Society 1960:575-579, 1960.

509. _____ Rock art of Owens Valley, California. UC-AS-R 65, 1965.

510. Walker, A. Judas of the Kern. Westways, p. 10, Mar. 1958. [Story of historical Indian pictographs near Keysville in southern Sierra Nevada site, Ker-19]

511. Walker, H. Rock art in the Coso Range. Desert Magazine 37(9): 26-29, 1974.

512. Waterman, T.T. The religious practices of the Diegueño Indians. UC-PAAE 8:271-358, 1910. [P. 293, rock paintings]

513. Weight, H.O. On Turtle Mountain trails. Desert Magazine, p. 23, July 1948. [Petroglyph photographs, map, environmental material for sites SBr 170-171]

514. _____ Puzzle rocks of the badlands. Desert Magazine 15: 18-22, 1952.

515. _____ Rock of the people from the sea. Westways, p. 18, May 1955. [The Hemet Maze in Reinhardt Canyon, Riv-20]

516. _____ Hidden Gold of Bicuner. Desert Magazine 18(6):10-13, 1955.

517. Whipple, A.W., et al. Indian pictographs. Pacific Railroad Reports 3:36-39, 1856.

518. Whitaker, K. Analytical interpretations of petroglyphs. SM-M 43:132-143, 1969.

519. Woodward, A. Gigantic intaglio pictographs in the Californian Desert. Illust. London News, Sept. 10:378-380, 1932.

520. Yates, L.G. Indian pictographs in California. Overland Monthly 28:657-661, 1896.

IX. CAVES AND ROCKSHELTERS

521. Baumhoff, M.A. Excavation of site Teh-1 (Kingsley Cave). UC-AS-R 30:40-73, 1955.

522. Beatty, M.E. More Indian caves discovered. YNN 12:7-8, 1933.

523. Bell, L. Victims of civilization. California Monthly 44(2): 12-46, 1953.

524. Bowers, S. A report on a cave in the San Martin Mountains. Pacific Science Monthly 4:1-7, 1885.

525. Elsasser, A. and Heizer, R.F. The archaeology of Bowers Cave, Los Angeles County, California. UC-AS-R 59:1-59, 1963.

526. Farmer, M.F. Tracing early man in Western Caves. Hobbies 40: 102-106, 1936.

527. Fenenga, F. and F.A. Riddell. Excavation of Tommy Tucker Cave, Lassen County, California. A. Ant. 14:203-213, 1949.

528. Harrington, M.R. A storage cave near Walker Pass (Kern Co.). SM-M 24:89-90, 1950.

529. Heizer, R.F. A cave burial in Kern County. UC-AS-R 10:22-36, 1951.

530. _____ A survey of cave archaeology in California. UC-AS-R 15:1-12, 1952.

531. Hilton, J. Crystals along shores of Salton Sea. Desert Magazine, p. 17, March 1940.
[Site at Hwy. 111 and Salt Cr. Wash, which contains shelter caves]

532. Lewis, W.S. Caverns of the Mohave. Rocks and Minerals 12:67-68, 1937.

533. Meighan, C.W. The Coville Rockshelter, Inyo County, California. UC-AR 12:171-224, 1953.

534. _____ Excavation of Isabella Meadows Cave, Monterey County, California. UC-AS-R 29:1-30, 1955.

535. Moseley, M. A small cave in Morongo Valley - El Grieta. SBCMA-Q 3:20-22, 1955.

536. Orr, P.C. Cave man hunt. SBMNH-MT 26:30-35, 1951.
[Cave of the Skulls, Vallecito and Moaning Cave]

537. Payen, L.A. A note on cupule sculptures in exogene caves from the Sierra Nevada, California. Caves and Karst 10(4): 33-39, Castro Valley, 1968.

538. Riddell, F.A. Final report on the archaeology of Tommy Tucker Cave. UC-AS-R 35:1-24, 1956.

539. Ryker, B.L. Silver Valley. Desert Magazine, p. 17, April 1966.

540. Short, H.W. The geology of Moaning Cave, Calaveras County, California. California Geology, California State Division of Mines and Geology, Sacramento, pp. 195-201. September 1975.

541. Smith, G.A. Preliminary report of the Schuiling Cave, Newberry, California. SBCMA-Q 3:2-12, 1955.

542. Smith, G.A., et al. Newberry cave, California. SBCMA-SS 1, 1957.

543. Van Valkenburgh, R. The rediscovery of Southern California's most famous Indian cave. Hobbies 12:93-95, 1934.

544. _____ We found the lost Indian cave of the San Martins. Desert Magazine 15:4-8, 1952.
[Bowers Cave]

545. Wallace, W.J. The mortuary caves of Calaveras County, California. Archaeology 4:199-203, 1951.

546. _____The archaeological deposit in Moaning Cave. UC-AS-R 12:29-39, 1951.

547. _____Rockshelter excavation in Death Valley National Monument. SM-M 31:144, 1957.

548. Wallace, W.J. and Lathrap, D.W. An early implement assemblage from a limestone cavern in California. A. Ant. 18:133-138, 1952.

549. Wallace, W.J. and Taylor, E.S. Excavation of Sis-13, a rock shelter in Siskiyou County, California. UC-AS-R 15:13-39, 1952.

550. Yarrow, H.C. A further contribution to the study of the mortuary customs of the North American Indians. BAE-AR 1879-80:87-203, 1881.

X. RAW MATERIALS AND SOURCES

551. Alliot, H. Pre-historic use of bitumen in Southern California. SCAS-B 41-44, 1917.
[Reprinted in SM-M 44:97-102, 1970]

552. Anonymous. Some of the ancient uses of asphaltum by the aborigines of California. Scientific American Supplement 994: 15085, 1894.

553. Belden, L.B. Jade mines of ancients found in desert area. San Bernardino Sun-Telegram, Feb. 12, 1961.

554. Berkolz, M.F. Toltec, Mohave Deseret [sic] mine of the ancients. Science of Man 1:10-11,34, 1960.

555. Dunn, H.H. Tracing the Pueblos to the Pacific. Touring Topics 22:48-50,53, 1930.
     [Turquoise mines]

556. Eisen, G. Long lost mines of precious gems [turquoise] are found again. San Francisco _Call_, March 18, 1927.

557. Farmer, M.F. An obsidian quarry near Coso Hot Springs, California. SM-M 11:7-9, 1937.

558. Grant, C. The Carpinteria tar pits. Santa Barbara Historical Society: Noticias 8:11-20, 1962.
     [Sources and uses of asphalt by the Santa Barbara Indians]

559. Harrington, M.R. A colossal quarry. SM-M 25:15-18, 1951.
     [Coso Hot Springs]

560. Heizer, R.F. Aboriginal use of bitumen by the California Indians. California State Division of Mines, Bulletin 118, Pt. 1, p. 74, 1940.

561. _____ Jade. Mineral Information Service 4:6. California State Division of Mines, 1951.
     [Occurrence of nephrite in Monterey County and its prehistoric use for hammer stones and cooking stones]

562. Heizer, R.F. and A.E. Treganza. Mines and quarries of the Indians of California. California Journal of Mines and Geology 40:291-359, 1944.

563. Hewett, D.F. Geology and mineral reserves of the Ivanpah quadrangle. USGS-P 275:165-166, 1956.
     [History of turquoise mining in Southern California]

564. Hilton, J. Turquoise on the Mojave. Desert Magazine, p. 9, Sept. 1938.
     [Turquoise Mountains]

565. Hohenthal, W.D. Southern Diegueño use and knowledge of lithic materials. KASP 2:9-15, 1950.

566. Lawbaugh, A.L.V. Where turquoise was mined by the ancients. Desert Magazine 14(10):9-12, 1951.

567. McGuire, J.D. Aboriginal quarries - soapstone bowls and the tools used in their manufacture. American Naturalist 17: 587-595, 1883.
     [Several references to California Indians]

568. Meighan, C.W. and Johnson, K.L. Isle of Mines: Catalina's ancient Indian quarries. CAS-PD 10(2):24-29, 1957.

569. Meighan, C.W. and Rootenberg, S. A prehistoric miner's camp on Catalina Island. SM-M 31:176-184, 1957.

570. Murdoch, J. and R.W. Webb. Minerals of California. California
      Division of Mines, Bulletin 136:13-15, 1948.
      [Ancient turquoise mines in the Halloran Springs area]

571. Rogers, M.J. California Indians mined turquoise. El Palacio
      27:185-186, 1929.

572. Schoolcraft, H.R. Evidence of ancient mining operations in
      California. Archives of Aboriginal Knowledge 1:105, 1860.

573. Schumacher, P. Ancient olla manufactory on Santa Catalina Is-
      land, California. American Naturalist 12:629, 1878.
      [See also his notes in PM-R 11:258-264, 1878]

574. Spencer, D.L. Notes on the Maidu Indians of Butte County.
      JAFL 21:242-245, 1908.
      [P. 243, obsidian mine at Table Mountain near Oroville;
      flint mines in Pinket Ravine, Plumas County]

575. Strong, M.B. Toltec revisited. Gems and Minerals, p. 19-22,
      Sept. 1963.
      [Ancient mines in Turquoise Mountains E. of Baker]

576. Walker, E.F. A prehistoric soapstone quarry. SM-M 9:178-180,
      1935.

577. Wallace, W.J. An aboriginal hematite quarry in Oakland, Calif-
      ornia. A. Ant. 12:272-273, 1947.

578. _____ Indian use of California's rocks and minerals.
      Journal of the West 10(1), 1971.

579. Weight, H.O. Mojave Desert opal diggings. Desert Magazine,
      p. 18, Nov. 1958.
      [Black and Inscription Canyons, near Barstow]

XI. TRADE AND TRAILS

580. Barber, E.A. Stone implements and ornaments from the ruins of
      Colorado, Utah, and Arizona. American Naturalist 11:
      264-275, 1877.

581. Berkholz, M.F. Golden Valley flower agate. Desert Magazine,
      p. 8, Dec. 1962.
      [Notes the intersection of two Indian trails in Golden
      Valley, between Blackwater Well and Johannesburg]

582. Brand, D.D. Southwestern trade in shell products. A. Ant. 2:
      300-302, 1937.

583. _____ Aboriginal trade routes for sea shells in the South-
      west. Yearbook of Association for Pacific Coast Geograph-
      ers 4:3-10, 1938.

584. Cooke, D.I. Indian trails. SBMNH-L 15:5-7, 1940.

585. Cox, S.C. An incident on the Old Road. Historical Society of
Southern California Annual, p. 258, 1925.
[Historical reference to an old Indian trail through
San Timoteo Canyon, then approximating California Hwy. 79,
from Beaumont via Hemet to Aguanga]

586. Davis, J.T. Trade routes and economic exchange among the Indians
of California. UC-AS-R 54, 1961.

587. Farmer, M.F. A Mojave trade route. SM-M 9:154-157, 1935.

588. Farrington, O.C. Dolomite used as Indian money, near Lakeport,
Lake County, California. New Mineral Occurrences: Field
Columbian Museum Publication No. 44, Geological Series 1:
230-231, 1900.

589. Fewkes, J.W. Pacific Coast shells from prehistoric Tusayan
pueblos. AA 9:359-367, 1896.

590. Gifford, E.W. Californian shell artifacts. UC-AR 9:1-132, 1947.
[Pp. 61-62, shell artifacts from California found in
ancient Anasazi sites]

591. _____ Early Central Californian and Anasazi shell artifact
types. A. Ant. 15:156-157, 1949.

592. Heizer, R.F. Aboriginal trade between the Southwest and California. SM-M 15:185-188, 1941.

593. _____The occurrence and significance of Southwestern
grooved axes in California. A. Ant. 11:187-193, 1946.

594. Heizer, R.F. and H. Rapoport. Identification of Distichlis
salt used by California Indians. SM-M 36:146-148, 1962.

595. Henderson, J. Ancient shell trade routes. The Nautilus 43:
109-110, 1930.

596. _____Old Indian waterhole. Desert Magazine, p. 10,
January 1954.
[Trail between Travertine Point and spring with palms to
west of it. Possible route from shore of Lake Cahuilla
into Santa Rosa Mts., for piñons]

597. Jackson, T.L. and P.D. Schulz. Typology, trade and trade analysis: a test of local manufacture of Sacramento Valley
obsidian tools. UCLA-JNWA 1:1-8, 1975.

598. Johnston, F.J. San Gorgonio Pass: Forgotten route of the
Californios. Journal of the West 8(1):125-136, 1969.
[Some material on Indian trail forerunners of a historical
and modern highway]

599. Johnston, F.J. and P.H. An Indian trail complex of the Central Colorado Desert: a preliminary survey. UC-AS-R 37:22-39, 1957.

600. Jones, L. Value of an ancient trail. Desert Magazine, p. 8-11, March 1966.
[Bee Rock Mesa, Riv-51,53,&54]

601. Latta, F.F. El Camino Viejo. Kern County Historical Society, Bakersfield, 1931.
[Indian trail, which became a historic trail, from Los Angeles to Oakland area, via Newhall, Lake Elizabeth, Lebec, San Emigdio, and up the Eastern foot of the Coast Range, recrossing the mountains via Livermore and Castro Valley]

602. Rogers, M.J. Aboriginal culture relations between Southern California and the Southwest. SDM-B 5:1-6, 1941.

603. Sample, L.L. Trade and trails in aboriginal California. UC-AS-R 8:1-30, 1950.

604. Schroeder, A.H. The significance of Willow Beach. Plateau 25:27-29, 1952.
[Trade route in ceramic times across Southern Calif.]

605. Stearns, R.E.C. Aboriginal shell ornaments, and Mr. E.A. Barber's paper thereon. American Naturalist 11:473-474, 1877.
[On trade in shells from California to the Southwest]

606. Tower, D.B. The use of marine mollusca and their value in re-constructing prehistoric trade routes in the American Southwest. Papers of the Excavators Club 2(3), 1945.

607. Van Dyke, D. Modern interpretation of the Garcés route. Historical Society of Southern California, Annual, p. 353, 1927.
[Field research on the Mojave Trail, location of rancherias, observations on the country involved]

608. Weaver, J.R. An Indian trail near Needles, California. UC-AS-R 70, p. 151-157, 1967.

609. Weight, H.O. Gold and roses on Garcés' trail. Desert Magazine, p. 8, Dec. 1950.
[Trail and shrine of E-Vee-Taw-Ash in Indian Pass]

610. _____Dark gold on the Tabaseca Trail. Desert Magazine 18(7):4-8, 1955.
["Indian trail", Riverside County]

611. _____Desert trails. Westways, p. 7, Oct. 1963.
[General discussion and good photograph of the Cocomaricopa Trail between Coachella Valley and the Colorado River]

612. Wilhelm, P. Trail of the fifty seven shrines. Desert Magazine 14(8):4-8, 1951.
[Description and photographs of the trail from Hidden Palms Oasis to Thousand Palms Oasis]

613. Wilkinson, V.P. Serrano old Indian trail. Desert Magazine 34(2):18-19, 1971.

XII. COMPOSITION OF ABORIGINAL SITES; DEMOGRAPHY

614. Ascher, R. A prehistoric population estimate using midden analysis. SWJA 15, 168-178, 1959.
[Zuma Creek site: LAn-174]

615. Chartkoff, J.L. Evaluating a midden sampling technique at the Big Tujunga site (LAn-167). UCLA-AS-AR 8:123-136, 1966.

616. Cook, S.F. The conflict between the California Indian and white civilization: I - IV. UC-IA 21-24, 1943.
[All reprinted by U.C. Press, Berkeley, 1976]

617. _____ A reconsideration of shellmounds with respect to population and nutrition. A. Ant. 12:50-53, 1946.

618. _____ Physical analysis as a method for investigating prehistoric occupation sites. UC-AS-R 7:2-5, 1950.

619. _____ The aboriginal population of Alameda and Contra Costa Counties, California. UC-AR 16:131-135, 1956.

620. _____ The aboriginal population of the North Coast of California. UC-AR 16:81-130, 1956.

621. _____ The nature of charcoal excavated at archaeological sites. A. Ant. 29:514-417, 1964.

622. _____ The population of the California Indians, 1769-1970. U.C. Press, Berkeley, 1976.

623. Cook, S.F. and R.F. Heizer. The quantitative investigation of aboriginal sites; analyses of human bones. AJPA 5:201-220, 1947.

624. _____ Chemical analysis of the Hotchkiss Site (CCo-138). UC-AS-R 57:1-25, 1962.

625. _____ The quantitative approach to the relation between population and settlement size. UC-AS-R 64, 1965.

626. _____ Relationships among houses, settlement areas and population in aboriginal California. In K.C. Chang (Ed.), Settlement archaeology, pp. 79-116. National Press, 1968.

41

627. Cook, S.F. and A.E. Treganza. The quantitative investigation of aboriginal sites: comparative physical and chemical analysis of two California Indian mounds. A. Ant. 13: 135-141, 1947.

628. Deetz, J. and E. Dethlefsen. Soil pH as a tool in archaeological site interpretation. A. Ant. 29:242-243, 1963.

629. Downs, T. and H. Howard. Summary of vertebrate remains. SBCMA-Q 3(2), 1955.
[Schuiling Cave, Newberry, California]

630. Drover, C.E. Seasonal exploitation of Chione clams on the Southern California coast. JCA 1(2):224-232, 1974.

631. Fitch, J.E. Fish remains recovered from a Corona Del Mar, California, Indian midden. PCAS-Q 6(2,3), 1970.

632. Follett, W.I. Fish remains from a shellmound in Marin County, California. A. Ant. 23:68-71, 1957.

633. _____ Fish remains from the Century Ranch Site (LAn-227), Los Angeles County, California. UCLA-AS-AR 5:259-319, 1963.

634. _____ Fish remains from Arroyo Sequit Shellmound (LAn-52), Los Angeles County, California. CDPR-AR 9, (Appendix), 1963.

635. _____ Fish remains from a sixteenth century site on Drake's Bay, California. UCLA-AS-AR 6:27-46, 1946.

636. _____ Fish remains from the Conejo Rock Shelter Site (Ven-69), Ventura County, California. UCLA-AS-AR 7:81-90, 1965.

637. _____ Fish remains from archaeological sites at Irvine, Orange County, California. UCLA-AS-AR 8:185-195, 1966.

638. _____ Fish remains from two submerged deposits in Tomales Bay, Marin County, California. CAS-OP 67(2), 1968.

639. _____ Fish remains from Century Ranch Site, LAn-229, Los Angeles County, California. UCLA-AS-AR 10:132-143, 1968.

640. _____ Fish remains from Mission La Soledad cemetery (Mnt-233), Monterey County, California. Monterey County Archaeological Society Quarterly 1(3):11, 1972.

641. Fredrickson, D.A. Technological change, population movement, environmental adaptation, and the emergence of trade: Inferences on culture change suggested by midden constituent analysis. UCLA-AS-AR 11:101-126, 1969.

642. Gifford, E.W. Composition of California shellmounds. UC-PAAE 12:1-29, 1916.

643. _____ Diet and the age of California shellmounds. A. Ant. 14:223-224, 1949.

644. Graham, T. Bone remains from the Kodani site. Monterey County Archaeological Soc. Quarterly 1(4):10-11, 1972.

645. Greengo, R.E. Molluscan species in California shell middens. UC-AS-R 13:1-23, 1951.

646. Greenwood, R.S. Quantitative analysis of shells from a site in Goleta, California. A. Ant. 26:416-420, 1961.

647. Heizer, R.F. California population densities, 1770 and 1959. UC-AS-R 50:9-12, 1960.

648. Heizer, R.F. and S.F. Cook. Some aspects of the quantitative approach in archaeology. SWJA 12:229-248, 1956.

649. Henn, W.G. Faunal analysis at 4-Mrn-216, a seasonal site on Limantour Sandspit, Point Reyes National Seashore. SFSC-TAMP 6:195-210, 1972, (1970).

650. Hester, T.R. The formation of a "burned rock midden": A California example. The Record 29(3): Dallas Archaeological Society, 1973.

651. Howard, D.M. Invertebrate remains from the Kodani site. Monterey County Arch. Soc. Quarterly 1(4):8-9, 1972.

652. Kennedy, K.A.R. The aboriginal population of the Great Basin. UC-AS-R 45:1-84, 1959.

653. Koloseike, A. The logic of midden analysis with respect to shell. UCLA-AS-AR 10:371-382, 1968.

654. _____ On calculating the prehistoric food resource value of molluscs. UCLA-AS-AR 11:143-160, 1969.

655. _____ Costs of shell analysis. A. Ant. 35(4):475-479, 1970.

656. Koloseike, A. and M. Peterson. Macro-column shell analysis. UCLA-AS-AR 5:439-462, 1963.
[Site SDi-603]

657. Loud, L.L. Ethnogeography and archaeology of the Wiyot territory. UC-PAAE 14:221-436, 1918.
[Composition of Humboldt Bay sites, pp. 349-356]

658. Martin, P.S. and F.W. Sharrock. Pollen analysis of prehistoric human feces: a new approach to ethnobotany. A. Ant. 30:168, 1964.

659. Morse, E.S. Shell-mounds and the changes in shells composing them. Scientific Monthly 21(4):429-440, 1925.

660. Schulz, P.D. Solar burial orientation and paleodemography in the Central California Windmiller Tradition. In Papers on California and Great Basin Prehistory. CARD Pub. No. 2, 1970.

661. Treganza, A.E. and S.F. Cook. The quantitative investigation of aboriginal sites: complete excavation with physical and archaeological analysis of a single mound. A. Ant. 13:287-297, 1948.

662. Warren, C.N. and M.G. Pavesic. Shell midden analysis of site SDi-603 and ecological implications for cultural development of Batiquitos lagoon, San Diego County, California. UCLA-AS-AR 5:407-438, 1963.

663. Weide, D.L. Soil pH as a guide to archaeological investigation. UCLA-AS-AR 8:151-164, 1966.

664. Wilson, S.C. Faunal analysis of 4-Mrn-298E: A perspective on 4-Mrn-216. SFSC-TAMP 6:211-221, 1972 (1970).

XIII. CHRONOLOGY: RADIOCARBON, BONE ANALYSIS, SOILS

665. Anonymous. La Brea samples dated. University of California: Bulletin 9:134-135, 1961.

666. Anonymous. UCLA and Los Angeles County Museum scientists find skeleton to be 9,000 years old with dating method. University of California: Bulletin 18:97-98, 1970.

667. Anonymous. Scientific redating of human bones. University of California: Bulletin 22(35):182, 1974. [Amino-acid dating of San Diego Paleo-Indian skull, dated at approx. 50,000 years BP]

668. Antevs, E. Comments on dating of Pluvial lakes in the Great Basin. AJS 251:237, 1935.

669. _____ Age of artifacts below peat bed in Lower Klamath Lake, California. Carnegie Institution of Washington, Yearbook 39:307, 1940.

670. _____ On division of the last 20,000 years. UC-AS-R 22: 5-8, 1953.

671. _____ The postpluvial or neothermal. UC-AS-R 22:9-23, 1953.

672. _____ Geologic-climate dating in the west. A. Ant. 20:325-328, 1955.

673. Bada, J.L. Amino acids and their use in dating fossil bone.

San Diego Society of Natural History: Environment Southwest No. 448:1-4, 1972.

674. Bada, J.L. and R. Protsch. Racemization reaction of aspartic acid and its use in dating fossil bones. Proceedings of the National Academy of Sciences 70(5):1331-1334, 1973.

675. Bada, J.L. et al. New evidence for the antiquity of man in North America deduced from aspartic acid racemization. Science 184:791-793, 1974.
[Laguna skull, Los Angeles Man, four other sets of remains tested - authors suggest man present in new world 50,000 years BP]

676. Barbour, E.P. A Study of the structure of fresh and fossil human bone by means of the electron microscope. AJPA n.s. 8:315-330, 1950.
[Bones from Topanga Canyon, Southern California]

677. Baumhoff, M.A. and J.S. Byrne. Desert side - notched points as a time marker in California. UC-AS-R 48:32-65, 1959.

678. Belous, R.E. The Central California chronological sequence re-examined. A. Ant. 18:341-353, 1953.
[Application of the Brainerd-Robinson method]

679. Borden, F.W. The use of surface erosion observations to determine chronological sequence in artifacts from a Mojave Desert site. ASASC-P 7, 1971.

680. Brainerd, G.W. A re-examination of the dating evidence for the Lake Mohave artifact assemblage. A. Ant. 18:270-271, 1953.

681. Bright, M. California radiocarbon dates. UCLA-AS-AR 7:363-376, 1965.

682. Carter, G.F. On soil color and time. SWJA 12:295-324, 1956.
[Southern California sites]

683. Clark, D.L. Archaeological chronology in California and the obsidian hydration method: Part I. UCLA-AS-AR 6:139-228, 1964.

684. Cook, S.F. and R.F. Heizer. The fossilization of bone: Organic components and water. UC-AS-R 17, 1952.

685. _____The present status of chemical methods for dating prehistoric bone. A. Ant. 18:354-358, 1953.

686. Cressman, L.S. Western prehistory in the light of carbon-14 dating. SWJA 7:289-313, 1951.

687. Cruxent, J.M. Phosphorus content of the Texas Street "hearths". A. Ant. 28:90-91, 1962.

688. Dixon, K.A. A brief report on radiocarbon and obsidian hydra-
     tion measurements from Ora-58, Orange County, California.
     PCAS-Q 6(4), 1970.

689. Ericson, J.E. and R. Berger. Late Pleistocene American obsid-
     ian tools. Nature 249:824-825, 1974.

690. Ezra, H.C. and Cook, S.F. Amino acids in fossil human bone.
     Science 126:80, 1957.
     [Loss and retention of certain amino acids after burial
     for various lengths of time]

691. Friedman, I., R.L. Smith and D. Clark. Obsidian dating. In
     Science and archaeology, D. Brothwell and E. Higgs, eds.,
     pp. 47-58. Thames & Hudson, London, 1963.

692. Gifford, E.W. Diet and age of the California shellmounds.
     A. Ant. 14:223-224, 1949.

693. Hare, P.E. Amino acid dating - a history and an evaluation.
     MASCA Newsletter 10(1), Philadelphia, 1974.
     [Discussion of J.L. Bada's work, etc.]

694. Harradine, F. Report on pedologic observations made at the
     "Capay Man" site in Western Yolo County. UC-AS-R 22:27,
     1953.

695. Haury, E.W. The stratigraphy and archaeology of Ventana Cave,
     Arizona. Albuquerque, University of New Mexico Press,
     1950.
     [Correlations with Southern California cultures]

696. Heizer, R.F. On the methods of chemical analysis of bone as an
     aid to prehistoric culture chronology. UC-AS-R 7:10-14,
     1950.

697. _____ Archaeology of CCo-137, the Concord Man site. UC-
     AS-R 9:6-19, 1950.

698. _____ An assessment of certain Nevada, California and
     Oregon radiocarbon dates. A. Ant. 17:23-25, 1951.

699. _____ Radiocarbon dates from California of archaeological
     interest. UC-AS-R 44:1-16, 1958.

700. _____ Problems in dating Lake Mohave artifacts. SM-M 39:
     125-134, 1965.

701. Heizer, R.F. and S.F. Cook. Archaeology of Central California:
     A comparative analysis of human bone from nine sites. UC-
     AR 12:2, 1949.

702. _____ Flourine and other chemical tests of some
     North American human and fossil bones. AJPA 10:289-303,
     1952.

703. Ho, T.Y., L.F. Marcus, and R. Berger. Radiocarbon dating of petroleum impregnated bone from tar pits at Rancho LaBrea, California. Science 164:1051-1052, 1969.

704. Hoover, R.L. Chumash typologies for dating and computer analysis. SLOCAS 2, 1971.

705. Howard, H. Significance of Carbon-14 dates for Rancho LaBrea. Science 131:712-714, 1960.

706. Hubbs, C.L. A discussion of the geochronology and archaeology of the California Islands. In Proceedings of the symposium on the biology of the California Islands, pp. 337-341, Santa Barbara, 1967.

707. Johnson, L. Obsidian hydration rate for the Klamath Basin of California and Oregon. Science 165:1354-1356, 1969.

708. Martin, P.S. and P.J. Mehringer. Pleistocene pollen analysis and biogeography of the Southwest. In The Quaternary of the United States, pp. 433-451, 1965.

709. Meighan, C.W. and C.V. Haynes. New studies on the age of the Borax Lake site. SM-M 42:4-9, 1968.

710. Michels, J.W. A progress report on the UCLA Obsidian Hydration Dating Laboratory. UCLA-AS-AR 7:377-388, 1965.

711. _____ Testing stratigraphy and artifact reuse through obsidian hydration. A. Ant. 34(1):15-22, 1969.

712. Moriarty, J.R. Culture phase divisions suggested by typological change, coordinated with stratigraphically controlled radiocarbon dating at San Diego. Anthropological Journal of Canada 4:20-21, 1966.

713. Oakley, K. Relative dating of Arlington Springs Dam. Science 141:1172, 1963.

714. Orr, P.C. Geochronology of Santa Rosa Island, California. In R.N. Philbrick (Ed.), p. 317-325, Proceedings of the symposium on the biology of the California Islands. Santa Barbara, 1967.

715. Owen, R.C. Early Milling Stone Horizon (Oak Grove), Santa Barbara County, California: Radiocarbon dates. A. Ant. 30: 210-213, 1964.

716. Ritter, E.W. and R.G. Matson. Form categories, cluster analysis and multidimensional scaling: A case study of projectile points. Southwestern Lore 37(4):102-116, 1972.

717. Shepard, F.P. Sea level changes in the past 6,000 years: possible archaeological significance. Science 143:574-576, 1964.

718. Storie, R.E. and F. Harradine. An age estimate of the burials unearthed near Concord, California, based on pedologic observations. In R.F. Heizer, Archaeology of CCo-137, the Concord Man site. UC-AS-R 9:15-19, 1950.

719. Warren, C.N. and J. DeCosta. Dating Lake Mohave artifacts and beaches. A. Ant. 30:206-209, 1964.

720. Woodward, J.A. and A.F. Woodward. The Carbon-14 dates from Lake Mohave. SM-M 40:96-102, 1966.

721. Wright, R.H. Map showing locations of samples dated by radiocarbon methods in the San Francisco Bay Region. U.S. Dept. Interior, Geological Survey: Basic Data Contribution No. 33, Menlo Park, 1971.

XIV. EARLY MAN

722. Amsden, C.A. The Pinto Basin artifacts. In E.W.C. and W.H. Campbell, pp. 33-51, (see No. 749), 1935.

723. Angel, J.L. Early skeletons from Tranquility, California. SI-CK 2(1), 1966.

724. Anonymous. Researches of M.R. Harrington. Carnegie Institution of Washington, Yearbook 37:345-347, 1938.

725. Anonymous. "Tools" made by nature. Science News Letter, Oct. 6, 1956.

726. Antevs, E. Age of the Lake Mohave Culture. In Campbell, E.W.C. et al, pp. 45-50, (see No. 751), 1937.

727. _____ Climate and early man in North America. In Early Man, Ed. by G.G. MacCurdy, p. 125-132, 1937.
[Pp. 126-129, Lake Mohave culture dating]

728. _____ Age of artifacts below peat bed at Lower Klamath Lake, California. Carnegie Institution of Washington, Yearbook 39:307-309, 1940.

729. _____ Climatic history and the antiquity of man in California. UC-AS-R 16:23-31, 1952.
[Lake Mohave, Pinto, Borax Lake complexes]

730. Ayres, W.O. The ancient man of Calaveras. American Naturalist 16:845-854, 1882.

731. Bancroft, H.H. The native races of the Pacific States of North America. Vol. IV. San Francisco, 1875.
[Pp. 697-708, mention of a large number of finds of artifacts in auriferous gravels. Important in that he cites contemporary newspaper notices of such discoveries]

732. Barbieri, J.A. Technique of the implements from Lake Mohave. In Campbell, E.W.C. et al, pp. 99-108, (see No. 751), 1937.

733. Becker, G.F. Antiquities from under Tuolumne Table Mountain in California. GSA-B 2:189-200, 1891.

734. Belden, L. 50,000 years ago. Desert Magazine, p. 8, Dec. 1968. [Reprinted in SBCMA-Q 19, 1968]

735. Black, W.P. Notice of a human skull found at depth of 250 feet below surface near Columbia, Tuolumne County. CAS-P 3: 291, 1868.

736. _____The Pliocene Skull of California and flint implements of Table Mountain. Journal of Geology 7:631-637, 1889.

737. Bode, F.D. Geology of the Lake Mohave outlet channel. In Campbell, E.W.C. et al, pp. 109-118, (see No. 751), 1937.

738. Boule, M. Découverte d'un squelette humain dans les asphaltes de Rancho LaBrea (Californie). L'Anthropologie 25:594-595. Paris, 1914.

739. Boutwell, J.M. The Calaveras Skull. In W. Lindgren, pp. 54-55, (see No. 837), 1911.

740. Bowden, O.A. and I.A. Lopatin. Pleistocene Man in Southern California. Science 84:507-508, 1936. [Printed also in El Palacio 41:121-123, 1936]

741. Brainerd, G.W. On the study of early man in Southern California. UC-AS-R 16:18-22, 1952.

742. Branco, W. Fragliche Reste und Fussfährten des tertiären Menschen. Zeitschrift d. Deutsch. Geol. Gesellschaft 56: 97-132, Berlin, 1904. [Pp. 102-104, Calaveras skull]

743. Brewer, W.H. Alleged discovery of an ancient human skull in California. American Journal of Science and Art 42:424, 1866.

744. Brewster, E.T. Life and letters of Josiah Dwight Whitney. Boston and N.Y., 1909. [P. 253, letter from Josiah to W.D. Whitney, July 18, 1866 reporting discovery of Calaveras skull]

745. Bryan, A.L. Paleo-American prehistory. Occasional Papers of Idaho State University Museum, No. 16, 1965. [Pp. 159-168, discussion of ancient California sites]

746. Campbell, E.W.C. Archaeological problems in the Southern California deserts. A. Ant. 1:295-300, 1936. [P. 297, Lake Mohave culture]

747. Campbell, E.W.C. Two ancient archaeological sites in the Great Basin. Science 109:340, 1949.
[Mohave, Pinto, Folsom artifacts from Owens Lake Region]

748. Campbell, E.W.C. and C. Amsden. The Eagle Mountain site. SM-M 8:170-173, 1934.
[Pinto Basin site, preliminary account]

749. Campbell, E.W.C. and W.H. The Pinto Basin Site. SM-P 9, 1935.

750. _____ A Folsom complex in the Great Basin. SM-M 14:7-11, 1940.

751. Campbell, E.W.C., et al. The archaeology of Pleistocene Lake Mohave, a Symposium. SM-P 11, 1937.

752. Carter, G.F. Evidence for Pleistocene Man at La Jolla, California. Transactions of the New York Academy of Sciences 2:254-257, 1949.

753. _____Evidence for Pleistocene Man in Southern California. Geographical Review 40:84-102, 1950.

754. _____An interglacial site at San Diego, California. SM-M 28:165-174, 1954.

755. _____Pleistocene Man at San Diego. Johns Hopkins Press, Baltimore, 1957.

756. _____Is there an American Lower Paleolithic? Miscellanea Paul Rivet 1:227-243. Mexico, 1958.

757. _____Man, time, and change in the far Southwest. Annals of the Association of American Geographers 49(3):8-33, 1959.

758. _____Pleistocene Man at San Diego: a reply. A. Ant. 24:319-320, 1959.

759. Clements, L. A preliminary study of some Pleistocene cultures of the California desert. SM-M 28:177-185, 1954.

760. _____Ancient inhabitation of Panamint Valley. SM-M 30:184-190, 1956.

761. Clements, T. Age of the "Los Angeles Man" deposits. AJS 36:137-141, 1938.

762. Clements, T. and L. Clements. Evidence of Pleistocene Man in Death Valley. GSA-B 64:1189-1204, 1953.

763. Cope, E.D. Pliocene Man. American Naturalist 14:60-62, 1880.

764. Cox, V. As far back as man. Westways 64(5):27-30,86, 1972.
[Calico Hills site]

765. Crabtree, D.E. Mastodon bones with artifacts in California.
AA 5:148-149, 1939.

766. Cressman, L.S. Early man and culture in South-central Oregon.
American Philosophical Society Yearbook 1939:194-196,
1940.

767. _____Archaeological researches in the Northern Great
Basin. Publication 538, Carnegie Institution of Washing-
ton, 1942.
[Chaps. XV-XIX, Lower Klamath Lake finds]

768. Cruxent, J.M. Phosphorus content of the Texas Street "hearths".
A. Ant. 28:90-91, 1962.

769. Curtis, F. The European reaction to American "paleoliths".
SM-M 30:140-145, 1956.

770. Dall, W.H. The Calaveras Skull. Proceedings of the Acad. of
Natural Sciences of Philadelphia, 1899:2-4, 1899.

771. Davis, E.L. How did they live and how long ago? In Ancient
Hunters of the Far West (R.F. Pourade, ed.), pp. 127-138.
Union Tribune Publ. Co., San Diego, 1966.

772. DeMay, I. An avifauna from sub-recent deposits at Lower Klamath
Lake, California. The Condor 43:295-296, 1941.

773. Desor, E. L'homme pliocène de la Californie. 16 pp., Nice,
1879.

774. Dixon, K.A. A "Sandia" point from Long Valley, Mono County,
California. SM-M 27:97-104, 1953.

775. Eaton, J.E. Divisions and duration of the Pleistocene in Southern California. Bulletin of the American Association of
Petroleum Geologists 12:111-141, 1928.

776. Furlong, E.L. Excavation in a recently explored Quaternary cave
in Shasta County, California. Science 20:53-55, 1904.

777. _____The exploration of Samwel Cave. AJS 172:235-247,
1906.

778. _____Reconnaissance of a recently discovered Quaternary
cave deposit near Auburn, California. Science 25:392-394,
1907.
[Hawver Cave]

779. _____Stone Man Cave, Shasta County, California. Science
94:414-415, 1941.

780. Gates, R.R. Human ancestry. Harvard University Press, Cambridge, 1948.
[P. 297-298, auriferous gravel finds]

781. Glennan, W.S. Concave-based lanceolate fluted projectile points from California. SM-M 45:27-36, 1971.

782. Goldschmidt, W. Introduction to a symposium on the antiquity of man in California. UC-AS-R 16:1-2, 1951.

783. Graham, G.M. Ancient man in Hidden Valley, California. SM-M 25:79-82, 1951.

784. Greenman, E.F. An American Eolithic? A. Ant. 22:298, 1957.

785. Hamy, E.T. Précis de paleontologie humaine. Paris, 1870. [Pp. 67-69, Calaveras skull]

786. _____ L'homme tertiare en Amérique et la théorie des centres multiples de création. Rev. Cours Scient. March 19, 1870.

787. Hanks, H.G. The deep lying auriferous gravels and table mountains of California. San Francisco, 1901.

788. Harrington, M.R. Folsom Man in California. SM-M 12:133-137, 1938.

789. _____ Pre-Folsom Man in California. SM-M 12:173-175, 1938.

790. _____ Early man at Borax Lake. Carnegie Institution of Washington, News Service Bulletin, School Edition 4: 259-261, 1938.

791. _____ The age of the Borax Lake finds. SM-M 13:208-209, 1939.

792. _____ Return to Borax Lake. SM-M 16:214-215, 1942.

793. _____ Farewell to Borax Lake. SM-M 19:181-184, 1945.

794. _____ New work at Borax Lake. SM-M 20:189-190, 1946.

795. _____ A new Pinto site. SM-M 22:116-118, 1948.

796. _____ America's oldest dwelling? SM-M 22:148-152, 1948.

797. _____ An ancient site at Borax Lake, California. SM-P 16, 1948.

798. _____ The Rattlesnake Island site. In An ancient site at Borax Lake, California. SM-P 16:127-131, 1948.

799. _____ A cave near Little Lake. SM-M 27:77-82, 1953.

800. Hastie, W.L. Early man in Southern California. SLOCAS-OP 5, 1971.

801. Hay, O.P. The geological age of Tuolumne Table Mountain, California. Journal of the Washington Academy of Sciences 16: 358-361, 1926.

802. _____ The Pleistocene of the western region of North America and its vertebrated fossils. Carnegie Institution of Washington Publication 322 B, 1927.
[Pp. 218-235, "Geology and paleontology of the Gold Belt"]

803. Haynes, V. The Calico site: artifacts or geofacts? Science 181:305-310, 1973.

804. Heizer, R.F. A Folsom-type point from the Sacramento Valley. SM-M 12:180-182, 1934.

805. _____ A note on Folsom and Nepesta points. A. Ant. 6: 79-80, 1940.

806. _____ Review of D.B. Rogers, "Prehistoric man of the Santa Barbara coast," 1929. A. Ant. 6:372-375, 1941.

807. _____ A bibliography of ancient man in California. UC-AS-R 2, 1948.

808. _____ Observations on early man in California. UC-AS-R 7:5-9, 1950.
[Also in KAS-P 1:28-35, 1950]

809. _____ A review of problems in the antiquity of man in California. UC-AS-R 16:3-17, 1952.

810. _____ Sites attributed to early man in California. UC-AS-R 22:1-4, 1953.

811. Heizer, R.F. and S.F. Cook. "Capay Man", an ancient Central California Indian burial. UC-AS-R 22:24-26, 1953.

812. Heizer, R.F. and E.M. Lemert. Observations on archaeological sites in Topanga Canyon, California. UC-PAAE 44:237-252, 1947.

813. Heizer, R.F. and T.D. McCown. The Stanford Skull, a probable early man from Santa Clara County, California. UC-AS-R 6, 1950.

814. Hewes, G.W. Reconnaissance of the Central San Joaquin Valley. A. Ant. 7:123-133, 1941.
[P. 132, Tranquillity]

815. _____ Camel, horse, and bison associated with human burials and artifacts near Fresno, California. Science 97:328-329, 1943.

816. _____ Early man in California and the Tranquillity site. A. Ant. 11:209-215, 1946.

817. Hitchcock, C.H. The Calaveras Skull. Engineering and Mining
          Journal 9:345-346, 1870.

818. Hittell, J.S. The resources of California. S.F., 1863.
          [P. 70, various auriferous gravel finds of artifacts and
          skeletons in Nevada, El Dorado and Los Angeles Counties]

819. Hodge, F.W. Work of Mr. Harrington (at Borax Lake). SM-M 13:
          61-62, 1939.

820. Holmes, W.H. Preliminary revision of the evidence relating to
          Auriferous Gravel Man in California. AA 1:107-121,614-
          645, 1899.

821. _____ Review of the evidence relating to Auriferous Gravel
          Man in California. SI-AR 1899:419-472, 1901.
          [Pp. 454-469, the definitive study on the subject of the
          Calaveras skull]

822. _____ Anthropological studies in California. USNM-AR
          1900:155-187, 1902.
          [Pp. 166-172, observations on auriferous gravel artifact
          discoveries]

823. _____ Calaveras Man. Handbook of American Indians. BAE-B
          30(1):188, 1912.

824. _____ Handbook of aboriginal American antiquities. BAE-B
          60, 1919.
          [Pp. 61-68, Calaveras skull; Table Mountain auriferous
          gravel artifacts]

825. Howard, H. and A.H. Miller. The avifauna associated with human
          remains at Rancho LaBrea, California. Carnegie Institu-
          tion of Washington, Publ. 514:39-48, 1939.

826. Hrdlicka, A. Skeletal remains suggesting or attributed to
          early man in North America. BAE-B 33, 1907.
          [Pp. 21-28, Calaveras skull]

827. _____ Recent discoveries attributed to early man in Amer-
          ica. BAE-B 66, 1966.
          [Pp. 17-22, LaBrea skeleton]

828. _____ The origin and antiquity of the American Indian.
          SI-AR 1923:487, 1924.
          [Mention of Los Angeles Man found and reported upon by
          J.C. Merriam]

829. _____ Early man in America: What have the bones to say?
          In Early Man, Ed. by G.G. McCurdy, 1936, pp. 93-104.
          [Pp. 99-100, discussion of Los Angeles Man remains]

830. Johnson, F. and J.P. Miller. Review of G. Carter's Pleistocene
          Man at San Diego. A. Ant. 24:209-210, 1958.

831. Koch, F.J. The Calaveras Skull. American Antiquarian 33:199-202, 1911.

832. Kroeber, A.L. Discussion of "Lodi Man." Science 87:137-138, 1938.

833. _____The Rancho LaBrea Skull. A. Ant. 27:416-417, 1962.

834. Leakey, L.S.B., R.D. Simpson, and T. Clements. Archaeological excavations in the Calico Mountains, California. Preliminary report. Science 160:1022-1023, 1968.

835. Leakey, L.S.B., et al. Pleistocene Man at Calico. San Bernardino County Museum Association, 1972.

836. Lee, T.E. Calico Mountains Conference. Anthropological Journal of Canada 9(4):11-12, 1971.

837. Lindgren, W. The tertiary gravels of the Sierra Nevada of California. USGS-P 73, 1911.
     [Pp. 52-53, Calaveras skull]

838. Lopatin, I.A. Fossil man in the vicinity of Los Angeles, California. Proceedings of the Sixth Pacific Science Congress 4:177-181, 1940.

839. Lucas, B.J. Tree-holes at the Stahl site. SM-M 25:190-193, 1951.

840. MacCurdy, G.G. (Ed.). Early Man: As depicted by leading authorities at the International Symposium. The Academy of Natural Sciences. Philadelphia and New York, 1937.

841. Marcou, J. La crâne humain du Calaveras. Bulletin Société Géologique 11:419-420. Paris, 1883.

842. McCown, T.D. The Stanford Skull, a probable early man from Santa Clara County, California. UC-AS-R 6, 1950.

843. McGee, W.J. Geology and archaeology of the California Gold Belt. American Geologist 23:96-99, 1899.

844. McGee, W.J. and W.H. Holmes. The geology and archaeology of California. American Geologist 23:96-99, 1899.

845. Meighan, C.W. and C.V. Haynes. New studies on the age of the Borax Lake site. SM-M 42:4-9, 1968.

846. _____Further investigations of Borax Lake. SM-M 44:112-117, 1970.

847. _____The Borax Lake site revisited. Science 167:1213-1221, 1970.

848. Merriam, C.H. Ethnological evidence that the California cave skeletons are not recent. Science 29:805-806, 1909.
[Also in the American Antiquarian and Oriental Journal 31: 152-153, 1909; reprinted in..Various Papers on California Archaeology, Ethnology, and Indian History, UC-ARF, 1973]

849. Merriam, J.C. The fossil human remains of Table Mountain. Lenox Nutshell, Hopkinson, Iowa, 1898.
[Reprinted in Carnegie Institution of Washington, Publication 500, Vol. III:1556-1559, 1938]

850. _____ Recent cave exploration in California. AA 8:221, 1906.

851. _____ Note on the occurrence of human remains in Californian caves. Science 30:531-532, 1909.
[Reprinted in..Various Papers on California Archaeology, Ethnology, and Indian History. UC-ARF, 1973]

852. _____ The true story of the Calaveras Skull. Sunset Magazine, pp. 153-158, Feb. 1910.
[Reprinted in..Various Papers on California Archaeology, Ethnology, and Indian History, UC-ARF, 1973]

853. _____ Preliminary report on the discovery of human remains in an asphalt deposit at Rancho LaBrea. Science 40:198-203, 1914.

854. _____ The Brea maid. SCAS-B 13(2):27-29, 1914.

855. _____ Antiquity of man in California from the point of view of the paleontologist. Science 42:543-544, 1915.

856. _____ Present status of investigations concerning antiquity of man in California. Science 60:1-2, 1924.

857. _____ The Cave of the Magic Pool. Scribners Magazine 82: 264-272, 1927.
[Reprinted in The Living Past, New York, 1930, Chapter 1; and in Carnegie Institution of Washington, Pub. 500, Vol. III, 1938: Narrative account of the exploration of Samwel Cave, details the finding of the skeleton of an "Indian maiden"]

858. _____ Present status of knowledge relating to the antiquity of man in America. Sixteenth International Geolog. Cong. Report 2:1313-1323. Washington, 1936.
[P. 1315, Calaveras skull]

859. Miller, G.J. Man and Smilodon: A preliminary report on their possible coexistence at Rancho LaBrea. Los Angeles County Museum Contrib. in Science 163:1-8, 1969.

860. Minshall, H.L. Early man sites at Texas Street and Buchanan Canyon in San Diego, California. Anthropological Journal of

Canada 12:18, 1974.

861. Mitchell, L.L. Coyote Canyon Cave, 4-Ora-236, and "Clovis points". PCAS-S 14:5, 1975.

862. Moriarty, J.R. The San Dieguito Complex: Suggested environmental and cultural relationships. Anthropological Journal of Canada 7(3):2-18, 1969.

863. Munro, R. Archaeology and false antiquities. London, 1905. [Pp. 81-109, Calaveras skull]

864. Musgrave, L.C. Big dig at Calico. Westways 63(6):28-32, 1971.

865. _____The first Californians. Americas 25:25-30, 1973. [Calico site]

866. de Nadaillac, M. Les premiers hommes et las temps préhistoriques. Paris, 1881. [Pp. 435-439, Calaveras skull]

867. _____L'Amérique préhistorique. Paris, 1883. [Pp. 42-46, Fig. 14, Calaveras skull]

868. _____Le Crâne de Calaveras. Revue des Questions Scientifique 18:341-358. Louvain, 1900.

869. Newton, E.T. The evidence for the existence of man in the Tertiary Period. Proc. Geol. Assn. 15:63-82. London, 1899. [Pp. 77-79, Calaveras skull]

870. Oakley, K.P. Review of G.F. Carter: Pleistocene Man at San Diego. Man 59:183, 1959.

871. Orr, P.C. Arlington Springs Man. Science 135:219, 1962.

872. Owen, R.C. Assertions, assumptions and Early Horizon (Oak Grove) settlement patterns in Southern California: A rejoinder. A. Ant. 32:236-241, 1967.

873. Payen, L.A. Potter Creek Cave, 1903-1965. Cave Notes 7(5), 1965.

874. Payen, L.A. and R.E. Taylor. Man and Pleistocene fauna at Potter Creek Cave, California. JCA 3(1):51-58, 1976.

875. Pourade, R.F. (Ed.). Ancient hunters of the Far West. Union Tribune Publications Co. San Diego, 1966.

876. _____Foreword - A journey into man's past: discovering the San Dieguito people. In Ancient Hunters of the Far West, pp. 3-20, San Diego, 1966.

877. Putnam, F.W. Evidence of the work of man on objects from Quat-

ernary caves in California. AA 8:229-235, 1906.
[Pp. 230-234, Potter Creek Cave bone "tools"]

878. Putnam, F.W. Statement on Calaveras Skull. In W.J. Sinclair,
1908:128-129 (see No. 910).

879. Quenstedt, W. and A. Fossilium Catalogus 1: Animalia, Pars 74,
Hominidae fossiles. s'Gravenhage, 1936.
[Pp. 412-414, documentation in anthropological literature
up to 1933 of Calaveras skull]

880. Riddell, F.A. and W.H. Olsen. An early man site in the San
Joaquin Valley, California. A. Ant. 34:121-130, 1969.

881. Roberts, F.H.H., Jr. Recent developments in the problem of the
North American paleo-Indian. SI-MC 100:51-116, 1940.
[Pp. 86-94, California cultures]

882. Roehr, P. and A. Wilwand. Early man in California. The Digger's
Digest 6(2):2-3, 1968.

883. Rogers, D.B. Prehistoric man of the Santa Barbara Coast.
Santa Barbara, 1929.

884. Rogers, M.J. The stone art of the San Dieguito Plateau. AA 31:
454-467, 1929.

885. _____Archaeological and geological investigations of the
cultural levels in an old channel of San Dieguito Valley.
Carnegie Institution of Washington, Yearbook 37:344-345,
1938.

886. _____Early lithic industries of the lower basin of the
Colorado River and adjacent desert areas. SDM-P No. 3,
1939.

887. _____An outline of Yuman prehistory. SWJA 1:167-198,
1945.

888. _____The ancient hunters - who were they? In Ancient
hunters of the Far West (R.F. Pourade, ed), pp. 23-108,
Union Tribune Publ. Co. San Diego, 1966.

889. Rogers, S.L. 100,000 Years. SDM: El Museo 1(4):24-27, 1953.
[Critical analysis of G.F. Carter's work on early man]

890. Roosa, W.B. and Peckham, S. Notes on the Third Interglacial
artifacts. A. Ant. 19:280-281, 1954.

891. Sauer, C.O. Early relations of man to plants. Geographical
Review 37:1-25, 1947.

892. Scharf, D. The Quaternary history of the Pinto Basin. In E.W.C.
and W.H. Campbell, pp. 11-20 (see No. 749), 1935.

893. Schmidt, E. Zur Urgeschichte nordamerikas. Archiv für Anthropologie 5:153-172,222-259, 1872.
[Pp. 253-259, Calaveras skull]

894. _____Die ältesten Spuren des Menschen in Nordamerika. Sammlung gemeinverst. wissenschaftl. Vortrage, 2nd Ser., Vol. 38-39:1-58. Hamburg, 1887.
[Pp. 43-50, Calaveras skull]

895. Schoolcraft, H.R. Indian tribes of the United States. Philadelphia, 1851.
[Vol. 1, p. 101 - mention of the discovery, in August, 1849, of a shaft 210 feet deep at whose bottom was found a human skeleton]

896. Schuiling, W.C. (Ed.). Pleistocene Man at Calico. A report on the International Conference on the Calico Mountains Excavations, San Bernardino County, California. San Bernardino County Museum Association, 1972.

897. Scoggin, C. Folsom and Nepesta points. A. Ant. 5:290-298, 1940.

898. Sellards, E.H. Early man in America: Index to localities and selected bibliography. GSA-B 51(3):377-379, 1940.

899. Simpson, R.D. A classic "Folsom" from Lake Mohave. SM-M 21:24, 1947.

900. _____The plot thickens at Little Lake. SM-M 23:19, 1949.

901. _____A friendly critic visits Texas Street. SM-M 28:174-176, 1954.

902. _____An introduction to early Western American prehistory. SCAS-B 55(2):61-71, 1956.

903. _____The Manix Lake archaeological survey. SM-M 32:4-10, 1958.

904. _____Ice Age archaeology in the Calicos. PCAS-Q 5(4), 1969.

905. _____A search for Pleistocene archaeological evidence in the Calico Mountains of Eastern California. NGS-RR:219-225, (for 1964), 1969.

906. _____A search for Pleistocene archaeological evidence in the Calico Mountains of Eastern California. NGS-RR:231-237 (for 1965), 1971.

907. _____A search for Pleistocene archaeological evidence in the Calico Mountains of Eastern California. NGS-RR:225-233 (for 1966), 1973.

908. Simpson, R.D. A search for Pleistocene archaeological evidence
      in the Calico Mountains of Eastern California. NGS-RR:
      267-270 (for 1967), 1974.

909. Sinclair, W.J. The explorations of the Potter Creek Cave. UC-
      PAAE 2:1-27, 1904.

910. _____ Recent investigations bearing on the question of
      the occurrence of Neocene Man in the auriferous gravels
      of the Sierra Nevada. UC-PAAE 7:107-131, 1908.

911. Skertchley, S.B.J. On the occurrence of stone mortars in the
      ancient (Pliocene) river gravels of Butte County, Calif-
      ornia. JRAI 17:332-337, 1888.

912. Smith, G.A. Traces of ancient man at Bloomington, California.
      SM-M 17:124-127, 1942.

913. _____ Early man in the California desert. L.A. Westerner's
      Brand Book, No. 11, p. 32, 1964.

914. Southall, J.C. Pliocene Man in America. Victoria Institute,
      Transactions 15:191-220, 1882.

915. _____ Recent origin of man. Philadelphia, 1875.
      [P. 558, recital of original testimony that Calaveras
      skull was planted as a hoax]

916. Spinner, J. Steinzeitfunde paleolithischen Typs in Chile und
      ein Versuch ihrer Eingliederung in ein Besiedlungs-
      geschichte Südamerikas. Akten des 34 Internationalen
      Amerikanisten Kongresses. Pp. 451-464. Wien, 1960.

917. Stephenson, R.L. Thoughts on the Calico Mountains site. Univ-
      ersity of South Carolina: Institute of Archaeology and
      Anthropology, Notebook 3(1):3-9, 1971.

918. Stock, C. The Pleistocene fauna of Hawver Cave. UC-PG 10:461-
      515, 1918.

919. _____ A recent discovery of ancient human remains in Los
      Angeles, California. Science 60:2-4, 1924.

920. _____ Rancho LaBrea: a record of Pleistocene life in Calif-
      ornia. Los Angeles Museum, Publication 1, Science Series
      1, 1930.
      [Pp. 28-30, LaBrea skeleton; - Revised edition, issued in
      1946 and renumbered as Science Series No. 11, contains
      section (pp. 24-26) entitled "Occurrence of Human Remains"]

921. _____ Prehistoric archaeology. In Geology: 1888-1938. Fif-
      tieth Anniversary Volume of the Geological Society of
      America, pp. 139-158, 1941.
      [P. 149, LaBrea skeleton]

922. Taylor, G. Environment, race, and migration. Chicago, 1937.
[P. 224, Angeles Mesa finds]

923. Treganza, A. An archaeological reconnaissance of Northeastern
Baja California and Southeastern California. A. Ant. 8:
152-163, 1942.

924. _____Notes on the San Dieguito lithic industry of Southern California and Northern Baja California. In R.F.
Heizer and E.M. Lemert, pp. 253-255, 1947.

925. _____An ethno-archaeological examination of Samwel Cave.
Cave Studies, No. 12, 1964.

926. Treganza, A.E. and Bierman, A. The Topanga Culture: Final report on excavations, 1948. UC-AR 20:45-86, 1958.

927. Treganza, A.E. and C.G. Malamud. The Topanga Culture: First
season's excavation of the Tank site, 1947. UC-AR 12:
129-170, 1950.

928. True, D.L. An early complex in San Diego County, California.
A. Ant. 23:255-263, 1958.

929. Vayson de Pradenne, A. Les fraudes en archeologie prehistori-
que. Paris, 1932.
[Chap. 7, "Les crânes de Calaveras"]

930. Wade, M.P.M. Artifacts of early man in the New World. Science
182:1371, 1973.
[Calico site]

931. Walker, E.F. Sequence of prehistoric material culture at
Malaga Cove, California. SM-M 11:210-214, 1937.

932. Wallace, W.J. and E.S. Taylor. Early man in Death Valley.
Archaeology 8:82-92, 1955.

933. Walters, P. Early man in California. El Palacio 50:115-116,
1943.

934. Whitney, J.D. Geological survey of California. Vol. 1, Report
of Progress and Synopsis of the Field-Work from 1860-1864.
Philadelphia, 1865.
[P. 252, statement by Whitney that man, mastodon, and
elephant were contemporaneous in California. This observation was published before the discovery of the Calaveras
Skull]

935. _____ Notice of a human skull, recently taken from a
shaft near Angels, Calaveras County. CAS-P 3:277-278,
1867.
[Reprinted in American Journal of Science and Arts 43:
265-267, 1867]

936. Whitney, J.D. A cave in Calaveras County, California. SI-AR 1867:406-407, 1868.
   [Cave of skulls]

937. _____ On the Calaveras Skull and its geological position. American Naturalist 2:445-447, 1868.

938. _____ The auriferous gravels of the Sierra Nevada of California. Memoirs of the Harvard Museum of Comparative Anatomy 6:258-288, 1879.
   [Calaveras skull]

939. Whittlesey, C. On the evidence of the antiquity of man in the United States. American Association for the Advancement of Science, Proceedings 17:286-287, 1869.

940. Wilder, H.H. Man's prehistoric past. New York, 1923.
   [Argues that Calaveras skull may be reinstated as an ancient specimen]

941. Willis, B. Out of the long past - a story of the Stanford skull. The Stanford Cardinal 32:8-12, Oct. 1922.

942. Wilson, T. La haute ancienneté de l'homme dans l'Amérique du Nord. L'Anthropologie 12:297-339, 1901. Appears also in C.R. Congr. Internat. Anthr. Arch. Preh., 12th Session, Paris 1900:149-191, Paris, 1902.
   [Pp. 306-317, Calaveras skull]

943. Winslow, C.F. On human remains along with those of mastodon in the drift of California. Boston Society of Natural History Proceedings 6:278-279, 1857.
   [Also in American Journal of Science 96:407-408, 1868]

944. _____ Particulars relating to the discovery of human remains in Table Mountain. Boston Society of Natural History Proceedings 15:257-259, 1873.

945. Woodward, A. Atlatl dart foreshafts from the LaBrea Pits. SCAS-B 36:41-60, 1937.

946. Wormington, H.M. When did man come to North America? In Ancient hunters of the Far West (R.F. Pourade, ed), pp. 111-124, Union Tribune Publ. Co. San Diego, 1966.

947. Wright, G.F. The Ice Age in North America. New York, 1890.
   [Pp. 561-567, Calaveras skull and other auriferous gravel finds]

948. _____ Prehistoric man on the Pacific Coast. Atlantic Monthly 67:501-513, 1891.

949. _____ The Lava Beds of California and Idaho and their relation to the antiquity of man. British Association for the Advancement of Science, Report 61:651, 1892.

950. Wright, G.F. The latest concerning prehistoric man in California. Records of the Past 7:183-187, 1908.

951. Wyman, L.E. Notes on the Pleistocene fossils obtained from
Rancho LaBrea Asphalt Pits. Los Angeles Museum of History,
Science, and Art, Miscell. Publ. No. 2, 1926.

952. Yates, L.G. Prehistoric man in California. Bulletin of the
Santa Barbara Society of Natural History 1:23-29, 1887.
[Calaveras skull]

XV. HISTORIC ARCHAEOLOGY

953. Anonymous. Reading the Agua Mansa cemetery. SBCMA-Q 21:83-94,
1973.

954. Aga-Oglu, K. Late Ming and Early Ch'ing porcelain fragments
from archaeological sites in Florida. Florida Anthropologist 8:106, 1955.
[Mentions porcelain found at Drakes Bay]

955. Barnes, M.R. and R.V. May. Mexican majolica in Northern New
Spain. PCAS-OP 2, 1972.

956. Beardsley, R.K. The Monterey Custom House flag-pole; archaeological findings. California Historical Quarterly 25:204-
218, 1946.

957. Belden, L.B. Agua Mansa. SBCMA-Q 21:4-6, 1973.

958. Belden, L.B., et al. Agua Mansa. SBCMA-Q 8(4), 1961.

959. Bennyhoff, J.A. and A.B. Elsasser. Sonoma Mission: An historical and archaeological study of primary constructions,
1823-1913. UC-AS-R 27, 1954.

960. Broadbent, S.M. Historic ceramics at Sutter's Fort. CDPR-AR
1, 1961.

961. Chace, P.G. The archaeology of "Cienega", the oldest historic
structure on the Irvine Ranch. PCAS-Q 5(3), 1969.

962. Deetz, J.J.F. Archaeological investigations at La Purísima
Mission. UCLA-AS-AR 5:161-244, 1963.

963. Drake, R.J. Samplings in history at the Sanchez Adobe, San
Mateo County. El Palacio 59:19-29, 1952.

964. Elsasser, A.B. The crowning of Sir Francis Drake and others
according to early engravers. JCA 3(1):72-80, 1976.

965. Ezell, P.H. and N.D. Broadbent. Archaeological investigations
at the Casa de José Manuel Machado (the Stewart House).
PCAS-Q 8:1-34, 1972.

966. Fages, I.L. Doomed adobe landmarks. SM-M 24:188-190, 1950.

967. Fenenga, F. Artifacts from excavation of Sutter's sawmill. California Hist. Society Quarterly 26:160-162, 1947.

968. Greenwood, R.S. and N. Gessler. The Mission San Buenaventura aqueduct, with particular reference to the fragments at Weldon Canyon. PCAS-Q 4(4):61-86, 1968.

969. Hamlin, N. Reading the Agua Mansa cemetery-grave records. SBCMA-Q 21:95-115, 1973.

970. Harrington, M.R. Digging up the past at San Luis Rey. SM-M 32:55-57, 1958.

971. Haselden, R.B. Is the Drake Plate of Brass genuine? California Historical Society Quarterly 16:271-274, 1937.

972. Heinsen, V. Constructing the town of Jolon. Monterey County Archaeological Society Quarterly 4(2):9-10, 1975.

973. Heizer, R.F. Archaeological investigation of Sutter Sawmill site. California Hist. Quarterly 26:134-159, 1947.

974. _____Observations on historic sites and archaeology in California. UC-AS-R 9:1-5, 1950.

975. _____California's oldest historical relic? R.H. Lowie Museum of Anthropology. UC Berkeley, 1972.

976. _____ A probable relic of Juan Rodriques Cabrillo. SM-M 47:62-68, 1973.

977. _____Elizabethan California. Ballena Press, 101 pp., Ramona, 1974.

978. Hinkley, H.P. Restoration of the San Bernardino Asistencia. SBCMA-Q 13(1), 1965.

979. Howard, D.M. Archaeological investigation of the Royal Presidio of Monterey. Monterey County Archaeological Society Quarterly 1(2):1-11, 1971.

980. _____ Archaeological investigations at Mission Nuestra Señora de la Soledad, Mnt-233, Monterey County, California. Monterey County Archaeological Society Quarterly 1(3):1-10, 1972.

981. _____Lost adobes of Monterey County. Monterey County Archaeological Society. 105 pp. 1973.

982. Humphrey, R.V. The La Purísima Mission cemetery. UCLA-AS-AR 7:179-192, 1965.

983. Jones, C.H. Agua Mansa settled by those who spoke Spanish. SBCMA-Q 21:29-47, 1973.

984. King, T.F. and W. Upson. Protohistory on Limantour sandspit: Archaeological investigations at 4-Mrn-216 and 4-Mrn-298. SFSC-TAMP 6:115-194, 1972.

985. Lyhne, B. S.F. Bay discovery: The case for Drake. Redwood City Tribune, Apr. 3, (Weekly Suppl., pp. 8-10), 1971.

986. Mannion, M.C. A report on three archaeological sites with historic components. SFSC-TAMP 5(6), 1969.

987. May, R.V. An evaluation of Mexican majolica in Alta California: employing preliminary data from the San Diego Presidio. PCAS-OP 2:25-50, 1972.

988. _____Mexican majolica at the Presidio of Monterey. Monterey County Archaeol. Soc. Quarterly 3(4):1-6, 1974.

989. McGinty, B. A grave discovery. Westways 66(4):25-27, 1974. [J.R. Cabrillo grave stone from Lowie Museum]

990. Meighan, C.W. and Heizer, R.F. Archaeological exploration of 16th Century Indian Mounds at Drakes Bay. California Historical Quarterly 31:99-106, 1952.

991. Moriarty, J.R. Historic site archaeology at Mission San Diego de Alcalá. SM-M 43:100-108, 1969.

992. _____"With his boots on." SM-M 47:55-61, 1973. [Burials of soldiers at Mission San Diego]

993. Moriarty, J.R. and W.L. Crocker. A small iron cannon recovered from San Diego Bay. The Journal of San Diego History 11(4):37-42, 1965.

994. Moriarty, J.R. and W.R. Weyland. Excavations at San Diego Mission. SM-M 45:124-137, 1971.

995. Neasham, V.A. Drake's California landing: the evidence for Bolinas Lagoon. SCA-N 8:9, 1974.

996. Neasham, V.A. and W.E. Pritchard. Drake's California landing: The evidence for Bolinas Lagoon. Western Heritage Inc. Sacramento, 1974.

997. Oko, A.S. Francis Drake and Nova Albion. California Historical Society Quarterly 43:1-24, 1964.

998. Olsen, W.H. Archaeological investigations at Sutter's Fort State Historical Monument. California State Division of Beaches and Parks, Interpretive Services. Archaeological Report, 1961.

999. Payen, L.A. Excavations at Sutter's Fort. California State Division of Beaches and Parks, Interpretive Services. Archaeological Report, 1960.

1000. Pilling, A.R. Eight historic artifacts from 4-Mnt-12. Monterey County Archaeol. Soc. Quarterly 4(1), 1974.

1001. _____ Eight historic artifacts from 4-Mnt-12. Monterey County Archaeol. Soc. Quarterly 4(2):1-5, 1975.

1002. Reck, D.G. and Moriarty, J.R. Preliminary report on the discovery of a U.S. Army cemetery at the Mission San Diego de Alcalá. Anthropological Journal of Canada 10:2-12, 1972.

1003. Reed, E.K. Review of A.E. Treganza, "Fort Ross: A study in historical archaeology." In UC-AS-R 23, 1954. American Journal of Archaeology 58:352, 1954.

1004. Riddell, F.A. Archaeological excavations on the Farallon Islands, California. UC-AS-R 32:1-18, 1955.

1005. Schumacher, P. Historic archaeology. SCA-N 6:8-10, 1972.

1006. _____ Historical archaeology state-wide. SCA-N 9:8, 1975.

1007. Starr, W.A. Drake landed in San Francisco Bay in 1579: The testimony of the plate of brass. California Historical Society Quarterly 41:1-29, 1962.

1008. Stickel, E.G. and A.E. Cooper. The Chumash revolt of 1824: A case for an archaeological application of feedback theory. UCLA-AS-AR 11:5-21, 1969.

1009. Treganza, A.E. Fort Ross: a study in historical archaeology. UC-AS-R 23, 1954.

1010. _____ Sonoma Mission: an archaeological reconstruction of the Mission San Francisco de Solano Quadrangle. KASP 14:1-18, 1956.

1011. Von der Porten, E.P. Our first New England. U.S. Naval Institute Proceedings. P. 62-66, December 1960.

1012. _____ The porcelains and terra cottas of Drake's Bay. SFSC-TAMP 6:223-256, 1970.

1013. _____ Drake and Cermeño in California: Sixteenth Century Chinese porcelains. Historical Archaeology 6: 1-22, 1972.

1014. Wallace, W.J. Historic artifacts from the Hugo Reid Adobe. Lasca Leaves 8(2):74-80, 1958.

1015. Wallace, W.J. Historical materials pertaining to the Hugo Reid Adobe. Lasca Leaves 9(1):14-23, 1959.

1016. _____ Los Encinos State Historical Monument: The archaeological record. Journal of the West 1(2):170-192, 1962.

1017. Wallace, W.J., R.J. Desautels and G.Kritzman. The house of the Scotch paisano: Archaeological Investigations at the Hugo Reid Adobe, Arcadia, California. Lasca Leaves 8(1), 1958.

1018. Wallace, W.J. and E.T. Wallace. Indian artifacts from the Hugo Reid Adobe. Lasca Leaves 8(4), 1958.

1019. _____ Archaeological Investigations in the "patio" of the Hugo Reid Adobe. Lasca Leaves 9(3):55-60, 1959.

1020. _____ Historic objects from the Hugo Reid Adobe. Lasca Leaves 11 (2 and 3):39-65, 1961.

1021. Walker, H. Camp middens. Desert Magazine 35(2):8-11, 1972. [Brief mention of aboriginal kitchen middens mostly deals with later historic refuse]

1022. Webb, E.B. Indian life at the Old Missions. W.F. Lewis, Los Angeles, 1952. [P. 166, pl. opp. p. 191 - archaeological investigations of mill at Mission San Gabriel in 1894 and 1934]

1023. Williams, L.A. Digging for history at Drakes Bay. CAS-PD 6: 10-17, 1953.

1024. Wood, M. Agua Mansa Today. SBCMA-Q 21:57-82, 1973.

1025. Woodward, A. Archaeological notes and domestic fowl as ceremonial offerings. A. Ant. 6:284-285, 1941. [Reprinted UCLA-AS-AR 1:151-152, 1959]

XVI. GENERAL CALIFORNIA PREHISTORY

1026. Bancroft, H.H. The native races of the Pacific states of North America. Vol. IV, Antiquities, 1875. [Pp. 688-712, California archaeology]

1027. Baumhoff, M.A. Ecological determinants of population. UC-AS-R 41:34-39, 1957.

1028. Baumhoff, M.A. and J.S. Byrne. Desert Side-notched points as a time marker in California. UC-AS-R 48:32-65, 1959.

1029. Baumhoff, M.A. and A.B. Elsasser. Summary of archaeological survey and excavation in California. UC-AS-R 33:1-27, 1956.

1030. Bennyhoff, J.A. Californian fish spears and harpoons. UC-AR 9:295-329, 1950.

1031. Bennyhoff, J.A. Certain harpoons and fish spears from California. UC-AR 12:265-272,294-300, 1950.

1032. Blake, J. On some recently discovered aboriginal implements. CAS-P 4:221-222, 1873.
[Sacramento Valley and Coast Range]

1033. Carter, G.F. California as an island. SM-M 38:74-78, 1964.

1034. Curtis, E. (Ed.). Symposium on Central California archaeology. SAS-P 3, 1965.

1035. Davis, E.L., C.W. Brott, and D.L. Weide. The Western lithic co-tradition. SDM-P 6, 1969.

1036. Dixon, R.B. Some aspects of North American archaeology. AA 15:549-577, 1913.
[California pp. 558-559]

1037. Eberhart, H. Published archaeological site and surveys in Southern California. ASASC-N 17(2):4-21, 1970.

1038. Elsasser, A.B. The history of culture classification in California. UC-AS-R 49:1-10, 1960.

1039. _____ Archaeological evidence of shamanism in California and Nevada. KASP 24:38-48, 1961.

1040. Fenenga, F. Methods for archaeological site survey in California. UC-AS-R 5, 1949.

1041. Gates, G.R. Does long-term flooding harm sites? SCA-N 7:6-7, 1973.

1042. Gerow, B.A. Co-traditions and convergent trends in prehistoric California. SLOCAS-OP 8:1-55, 1974.

1043. Glassow, M.A. Considerations in estimating prehistoric California coastal populations. A. Ant. 32:354-359, 1967.

1044. Gould, R.A. Aboriginal California burial and cremation practices. UC-AS-R 60:149-168, 1963.

1045. _____ Exploitative economics and culture change in Central California. UC-AS-R 62:123-163, 1964.

1046. Harrington, J.P. Culture element distribution: Central California coast. UC-AR 7:1-46, 1942.

1047. Heizer, R.F. The direct historical approach in California archaeology. A. Ant. 7:98-122, 1941.

1048. _____ Remarks on the prone burial position in China and North America. A. Ant. 13:249-250, 1948.

1049. Heizer, R.F. The California Archaeological Survey. UC-AS-R 1, 1949.

1050. _____The California Archaeological Survey. A. Ant. 14: 222-223, 1949.

1051. _____A bibliography of the archaeology of California. UC-AS-R 4, 1949.

1052. _____Prehistoric Central California: A problem in historical-developmental classification. UC-AS-R 41:19-26, 1958.

1053. _____Village shifts and tribal spreads in California prehistory. SM-M 30:60-67, 1962.

1054. _____California archaeology: its development, present status, and future needs. SM-M 38:84-90, 1964.

1055. _____The western coast of North America. In Jennings and Norbeck (Eds.), Prehistoric man in the New World: 117-148. Chicago, 1964.

1056. _____Salvage and other archaeology. SM-M 40:54-60, 1966.

1057. _____A question of ethnics in archaeology - one archaeologist's view. JCA 1(2):145-151, 1974.

1058. _____Some thoughts on California archaeology at the moment. UCLA-JNWA 1, 1975.

1059. _____Index to the Reports of the University of California Archaeological Survey, Nos. 1-30. UC-AS-R 31, 1955.

1060. _____Check list and index to the University of California Archaeological Survey 32-74; check list of Contributions of the Archaeological Research Facility, Nos. 1-14; other information on activities (1948-1972). UC-AS-R 75:1-80, 1972.

1061. _____Reprints of various papers on California archaeology, ethnology and Indian history. UC-ARF, 1973.

1062. Heizer, R.F. and M.A. Baumhoff. California settlement patterns. In G.R. Willey (Ed.), Prehistoric settlement patterns in the New World (pp. 32-44). N.Y., 1956.

1063. Heizer, R.F. and A.B. Elsasser (with assistance of C.W. Clewlow). A bibliography of California archaeology. UC-C-ARF 6:1-78, 1970.

1064. Holman, M.P., et al. Archaeological survey of selected beaches and parks from District 2. Report to the Calif. State Department of Parks and Recreation, 1969.

69

1065. Holmes, W.H. Anthropological studies in California. USNM-AR 1900:1-187, 1902.

1066. King, T.F. A conflict of values in American archaeology. A. Ant. 36:255-274, 1971.

1067. _____New views of California Indians societies. The Indian Historian 5(4):12-17, 1972.

1068. _____Mitigation of mammoths in California and other bizarre stories. The Missouri Archaeologist 35:32-35, 1973.

1069. Klimek, S. Culture element distributions: 1. The structure of California Indian culture. UC-PAAE 37:1-70, 1935.

1070. Krause, F. Die Kultur der kalifornischen Indianer. Leipzig, 1921.

1071. Krieger, A.D. New World culture history: Anglo-America. In Anthropology Today, Chicago, 1953. [Pp. 247-248, Pacific Coast]

1072. Kroeber, A.L. The archaeology of California. Putnam Anniversary Volume, pp. 1-42. New York, 1909.

1073. _____California archaeological work in 1921. AA 24:235, 1922.

1074. _____California archaeological work in 1922. AA 25:111, 1923.

1075. _____The history of native culture in California. UC-PAAE 20:125-142, 1923.

1076. _____California archaeological work in 1924. AA 27:582, 1925.

1077. _____Handbook of the Indians of California. BAE-B 78, 1925. [Chapter 60, general survey of California archaeology]

1078. _____California archaeological work in 1927. AA 30:504, 1928.

1079. _____Prospects in California prehistory. A. Ant. 2:108-116, 1936.

1080. Lister, R.H. The stemmed, indented base point, a possible horizon marker. A. Ant. 28:264-265, 1953.

1081. MacLeod, W.C. California mortuaries. AA 31:772-776, 1929.

1082. Martin, P.S., G.I. Quimby, D. Collier. Indians before Columbus. Chicago: University of Chicago Press, 1947.

1083. Mason, O.T. Aboriginal American harpoons. USNM-AR 1900:189-304, 1902.
[California:Pp. 221-224]

1084. Meighan, C.W. Observations on the efficiency of shovel archaeology. UC-AS-R 7:15-21, 1950.

1085. _____Californian cultures and the concept of an Archaic stage. A. Ant. 24:289-305, 1959.

1086. _____Pacific Coast archaeology. In the Quaternary of the United States. H.E. Wright, Jr. and D.G. Frey, eds. (Pp. 709-719). Princeton University Press, 1965.

1087. Meredith, H.C. Archaeology of California: Central and Northern California. In W.K. Moorehead, Prehistoric implements, Sec. ix, pp. 258-295. Cincinnati, 1900.

1088. Merriam, J.C. Recent cave exploration in California. International Congress of Americanists. (XVth), 1906, Vol. II, pp. 139-146, Quebec, 1907.

1089. Moorehead, W.K. Prehistoric implements. Cincinnati. 1900.
[Northern, Central and Southern California, pp. 230-294]

1090. Moratto, M.J. California's vanishing past: Urban sprawl and the destruction of prehistory. In Death of the Past: 1-6, Society of California Archaeology, S.F., 1970.

1091. _____The status of California archaeology. Special report of the Society for California Archaeology 3:1-31, 1973.

1092. _____Archaeology in the Far West. In C. Chapman (Ed.), Archaeology in the 1970's. Univ. of Missouri Press, 1974.

1093. _____Conservation archaeology: A bibliography. Conservation Archaeology Papers 1, 20 pp. Archaeological Research Laboratory, S.F. State University, 1975.

1094. Musgrave, L.C. The first Californians? Americas 25(4):25-30, 1973.

1095. Oak, H.L. Antiquities of the Pacific States. Overland Monthly 15:305-318, 1875.

1096. Olson, R.L. Recent archaeological work on the Pacific Coast. Proceedings, 5th Pacific Science Congress, Canada, 1933, 4:2841-2846. Toronto, 1934.

1097. Osborne, D. Western American prehistory - an hypothesis. A. Ant. 24:47-52, 1958.

1098. Pastron, A.G., C.W. Clewlow, and P.T. Atkinson. Aboriginal

71

warfare in Northern California: Preliminary observations from skeletal materials. SM-M 47:136-142, 1973.

1099. Pourade, R.F. (Ed.). Ancient hunters of the Far West. San Diego Union Tribune Public., 1966.

1100. Putnam, F.W. On a collection of perforated stones from California. Proceedings of the Boston Society of Natural History 23:356, 1888.

1101. Ragir, S.R. The Early Horizon in Central California prehistory. UC-ARF-C 15, 1972.

1102. Riddell, F. and D. McGeein. Atlatl spurs from California. A. Ant. 34:474-478, 1969.

1103. Ritter, E.W., et al (Eds.). Papers on California and Great Basin prehistory. CARD Publ. No. 2, 1970.

1104. Schumacher, P. Ancient graves and shellheaps of California. SI-AR 1874:337-350, 1875. Reprinted UC-ARF, 1973.

1105. _____Observations on kjökken möddings and the finds in ancient graves in Southern California. Archiv für Anthropologie8:217-221, 1875. Reprinted UC-ARF, 1973.

1106. _____The case for salvage archaeology in California. SM-M 40:61-66, 1966.

1107. Smith, G.A. Black-paint stones. SM-M 28:187-190, 1954.

1108. State Archaeological Task Force. The status of California's heritage. Resources Agency, Sacramento, 1973.

1109. Tadlock, W.L. Certain crescentic stone objects as a time marker in the Western United States. A. Ant. 31:662-675, 1966.

1110. Warren, C.N. California. In J.E. Fitting (Ed.), The Development of North American Archaeology: 213-250, Anchor Books, Garden City, 1973.

1111. Wheeler, B.I. and F.W. Putnam. Ethnological and archaeological survey of California. AA 5:727-729, 1903.

1112. Willey, G.R. An introduction to American archaeology (Pp. 361-380, California). Prentice Hall, Inc., New Jersey, 1966.

1113. Willey, G.R. and P. Phillips. Method and theory in American Archaeology. Univ. of Chicago Press, 1958. [Framework of historical-developmental stages in prehistoric California-Delta, Bay areas. See also AA 57(4), 1955]

1114. Wuertele, E. Bibliographical history of California anthropological research 1850-1917. UC-C-ARF 26, 1975.

1115. Yates, L.G. The relics of the mound builders of California. *Alameda County Independent.* P. 1, June 19, 1875.

1116. _____Prehistoric man in California. Santa Barbara Society of Natural History Bulletin, No. 1:23-30, 1887.

1117. _____California Indian relics. The Traveler (S.F.). P. 54, October 1896.

1118. _____Aboriginal weapons of California. Overland Monthly, 2nd ser., 27:337-342, 1896.

1119. _____Archaeology of California: Southern California. In W.K. Moorehead, Pre-historic implements, Sec. vii, pp. 230-252, Cincinnati, 1900.

1120. _____Prehistoric California. SCAS-B 4:26-27, 1905.

XVII. NORTHWESTERN COAST; KLAMATH MOUNTAINS

1121. Chartkoff, J. and K.K. Chartkoff. Michigan State University Klamath River project. SCA-N 6:10-11, 1972.

1122. _____Test excavations at the May site, Seiad Valley. SCA-N 7:12-13, 1973.

1123. _____Late Period settlement of the Middle Klamath River of Northwest California. A. Ant. 40: 172-179, 1975.

1124. Cressman, L.S. Archaeological work in the Iron Gate Reservoir, Siskiyou County, California. California Oregon Power Co. University of Oregon, 1960. [Mimeo]

1125. Elsasser, A.B. and R.F. Heizer. Excavation of two Northwestern California coastal sites. UC-AS-R 67:1-150, 1966.

1126. Goldschmidt, W.R. A Hupa "calendar". AA 42:176-177, 1940.

1127. Gould, R.A. Archaeology of the Point St. George site, and Tolowa prehistory. UC-PA 4, 1966.

1128. _____A radiocarbon date from the Point St. George site, Northwestern California. UC-C-ARF 14:41-44, 1972.

1129. Harrington, E. The driftwood witch and the Tolowa adze-handle. SM-M 45:14-16, 1940.

1130. Harrington, M.R. Trailing early Californians. SM-M 13:163-166, 1939. [Illustration of slate "slave killer" and obsidian blades from Crescent City]

1131. Heizer, R.F. An unusual decorated steatite slab from Northwestern California. A. Ant. 15:252-254, 1950.

1132. _____ A prehistoric Yurok ceremonial site. UC-AS-R 11: 1-4, 1951.

1133. _____ Sacred rain rocks of Northern California. UC-AS-R 20:33-38, 1953.

1134. _____ An unusual antler zooform club from Northwestern California. UC-AS-R 38:17-18, 1957.

1135. Heizer, R.F. and A.B. Elsasser. Archaeology of Hum-67, the Gunther Island site in Humboldt Bay, California. UC-AS-R 62:5-122, 1964.

1136. Heizer, R.F. and J. Mills. The four ages of Tsurai. U.C. Press, Berkeley, 1952.

1137. Kroeber, A.L. and S.A. Barrett. Fishing among the Indians of Northwestern California. UC-AR 21(1), 1960.

1138. Leonhardy, F.C. The archaeology of a late prehistoric village in Northwestern California. Museum of Natural History, University of Oregon, Bulletin No. 4, 1967.

1139. Loud, L.L. Ethnogeography and archaeology of the Wiyot territory. UC-PAAE 14:221-436, 1918.

1140. MacCurdy, G.G. The cult of the ax. Washington, 1916.

1141. MacLean, J.J. Remarks on shellmounds near Cape Mendocino, Humboldt County. In C. Rau, Prehistoric Fishing:254-256. Smithsonian Institution, 1884.

1142. Mason, O.T. The Ray Collection from Hupa Reservation. SI-AR 1886:205-239, 1889.

1143. Miles, C. The Gunther Island sites. SM-M 39:92-103, 1965.

1144. Mills, J.E. Recent developments in the study of Northwestern California archaeology. UC-AS-R 7:21-25, 1950.

1145. Moratto, M.J. An archaeological survey of selected areas within Redwood National Park, California. U.S. National Park Service. Tucson, 1971.

1146. _____ Archaeological investigations in the Redwood National Park Region, California. U.S. National Park Service. Tucson, 1972.

1147. Palais, H. and A.E. Treganza. Natural resources of Northwestern California; preliminary report on history and archaeology. National Park Service. S.F., 1958.

1148. Rust, H.N. The obsidian blades of California. AA 7:688-695, 1905.

1149. Strong, C.L. The amateur scientist. Scientific American 217: 134-138, 1967.

1150. Thomsen, H.H. and R.F. Heizer. The archaeological potential of the Coast Yuki. UC-AS-R 63:45-83, 1964.

1151. Wallace, W.J. and E.S. Taylor. Excavation of Sis-13, a rock shelter in Siskiyou County, California. UC-AS-R 15: 13-39, 1952.

1152. Woodward, A. Some Tolowa specimens. MAIHF-INM 4:137-150, 1927.

XVIII. NORTHEASTERN PLATEAU AREA

1153. Anderson, R. Clear Lake cremation. Klamath County Museum: Clearing House for News 1(2):2, 1957.

1154. Baumhoff, M.A. and D.L. Olmsted. Palainihan: Radiocarbon support for glottochronology. AA 65:278-284, 1963.

1155. _____Notes on Palainihan culture history: Glottochronology and archaeology. In W. Bright (Ed.), Studies in California Linguistics. UC-PL 34:1-12, 1964

1156. Cressman, L.S. Archaeological researches in the northern Great Basin. Carnegie Institution of Washington, Publ. 538, 1942.
[Chaps. xv-xix, Lower Klamath Lake artifacts]

1157. _____Artifacts from Lower Klamath Lake. In Archaeological Researches in the Northern Great Basin. Carnegie Instit. of Washington Publ. 538:99-102, 1942.

1158. Fenenga, F. and R.F. Heizer. Origin and authenticity of an atlatl dart from Lassen County, California. A. Ant. 7:134-146, 1941.

1159. Fenenga, F. and F.A. Riddell. Excavation of Tommy Tucker Cave, Lassen County, California. A. Ant. 14:203-214, 1949.

1160. Hardesty, D.L. and S. Fox. Archaeological investigations in Northern California. Nevada Archaeological Survey, Research Paper 4, 1974.

1161. Harrington, M.R. Treasures from Tule Lake. SM-M 28:97-103, 1954.

1162. Heizer, R.F. Massacre Lake Cave, Tule Cave and shore sites. In Archaeological researches in the Northern Great Basin. Carnegie Instit. of Washington, Publ. 538, 1942.

1163. Johnson, L. Obsidian hydration rate for the Klamath Basin of California and Oregon. Science 165:1354-1356, 1969.

1164. O'Connell, J.F. The prehistory of Surprise Valley. BP-PA 4, 1975.

1165. O'Connell, J.F. and R.D. Ambro. A preliminary report on the archaeology of the Rodriguez Site (CA-Las-194), Lassen County, California. UC-AS-R 73:95-194, 1968.

1166. O'Connell, J.F. and P.S. Hayward. Altithermal and Medithermal human adaptations in Surprise Valley, Northeast California. Desert Research Institute Publications in the Social Sciences 8:25-41, 1972.

1167. Pilling, A.R. An incised pebble from Lassen County, California. UC-AS-R 38:6, 1957.

1168. Riddell, F.A. Summary report of the excavation of the Karlo Site. UU-AP 26:63-73, 1956.

1169. _____ Archaeological research in Lassen County, California. UC-AS-R 33:44-49, 1956.

1170. _____ The Eastern California border: cultural and temporal affinities. UC-AS-R 42:41-48, 1958.

1171. _____ The archaeology of the Karlo Site (Las-7), California. UC-AS-R 53, 1960.

1172. _____ Fossilized California bone artifacts. SM-M 47:28-32, 1973.

1173. Squier, R.J. Recent excavation and survey in Northeastern California. UC-AS-R 33:34-38, 1956.

XIX. NORTH COAST RANGES

1174. Contreras, E. An extraordinary Central California burial in Marin County. UC-AS-R 38:29-33, 1957.

1175. Edwards, R.L. A settlement pattern hypothesis for the Coast Miwok based on an archaeological survey of Point Reyes National Seashore. SFSC-TAMP 6:105-113, 1972 (1970).

1176. Fredrickson, D.A. Mrn-27 shell beads. In T.F. King, The dead at Tiburon:28-29, 1970.

1177. _____ Cultural diversity in early Central California: a view from the North Coast Ranges. JCA 1(1):41-53, 1974.

1178. Gerow, B.A. Comments on Fredrickson's "Cultural diversity". JCA 1(2):239-246, 1974.

1179. Harrington, M.R. A glimpse of Pomo archaeology. SM-M 17:9-12, 1943.

1180. _____Dollar Island. SM-M 22:154-156, 1948.

1181. Heizer, R.F. The archaeology of the Napa Region. UC-AR 12: 225-358, 1953.

1182. Jackson, T.L. San Jose Village: A Northern Marin County site. MAPOM Papers, No. 1, 1974.

1183. King, T.F. A cache of stone artifacts having "musical" properties from Marin County, California. A. Ant. 31:739-740, 1966.

1184. _____ Antiquities legislation in Marin County, California. Archaeology 21:62, 1968.

1185. _____Archaeological problems and research in the Coast Miwok area. SFSC-TAMP 6:275-288, 1972 (1970).

1186. _____ A possible paleo-Indian cemetery and village site in Lake County. SCA-N 7:1, 1973.

1187. _____ Flight to new pigeonholes: comments on Fredrickson. JCA 1(2):233-239, 1974. [In JCA 1(1), 1974]

1188. King, T.F., et al. Archaeological investigations in the San Antonio Valley, Marin and Sonoma Counties, California. Northwestern California Archaeological Society, Occasional Papers No. 1, Petaluma, 1966.

1189. King, T.F. and W. Upson. Protohistory on Limantour Sandspit: Archaeological investigations at 4-Mrn-216 and 4-Mrn-298. SFSC-TAMP 6:115-194, 1970.

1190. MacLean, J.J. Remarks on shellmounds near Cape Mendocino, Humboldt County. In C. Rau, Prehistoric fishing. SI-CK 25:254-256, 1884.

1191. Mannion, M.C. and L. Mannion. Abstracts from the Kelley manuscript: Coast Miwok material culture. SFSC-TAMP 6: 65-96, 1970.

1192. Meighan, C.W. Excavations in Sixteenth Century shellmounds at Drake's Bay, Marin County. UC-AS-R 9:27-32, 1950.

1193. _____ Archaeology of sites Nap-129 and Nap-131. In R.F. Heizer (Ed.), The Archaeology of the Napa Region. UC-AR 12:315-317, 1953.

1194. _____ Archaeology of the North Coast Ranges, California. UC-AS-R 30:1-39, 1955.

1195. Meighan, C.W. Archaeology: An introduction. (pp. 137-146), Chandler: San Francisco, 1966.
[Drake's Bay midden site]

1196. Meighan, C.W. and C.V. Haynes. The Borax Lake site revisited. Science 167:1213-1221, 1970.

1197. Meighan, C.W. and R.F. Heizer. Archaeological exploration of Sixteenth Century Indian mounds at Drake's Bay. California Hist. Society Quarterly 31(2):98-108, 1952.

1198. Moratto, M.J. A history of archaeological research at Point Reyes, California. SFSC-TAMP 6:97-104, 1972 (1970).

1199. _____A prospectus for the archaeological future of Point Reyes Peninsula. SFSC-TAMP 6:257-274, 1972 (1970).

1200. Moratto, M.J., et al. Sam Alley: Excavations at 4-Lak-305 near Upper Lake, California. SFSC-TAMP 11, 1973.

1201. Moratto, M.J., L.M. Riley, and S.C. Wilson (Eds.). Shelter Hill: Archaeological investigations at 4-Mrn-14, Mill Valley, California. SFSC-TAMP 15, 1974.

1202. Novato Sr. High (School) Archaeology Club. Report on the excavation of Mrn-374. (J. McBeath, Advisor). Novato, 1967.

1203. Porter, L.C. and D.C. Watson. Excavating in California. Hobbies, July:131-132, 1933.
[Bodega Bay area]

1204. Rau, C. Shell-heaps, near Cape Mendocino, Humboldt County, California. UC-AS-R 50:25-27, 1960.
[Reprinted from C. Rau, Aboriginal fishing in Europe and North America. SI-CK 25:254-256, 1885]

1205. Robinson, E. A house floor in Napa County, California. CDPR-AR 10:41-65, 1964.

1206. Schenk, R.E. (Ed.). Contributions to the Archaeology of Point Reyes National Seashore: a compendium in honor of Adan E. Treganza. SFSC-TAMP 6, 1970.

1207. Stearns, R.E.C. On certain aboriginal implements from Napa County, California. American Naturalist 16:203-209, 1882.

1208. Strong, C.L. An Indian mound is excavated by high school archaeologists. Scientific American 217(6):134-138, 1967.
[Mrn-374]

1209. Thomsen, H.H. and R.F. Heizer. The archaeological potential of the Coast Yuki. UC-AS-R 63:45-83, 1964.

1210. Treganza, A.E. Salvage archaeology in the Trinity Reservoir area, Northern California. UC-AS-R 43, part 1, 1958.

1211. Treganza, A.E., C. Smith, and W. Weymouth. An archaeological survey of the Yuki area. UC-AR 12:113-124, 1950.

1212. Wilson, S.C. Faunal analysis of Mrn-298: A perspective on Mrn-216. SFSC-TAMP 6:211-222, 1970.

1213. Yates, L.G. Notes on the Indians of Clear Lake. Alameda County Independent. June 12, 1875, p. 1.

XX. SACRAMENTO VALLEY AND DELTA

1214. Beardsley, R.K. Culture sequences in Central California archaeology. A. Ant. 14:1-28, 1948.

1215. Beck, J.L. A chipped stone crescent from Tracy Lake, California. SM-M 45:154-156, 1971.

1216. Belous, R.E. The Central California chronological sequence re-examined. A. Ant. 18:341-353, 1953.

1217. Bennyhoff, J.A. An antler point from the Sacramento Valley. UC-AS-R 38:19-25, 1957.

1218. Casteel, R.W. Some archaeological uses of fish remains. A. Ant. 37:404-419, 1972.

1219. Chartkoff, J.L. and K.K. Chartkoff. Excavations at the Finch Site: Research strategy and procedures. UCLA-AS-AR 10:315-370, 1968.

1220. Cook, S.F. and A.B. Elsasser. Burials in sand mounds of the delta region of the Sacramento-San Joaquin River system. UC-AS-R 35:26-46, 1956.

1221. Cook, S.F. and R.F. Heizer. The physical analysis of nine Indian mounds of the lower Sacramento Valley. UC-PAAE 40:281-312, 1951.

1222. Cowan, R.A., et al. The unusual burial of a bear and child from the Sacramento delta. UCLA-JNWA 1(2):25-30, 1975.

1223. Davis, L.C. "Long ago in San Joaquin." Sunset, Vol. 19:533-538, San Francisco, 1907.

1224. Elsasser, A.B. A steatite dish and a fragmentary stone pipe from Butte County, California. UC-AS-R 38:14-16, 1957.

1225. Fenenga, F. The elk antler adze. New Mexico Anthropologist 3:23-26, 1940.

1226. Furlong, E.L. The exploration of Samwel Cave. AJS 22:235-247, 1906.

1227. Haag, W.G. and R.F. Heizer. A dog burial from Sacramento Valley. A. Ant. 18:263-264, 1953.

1228. Harradine, F. Report on pedologic observations made at the "Capay Man" site in western Yolo County. UC-AS-R 22: 27, 1953.

1229. Heizer, R.F. A unique type of fishhook from Central California. SM-M 11:96-97, 1937.

1230. _____ A Folsom-type point from Sacramento Valley. SM-M 12:180-182, 1938.

1231. _____ Some Sacramento Valley-Santa Barbara archaeological relationships. SM-M 13:31-35, 1939.

1232. _____ The direct historical approach in California archaeology. A. Ant. 7:98-122, 1941.

1233. _____ The archaeology of Central California I: The Early Horizon. UC-AR 12:1-84, 1949.

1234. Heizer, R.F. and S.F. Cook. "Capay Man" an ancient Central California Indian burial. UC-AS-R 22:24-26, 1953.

1235. Heizer, R.F. and F. Fenenga. Archaeological horizons in Central California. A. Ant. 41:378-399, 1939.

1236. Heizer, R.F. and G.W. Hewes. Animal ceremonialism in Central California in the light of archaeology. AA 42:587-603, 1940.

1237. Johnson, E.N. The serrated points of Central California. A. Ant. 6:167-169, 1940.

1238. _____ Stone mortars of Contra Costa County, California. A. Ant. 7:322-326, 1942.

1239. Johnson, J.J. The archaeology of the Camanche Reservoir locality, California. SAS-P 6:1-34, 1967.

1240. Jones, P.M. Mound excavations near Stockton. UC-PAAE 20: 113-122, 1922.

1241. Kroeber, A.L. "Lodi Man". Science 87:137-138, 1938.

1242. Lillard, J.B., R.F. Heizer, and F. Fenenga. An introduction to the archaeology of Central California. Sacramento Junior College, Dept. of Anthropology, Bull. 2, 1939.

1243. Lillard, J.B. and W.K. Purves. The archaeology of the Deer Creek-Cosumnes Area, Sacramento County, California. Sacramento Junior College, Dept. of Anthro., Bull. 1, 1936.

1244. Meredith, H.C. Aboriginal art in obsidian. Land of Sunshine 11:255-258, 1899.

1245. Nordenskiöld, E. Modifications in Indian culture through inventions and loans. Comparative Ethnographical Studies no. 8. Gothenburg, 1930.
[Pp. 35-39, Lower Sacramento Valley baked clay objects]

1246. Olsen, W.H. and F.A. Riddell. Salvage of the Rio Oso Site. CDPR-AR 6, 1962.

1247. Palumbo, P.J. The archaeology of Amador-23. SAS-P 6:1-33, 1967.

1248. Payen, L.A. A spearthrower (atlatl) from Potter Creek Cave. In Papers on California and Great Basin Prehistory. CARD Publ. No. 2, 1970.

1249. Pritchard, W.E., et al. The Porter Rock Shelter site (But-S177), Butte County, California. UCLA-AS-AR 8:287-315, 1966.

1250. Schenck, W.E. and E.J. Dawson. Archaeology of the northern San Joaquin Valley. UC-PAAE 25:289-413, 1929.

1251. Sinclair, W.J. The exploration of Potter Creek Cave. UC-PAAE 2:1, 1904.

1252. Smith, C.E. and W.D. Weymouth. Archaeology of the Shasta Dam area, California. UC-AS-R 19, 1952.

1253. Smith, P. Obsidian ceremonials from mounds in Northern California. Hobbies (August), 1941, pp. 100-101.

1254. Treganza, A.E. Salvage Archaeology in Nimbus and Redbank Reservoirs areas, Central California. UC-AS-R 26, 1954.

1255. Treganza, A.E. and M.H. Heicksen. Salvage archaeology in the Whiskeytown Reservoir and the Wintu Pumping plant, Shasta County, California. SFSC-TAMP 1, 1960.

XXI. SAN JOAQUIN VALLEY

1256. Anonymous. Where the vanished Yokuts buried their dead. Standard Oil Bulletin: February, 1937, pp. 10-13.
[Buena Vista Lake]

1257. Belding, L. Relics from an Indian burying ground (In San Joaquin County). Zoë 3:124,200, 1892.

1258. Coyle, J. Archaeology in the Southern San Joaquin Valley. ASASC-N 4(1-2):9-10, 1957.

1259. Fenenga, F. The archaeology of Slick Rock Village, Tulare County, California. A. Ant. 17:339-347, 1952.

1260. Gifford, E.W. and W.E. Schenck. Archaeology of the Southern San Joaquin Valley. UC-PAAE 23:1-123, 1926.

1261. Harrington, M.R. Treasures from Tule [Tulare] Lake. SM-M 28:97-103, 1954.

1262. Heizer, R.F. A cave burial from Kern County. UC-AS-R 10: 29-36, 1951.

1263. Hewes, G.W. Archaeological reconnaissance of the Central San Joaquin Valley. A. Ant. 7:123-133, 1941.

1264. King, T.F., R.E. Schenk, and L.E. Wildesen. Audio-visual techniques in emergency salvage archaeology. A. Ant. 35:220-223, 1970.

1265. Kroeber, A.L. At the bedrock of history. Sunset Magazine 25:255-260, 1910.
[Reprinted in UC-AS-R 11:5-10, 1951]

1266. Latta, F.F. San Joaquin primeval: Archaeology. The Tulare Daily Times: May 19-July 15, 1931.

1267. McAlexander, M. and W. Upson. Gewachiu (Fre-398). SFSC-TAMP 5(7), 1969.

1268. Mounday, L.H. and C.H. Jennings. Kern County dig. SCA-N 6:7-8, 1972.

1269. Moratto, M.J. The archaeology of the Jones Site, 4-Mad-159. SFSC-TAMP 5(5), 1969.

1270. _____Chowchilla River prehistory. Madera County Historian 12(2):1-8, 1972.

1271. _____Reviews of "Archaeology of the Grayson Site, Merced County, California," by W.H. Olsen and L. Payen, and "Archaeology of the Menjoulet Site, Merced County, California," by W.E. Pritchard. A. Ant. 37:556-558, 1972.

1272. Olsen, W.H. and L. Payen. Archaeology of the Little Panoche Reservoir, Fresno County, California. CDPR-AR 11, 1968.

1273. _____Archaeology of the Grayson Site, Merced, California. CDPR-AR 12, 1969.

1274. Olsen, W.H. and N. Wilson. The salvage archaeology of the Bear Creek Site (SJo-112), a terminal Central California Early Horizon site. SAS-P 1, 1964.

1275. Pendergast, D.M. and C.W. Meighan. The Greasy Creek Site, Tulare County, California. UCLA-AS-AR 1:1-10, 1959.
[San Joaquin Valley]

1276. Pilling, A.R. The archaeological implications of an annual coastal visit for Central Yokuts groups. AA 52: 438-440, 1950.

1277. Pritchard, W. Archaeology of the Menjoulet Site, Merced County, California. CDPR-AR 13, 1970.

1278. Riddell, F.A. Excavation of site Ker-74. UC-AS-R 10:1-29, 1951.

1279. Schenck, W. and E.J. Dawson. Archaeology of the Northern San Joaquin Valley. UC-PAAE 25:4, 1929.

1280. Steward, G.C. Mounds in California. American Antiquarian 12:26-27, 1890.

1281. Summers, R.W. Archaeology of the Kern National Wildlife Refuge: Site FSC-59. Fresno State College Department of Anthropology, 1971.

1282. Walker, E.F. A Yokuts cemetery at Elk Hills. SM-M 9:145-150, 1935.

1283. _____ Excavation of a Yokuts Indian cemetery. Kern County Historical Society, Bakersfield, 1947.

1284. Walker, W.S. Excavating ancient Yokuts shellmounds in California. Smithsonian Institution explorations and field-work (1934):73-76, 1935.

1285. Wallace, W.J. Archaeological resources of the Poso Creek Reservoir area. SM-M 41:88-97, 1967.

1286. _____ Archaeological investigations at Hidden Reservoir, Madera County, California. ARA-CCA 7, 1973.

1287. Warren, C.N. and M.B. McKusick. A burial complex from the Southern San Joaquin Valley. UCLA-AS-AR 1:15-24, 1959.

1288. Wedel, W.R. Archaeological investigations at Buena Vista Lake, Kern County, California. BAE-B 130, 1941.

1289. von Werlhof, J.C. Granite galleries. CAS-PD 11(4):16-22, 1958.

1290. _____ Six chert knives from Tulare County, California. UC-AS-R 50:37-41, 1960.

XXII. SIERRA NEVADA

1291. Allsop, R. California and its Gold Mines. London. 1853. [Pp. 51-53, early note on bedrock mortars]

1292. Anonymous. The A.J. Brown Collection donated to Yosemite

Museum. YNN 3:3-4, 1924.
[Notes on a collection of 622 Indian artifacts]

1293. Anonymous. Appraisal of the archaeological resources of Pine
       Flat Reservoir, Fresno County, California. SI-RBS
       (Columbia Basin), 1948.

1294. Avery, B.P. Chips from an Indian workshop. Overland Monthly
       11:489-493, 1873.

1295. Baumhoff, M.A. Excavation of site Teh-1 (Kingsley Cave). UC-
       AS-R 30:40-73, 1955.

1296. _____ An introduction to Yana archaeology. UC-AS-R
       40:1-61, 1957.

1297. Beck, J. Turtle-bone artifacts from Pinnacle Point Cave
       (4-Tuo-272), Tuolumne County, California. In Papers
       on California and Great Basin Prehistory. CARD Publ.
       2, 1970.

1298. Becker, G.F. Antiquities from under Tuolumne Table Mountain
       in California. GSA-B 2:189-200, 1891.

1299. Bennet, W. Obsidian arrowheads. YNN 21:61-63, 1942.

1300. Bennyhoff, J.A. High altitude occupation in the Yosemite
       Park region. UC-AS-R 21:31-32, 1953.

1301. _____ An appraisal of the archaeological resources of
       Yosemite National Park. UC-AS-R 34, 1956.

1302. Berryman, L. and A.B. Elsasser. Terminus Reservoir. U.S.
       Army Corps of Engineers. Sacramento, 1966.

1303. Caywood, L.R. An Indian medicine man's grave located. YNN
       33:48-49, 1954.

1304. Conger, O.D. The Witt Collection. Diggers Digest (Northwest-
       ern Calif. Archaeological Society) 11(6), 1963.

1305. Davis, J.O., et al. Coastal geomorphology of the South shore
       of Lake Tahoe. In Holocene Environmental Change. Nev-
       ada Archaeological Survey, Res. Paper No. 6:40-65, 1976.

1306. Douglas, I. Ancient campsites. YNN 15:22-23, 1936.

1307. Drucker, P. Appraisal of the archaeological resources of the
       Pine Flat Reservoir, Fresno County, California. SI-
       RBS, 1948.

1308. Elsasser, A.B. Aboriginal use of restrictive Sierran environ-
       ments. UC-AS-R 41:27-33, 1957.

1309. Elsasser, A.B. The archaeology of the Sierra Nevada in California and Nevada. UC-AS-R 51, 1960.

1310. Enfield, R. and G. Enfield. Mammoth Creek Cave, Mono County, California. UCLA-AS-AR 6:393-430, 1964.

1311. Engle, M. Caliente's big year. Desert Magazine, p. 10, Dec. 1969.
[Photo of bedrock mortars at intersection of Caliente-Bodfish Road and Bealville Road]

1312. Fitzwater, R.J. Final report on two seasons' excavations at El Portal, Mariposa County, California. UCLA-AS-AR 4: 235-282, 1962.

1313. _____ Big Oak Flat; Two Archaeological Sites in Yosemite National Park. UCLA-AS-AR 10:275-314, 1968.

1314. Fitzwater, R.J. and M. Van Vlissingen. Preliminary report on an archaeological site at El Portal, California. UCLA-AS-AR 2:155-200, 1960.

1315. Freed, S.A. Washo habitation sites in the Lake Tahoe area. UC-AS-R 66:73-83, 1966.

1316. Garrison, L. Indian Creek Rancheria. YNN 17:72, 1938.

1317. Gonsalves, W.C. Winslow Cave, a mortuary site in Calaveras County, California. UC-AS-R 29:31-45, 1955.

1318. Griffin, D.W. Prehistory of the Southern Sierra Nevada. SM-M 37:49-57,105-113, 1963.

1319. _____ Material culture imperatives: A method proposed for using ethnographic data in investigating prehistoric sites. UCLA-AS-AR 6:229-247, 1964.

1320. Guthrie, G. Southern Sierra Nevada archaeology. ASASC-N 4 (1-2):3-5, 1957.

1321. Hartesveldt, R.J. Indian sites' study adds to Yosemite's Story. YNN 32:53-59, 1953.

1322. Heizer, R.F. and A.B. Elsasser. Some archaeological sites and cultures from the Central Sierra Nevada. UC-AS-R 21, 1953.

1323. Heizer, R.F. and T.R. Hester. The archaeology of Bamert Cave, Amador County, California. UC-ARF, 1973.

1324. Henn, W.G. The archaeology of 4-Mad-158. SFSC-TAMP 5(3), 1969.

1325. _____ Excavations at 4-Tuo-279. SFSC-TAMP 9:45-65, 1971.

1326. Hindes, M.G. A report on Indian sites and trails, Huntington Lake Region, California. UC-AS-R 48:1-15, 1959.

1327. Hindes, M.G. The archaeology of the Huntington Lake Region in the Southern Sierra Nevada, California. UC-AS-R 58, 1962.

1328. Jensen, P.M. Notes on the archaeology of the Sutter Buttes. In Papers on California and Great Basin Prehistory. CARD Publ. 2, 1970.

1329. Jewell, D.P. Archaeology of the Oroville Dam Spillway. CDPR-AR 10:1-40, 1964.

1330. Johnson, J.J. The archaeology of the Camanche Reservoir locality, California. SAS-P 6, 1967.

1331. _____ Archaeological investigations at the Applegate Site (4-Ama-56). In Papers on California and Great Basin Prehistory. CARD Publ. 2, 1970.

1332. Johnston, R.L. An Indian village site near the Mariposa Grove. YNN 16:6, 1937.

1333. King, T.F. The archaeology of the Schwabacher Site, 4-Mad-117. In The archaeology of the Buchanan Reservoir Region, Madera County, California. SFSC-TAMP 4(2), 1968.

1334. _____ Three little settlements: Initial investigation of small Mariposa Complex middens at Buchanan Reservoir. SFSC-TAMP 5(4), 1969.

1335. King, T.F. (Ed.). Archaeology of the Buchanan Reservoir Region, Madera County, California. SFSC-TAMP 5(3-7), 1969.

1336. King, T.F. Buchanan Reservoir. SCA-N 6:4, 1972.

1337. King, T.F. and M.J. Moratto. Archaeology of the Buchanan Reservoir region, Madera County, California. Parts I and II. SFSC-TAMP 4(1-2), 1968.

1338. Lathrap, D.W. and D. Shutler, Jr. An archaeological site in the High Sierra of California. A. Ant. 20:227-240, 1955.

1339. Littlejohn, H.W. A Northeastern Californian dug-out canoe. AA 31:777-779, 1929.

1340. Mannion, M.L. A report on three archaeological sites with historic components. SFSC-TAMP 5(6), 1969.

1341. Matson, R.G. Pollen from the Spring Garden Ravine site (4-Pla-101). In Papers on Nisenan environment and subsistence. CARD Publ. 3, 1972.

1342. _____ Aspects of Nisenan ecology. In Papers on Nisenan environment and substance. CARD Publ. 3, 1972.

1343. McLellan, P.M. The 7,000 year mistake. YNN 31:110-115, 1952.

1344. Merriam, C.H. Ethnological evidence that the California cave skeletons are not recent. Science 29:805-806, 1909.

1345. _____ Human remains in California caves. American Antiquarian and Oriental Journal 31:152-153, 1909.

1346. _____ Indian village and camp sites in Yosemite Valley. Sierra Club Bulletin 10:202-209, 1917.

1347. Merriam, J.C. Recent cave explorations in California. AA 8: 221-228, 1906.
[Appears also in ICA, 15th Session, 1906 2:139-146, 1907, Quebec]

1348. Moratto, M.J. A reconstruction of proto-Miwok Culture. In T.F. King (Ed.), Buchanan Reservoir background and pre- liminary data. U.S. Nat. Park Serv., S.F., Tucson, 1967.

1349. _____ A Survey of the archaeological resources of the Buchanan Reservoir Region, Madera County, California. SFSC-TAMP 4(1), 1968.

1350. _____ The archaeology of the Jones site, 4-Mad-159. SFSC-TAMP 5(5), 1969.

1351. _____ Archaeology of the Buchanan Reservoir Region, Madera County, California. SFSC-TAMP 7(8), 1970.

1352. _____ Archaeological investigations at 4-Tuo-300, Tuo- lumne County, California. SFSC-TAMP 9:78-111, 1971.

1353. _____ Chowchilla River prehistory. Madera County Hist- orian 12(2):1-8, 1972.

1354. _____ Large structure excavated. SCA-N 6:5, 1972.
[Buchanan Reservoir]

1355. _____ Archaeological investigations of site 4-Cal-414, a rockshelter in Calaveras County, California. Archaeol. Res. Laboratory, S.F. State Univ., 1976.

1356. _____ New Melones archaeological project - Stanislaus River, Calaveras and Tuolumne Counties, California. Phase VI, 5 parts. Conservation Archaeology Papers, No. 3, Archaeol. Res. Lab., S.F. State Univ., 1976.

1357. Moratto, M.J. (Ed.). A study of prehistory in the Tuolumne River Valley, California. SFSC-TAMP 9, 1971.

1358. Olsen, W.H. and F.A. Riddell. The archaeology of the Western Pacific Railroad relocation, Oroville Project, Butte County, California. CDPR-AR 7, 1963.

1359. Orr, P.C. Cave man hunt. SBMNH-MT 26:30-35, 1951.

1360. Palumbo, P.J. The archaeology of 4-Ama-23. SAS-P 6(2), 1967.

1361. Payen, L.A. "Pipe" artifacts from Sierra Nevada mortuary caves. Cave Notes 6(4):25-31, 1964.

1362. Payen, L.A. and D.S. Boloyan. Archaeological excavations at Chilcoot Rockshelter, Plumas County, California. CDPR-AR 4, 1961.

1363. Payen, L.A. and J.J. Johnson. Current cave research in the Central Sierra Nevada Mountains: A progress report. SAS-P 3:26-36, 1965.

1364. Pendergast, D.W. and C.W. Meighan. The Greasy Creek Site, Tulare County, California. UCLA-AS-AR 1:1-10, 1959.

1365. Price, J.A. Washo prehistory: A review of research. UU-AP 67:78-95, 1963.

1366. Rackerby, F.E. An archaeological survey on the Chowchilla River, Madera County, California. UCLA-AS-AR 7:303-322, 1965.

1367. Rasson, J. Excavations at Ahwahnee, Yosemite National Park, California. UCLA-AS-AR 8:165-183, 1966.

1368. Riddell, F.A. Archaeological reconnaissance of Frenchman Dam and Reservoir, Plumas County, California. Calif. Dept. of Water Resources, Archaeological Rpt. A-3, 1960.

1369. Riddell, F.A. and W.E. Pritchard. Archaeology of the Rainbow Point site (4-Plu-594), Bucks Lake, Plumas County, California. University of Oregon Anthropological Papers 1: 59-102, 1971.

1370. Ritter, E.W. Northern Sierra foothill archaeology: Culture history and culture process. CARD Publ. 2:171-184, 1970.

1371. _____ The archaeology of Placer 101. CARD Publ. 3, 1971.

1372. Ritter, E.W. and P.D. Schulz (Eds.). Papers on Nisenan environment and subsistence. CARD Publ. 3, 1972.

1373. Russell, C.P. Interesting Indian artifacts come to light. YNN 4:62, 1925.

1374. Schulz, P.D. and D.D. Simons. Prehistoric bighorn sheep in the Northern Sierra Nevada, California. Great Basin Naturalist 33:221-224, 1973.

1375. Sheets, P.D. Surface collection analysis. SCA-N 7:12, 1973. [Sierra National Forest]

1376. Sinclair, W.J. Recent investigations bearing on the question of Neocene man in the auriferous gravels òf the Sierra Nevada. UC-PAAE 7:107-132, 1908.

1377. Treganza, A.E. Archaeological investigations in the Farm-ington Reservoir area, Stanislaus County, California. UC-AS-R 14, 1952.

1378. Treganza, A.E., M.H. Heickson, and W.B. Woolfenden. The archaeology of the Black Butte Reservoir region. Glenn and Tehama Counties, California. SFSC-TAMP 2, 1969.

1379. Treganza, A.E. and R.F. Heizer. Additional data on the Farm-ington Complex, a stone implement assemblage of probable early postglacial date from Central California. UC-AS-R 22:28-38, 1953.

1380. Wallace, W.J. The archaeological deposit in Moaning Cave, Calaveras County. UC-AS-R 12:29-41, 1951.

1381. _____ The mortuary caves of Calaveras County. Archaeology 4:199-203, 1951.

1382. _____ Seasonal Indian campsites in the Lake Isabella area, California. SM-M 44:84-96, 1970.

1383. Wallace, W.J. and D.W. Lathrap. An early implement assemblage from a limestone cavern in California. A Ant 18:133-138, 1952.

1384. von Werlhof, J. What we found at Hospital Rock. The Kaweah Magazine, September, p. 17-22, 1960.

XXIII. SAN FRANCISCO BAY

1385. Anonymous. Shellmound in California.. American Antiquarian. 7:159-162, 1885.
        [Emeryville shellmound]

1386. Anonymous. Records of the past. 2:351, 1903.
        [A brief note on shell mound opened at Port Richmond, California by C.P. William of the Golden Gate Park Memorial Museum]

1387. Anonymous. Indians of the San Francisco Bay region. Science, Supplement XII, Sept. 11, 1925.

1388. Asturias, M. A brief account of archaeology at 4-SMa-110. SFSC-TAMP 8:49-55, 1971.

1389. Bancroft, H.H. The native races of the Pacific states. Vol. 4:709-712, 1882-1883.

1390. Beardsley, R.K. Culture sequences in Central California archaeology. A Ant 14:1-28, 1948.

1391. Beardsley, R.K. Temporal and areal relationships in Central California Archaeology. UC-AS-R 24,25, 1954.

1392. Brown, A.K. Before the Sanchez Adobe. La Peninsula, San Mateo County Historical Society, 1957.

1393. Brown, A.K. and F. Stanger. Who discovered the Golden Gate? San Mateo County Historical Society, 1969.

1394. Bush, F.R. Prehistoric implements of the Rivers Coyote and Guadalupe, Santa Clara County, California. American Naturalist 13:715-716, 1879.

1395. Coberly, M.B. The archaeology of the Ryan Mound, Site Ala-329, A Central California coastal village site. Univ. of Northern Colorado, Occasional Publ. in Anthropology, Archaeology Series, No. 4, 114 pp., 1973.

1396. Davidson, E.C. Notes on California Indian shellmounds. National Society of Colonial Dames of America in the State of California, 1930.

1397. Davis, J.T. The archaeology of the Fernandez site, a San Francisco Bay region shellmound. UC-AS-R 49:11-74, 1960.

1398. Davis, J.T. and A.E. Treganza. The Patterson Mound: A comparative analysis of the archaeology of Site Ala-328. UC-AS-R 47, 1959.

1399. Deans, J. Kithchen middens or shell mounds on the shores of the Bay of San Francisco. Journal of the Anthropological Institute 5:489-490, 1876.

1400. Dodge, R.E. California shellmounds. Records of the past 13: 120, 1914.

1401. Drake, R.J. Archaeological investigations of the San Bruno Shellmound, San Mateo County, California. El Palacio 55:317-323, 1948.

1402. Elsasser, A.B. A charmstone site in Sonoma County, California. UC-AS-R 28:28-33, 1955.

1403. Fredrickson, D. Recent excavations in the interior of Contra Costa County, California. SAS-P 3:18-25, 1965.

1404. _____ Archaeological investigation at CCo-30, near Alamo, Contra Costa County, California. CARD Publ. 1, 1968.

1405. Gerow, B.A. and R.W. Force. An analysis of the University Village Complex. Stanford University, 1968.

1406. Gould, R.A. Exploitative economics and culture change in Central California. UC-AS-R 62:123-163, 1964.

1407. Graham, G.M. Ancient man in Hidden Valley, California. SM-M 25:79-82, 1951.

1408. Greengo, R.E. Molluscan species in California shell middens. UC-AS-R 13, 1951.

1409. Hammel, E.A. An unusual burial from Contra Costa County. UC-AS-R 45:47-55, 1956.

1410. Heizer, R.F. Archaeological evidence of Sebastian Rodriguez Cermeño's California visit in 1595. California Historical Society, Special Publication, 1941.
[Reprinted, with additions, from California Historical Society Quarterly 20:315-328]

1411. _____ Archaeology of CCo-137, the "Concord Man" site. UC-AS-R 9:6-19, 1950.

1412. _____ Indians of the San Francisco Bay Area. Geologic Guidebook of the San Francisco Bay Counties. Bulletin 154, California State Division of Mines, 1951.

1413. _____ The Archaeology of the Napa region. UC-AR 12: 225-358, 1953.

1414. Heizer, R.F. and G.W. Hewes. Animal ceremonialism in Central California in the light of archaeology. AA 42:587-603, 1940.

1415. Heizer, R.F. and T.D. McCown. The Stanford Skull, a probable early man from Santa Clara County, California. UC-AS-R 6, 1950.

1416. Henn, W., T. Jackson, and J. Schlocker. Buried human bones at the "Bart" Site, San Francisco. California Geology 25: 208-209, 1972.
[C-14 dated 4900+ 250 BP]

1417. Howard, H. The avifauna of Emeryville shellmound. UC-PZ 32: 301-394, 1929.

1418. Hudson, A.S. On shell mounds in Oakland, California. CAS-P 5:302,303, 1875.
[Also in "Reprints of various papers on California Archaeology, Ethnology, and Indian History." UC-ARF, 1973]

1419. Jackson, T.L. The geographical source of obsidian from SMa-140. SFSC-TAMP 8:68-69, 1971.

1420. _____ An archaeological reconnaissance of a portion of the San Mateo County coastside. SFSC-TAMP 9:11-20, 1971.

1421. Kemnitzer, L. A survey of archaeological sites in Contra Costa County. CARD Publ. 1:173-183, 1968.

1422. King, C.D. and L. King. General research design: Bay Area Archaeological Cooperative. In T.F. King and P.P. Hickman, The Southern Santa Clara Valley: A general plan for archaeology: Appendix 3:1-4. Report to U.S. National Park Service, Tucson, 1973.

1423. King, T.F. The dead at Tiburon. Northwestern California Archaeological Society Occasional Paper 2, 1970.

1424. King, T.F. and P.P. Hickman. The Southern Santa Clara Valley: A general plan for archaeology. Report to U.S. National Park Service, Tucson, 1973.

1425. Kroeber, A.L. Shellmounds at San Francisco and San Mateo. Records of the Past 10:227-228, 1911.

1426. Laidlaw, G.E. Shell mound in [Oakland] California. American Antiquarian 7:159-162, 1885.

1427. Loud, L.L. The Stege mounds at Richmond, California. UC-PAAE 17:355-372, 1924.

1428. Lyhne, R. Probing for Peninsulans past. In "Peninsula Living": Advance Star, Burlingame, June 1, 1969.

1429. McChesney, ___. Notice of a mound 2.5 miles from Broadway Station, Oakland. CAS-P 5:202, 1875.

1430. Mannion, L. The Tucker Collection from San Mateo County. SFSC-TAMP 8:74, 1971.

1431. McGeein, D.J. and W.C. Mueller. A shellmound in Marin County, California. A. Ant. 21(1):52-66, 1955.

1432. Meighan, C.W. Preliminary excavation at the Thomas Site, Marin County. UC-AS-R 19:1-14, 1953.

1433. Moratto, M.J. Archaeological investigations at 4-SMa-140. SFSC-TAMP 8:56-70, 1971.

1434. _____ Ethnology, ethnohistory, and archaeology in the Southern San Francisco Bay Region: A bibliography. Type Ink Press, Berkeley, 1973.

1435. _____ The Peninsula's Indian past. Santa Cruz Sentinel January 14:17, 1973.

1436. Moratto, M.J. (Compiler). Anthropological and ethnohistorical sources for the San Francisco Bay Region. SFSC-TAMP 13, 1974.

1437. Moratto, M.J. (Ed.). Contributions to the Archaeology of San Mateo County, California. SFSC-TAMP 8, 1971.

1438. Moratto, M.J. and L.M. Riley. A cultural inventory of the Devil's Slide locality (San Mateo County, California). Conservation Archaeology Papers No. 2, 20 pp. Archaeological Research Laboratory, S.F. State Univ., 1975.

1439. Moratto, M.J. and B. Singh. Prior archaeological work in the San Francisco Bay Region. SFSC-TAMP 8:1-8, 1971.

1440. Nelson, N.C. Shellmounds of the San Francisco Bay region. UC-PAAE 7:309-356, 1909.

1441. _____ The Ellis Landing shellmound. UC-PAAE 7:357-426, 1910.

1442. Oliphant, R.L. The Archaeology of 4-SMa-101. SFSC-TAMP 8: 37-48, 1971.

1443. Phebus, G.E., Jr. Contributions to Costanoan archaeology: Archaeological investigations at 4-Ala-330 and 4-SMa-22. In J. Dotta (Ed.), SFSC-TAMP 12, 1973.

1444. Porter, L.C. and C.D. Watson. Excavating in California. Hobbies, pp. 131-132, July 1933.

1445. Powell, J.W. Notes on examination of San Francisco Bay Shell-heaps. In C. Rau, Prehistoric Fishing. SI-CK:254, 1884.

1446. Rackerby, F. The archaeological salvage of two San Francisco Bay shellmounds. SFSC-TAMP 3:1-86, 1967.

1447. Rackerby, F. and J.P. Whelan. Contributions to the archaeology of Southern San Francisco Bay. SFSC-TAMP 3, 1967.

1448. Ransom, L. Shellmounds. CAS-P 4:86-87, 1873. Also in Reprints of Various Papers on California Archaeology, Ethnography and Indian History. UC-ARF, 1973. [San Francisco Bay area]

1449. Riddell, F.A. Archaeological excavation in the Farallon Islands, California. UC-AS-R 32:1-18, 1955.

1450. _____ Archaeological reconnaissance of the South Bay Aqueduct Project, Alameda County, California. California Department of Water Resources, Archaeological Report No. A-1. Sacramento, 1960.

1451. Schenck, W.E. The Emeryville shellmound: Final report. UC-PAAE 23:147-282, 1926.

1452. Schenk, R. Coyote Hills Park report. SCA-N 3(6), 1970.

1453. Schenk, R. and S. Van Dyke. Archaeological investigations on San Bruno Creek. La Peninsula, San Mateo County Historical Society, 1970.

1454. Slaymaker, C. The material culture of Cotomko'tca. MAOPM
      Papers, No. 3, 1977.

1455. Smith and Elliot. History of Contra Costa County. 1878.

1456. Suggs, R.C. The archaeology of San Francisco. Thomas Y.
      Crowell, New York, 1965.

1457. Sumner, F.B., et al. A report upon the physical conditions in
      San Francisco Bay. UC-PZ 14:1-198, 1914.

1458. Treganza, A.E. The examination of Indian shellmounds within
      San Francisco Bay with reference to the possible 1579
      landfall of Sir Francis Drake. Nova Albion Explorations
      Project No. 1. Reporter Pub. Co. Vacaville, 1957.

1459. Treganza, A.E. and S.F. Cook. The quantitative investigation
      of aboriginal sites: Complete excavation with physical
      and archaeological analysis of a single mound. A. Ant.
      13:287-297, 1948.

1460. Uhle, M. The Emeryville shellmound. UC-PAAE 7:1-106, 1907.

1461. _____ El problema paleolítica Americana. Quito, 1923.
      [P. 9 mentions Emeryville shellmound]

1462. Van Dyke, S. The archaeology of site 4-SMa-100. SFSC-TAMP 8:
      21-36, 1971.

1463. Wallace, W.J. and D.W. Lathrap. Ceremonial bird burials in
      San Francisco Bay Shellmounds. A. Ant. 25:262-264, 1959.

1464. _____West Berkeley (Ca-Ala-307): A culturally
      stratified shellmound on the east shore of San Francisco
      Bay. UC-C-ARF 29, 1975.

1465. Whelan, J. A partial faunal analysis of Ala-12 and 13, two
      San Francisco Bay shellmounds. SFSC-TAMP 3:1-24, 1967.

1466. Wildesen, L. Ohlone prehistory. The Indian Historian 2(1):25-
      28, The American Indian Historical Society, 1969.

1467. Yates, L.G. Localities of mounds in Alameda County, Washington
      Township. Alameda County Independent, June 26, July 3,
      July 10, 1875.

XXIV. SOUTH COAST RANGES

1468. Baldwin, M.A. Archaeological evidence of cultural continuity
      between Chumash and Salinan Indians in California. SLOCAS-
      OP 6, 1972.

1469. Barnes, M.S. Some primitive Californians. Appleton's Popular
      Science Monthly 50:486-495, 1897.
      [Excavation in a Santa Clara Valley site]

1470. Breschini, G.S. Archaeological excavations at Mnt-436, the Kodani Site. Monterey County Archaeological Society Quarterly 1(4):1-2, 1972.

1471. _____ Excavations at the Church Creek Rockshelter, Mnt-44. Monterey County Archaeological Society Quarterly 2(4):1-9, 1973.

1472. Clemmer, J.S. Archaeological notes on a Chumash house floor at Morro Bay. Central California Archaeological Foundation, Report for P.G. & E., 1962.

1473. Cole, D. Ancient secrets of Indian life unlocked in Big Sur dig. PCAS-S 12:5-7, 1973.

1474. Dalton, O.M. Note on a specimen of basketwork from California recently acquired by the British Museum. Man 1901:23-24, 1901.

1475. Davidson, E.C. Notes on California Indian shellmounds. National Society of Colonial Dames of America in the State of California, 1930.

1476. Deans, J. Note on shellmounds between Point Bruno and Visitacion Valley. JRAI 5:489, 1876.

1477. Dodge, R.E. California shellmounds. Records of the Past 13: 120, 1914.

1478. Follett, W.I. Fish remains from the Kodani Site. Monterey County Archaeological Society Quarterly 1(4):3-4, 1972.

1479. _____ Fish remains of the Church Rockshelter, Mnt-44, Monterey County, California. Monterey County Archaeological Society Quarterly 2(4):10-11, 1973.

1480. Gates, M.J. Contributions to local history. Mountain View, California, 1894.
[Notes on local archaeology]

1481. Glennan, W.S. An unusual steatite pipe: from the Tehachapi Mountains, California. SM-M 46:152-154, 1972.

1482. Greenwood, R.S. 9,000 years of prehistory at Diablo Canyon, San Luis Obispo County, California. SLOCAS-SP 7, 1972.

1483. Howard, D.M. Archaeological investigations in the Monterey Big Sur Area. The Indian Historian 2(3):41-48, 1969.

1484. _____ Excavations at Tes-haya: The Indian rancheria at Mission San Antonio de Padua (Mnt-100). Monterey County Archaeological Society Quarterly 2(1):1-11, 1972.

1485. _____ Test archaeology at the Smith site, Mnt-463.

Monterey County Archaeological Society Quarterly 2(2): 7-11, 1973.

1486. _____The archaeology of the Uriah Ray rockshelter No. 1. (Mnt-483). Monterey County Archaeological Society Quarterly 2(3):1-11, 1973.

1487. _____The Gamboa site (Mnt-480) - An Esselen village with a review of Esselen ethnography. Monterey County Archaeological Society Quarterly 3(1):1-11, 1973.

1488. _____The Francis Doud site (Mnt-298). Monterey County Archaeological Society Quarterly 3(4):8-11, 1974.

1489. _____Big Sur archaeology at 4-Mnt-88. Popular Archaeology 3(9-10):31-37, 1974.

1490. _____Jolon-an introduction. Monterey County Archaeological Society Quarterly 4(2):6-8, 1975.

1491. Howard, D.M. and S.F. Cook. The archaeology of the Hudson Mound. Monterey County Archaeological Society Quarterly 1(1):1-10, 1971.

1492. LaMonk, C. Painted rock. ASASC-N 2(4):3-5, 1955.

1493. Meighan, C.W. Excavation of Isabella Meadows Cave, Monterey County, California. UC-AS-R 29:1-30, 1955.

1494. Pilling, A.R. The surface archaeology of the Pecho Coast, San Luis Obispo County, California. SM-M 25:196-200, 1951.

1495. _____Relationships of prehistoric cultures of coastal Monterey County, California. KAS-P 12:70-87, 1955.

1496. Rashkin, P. Monterey Peninsula shell mounds - some general remarks. Monterey County Archaeological Society Quarterly 1(4):5-7, 1972.

1497. Reddell, D. Harrigan site: Shell Beach. SLOCAS-OP 1, 1970.

1498. Reinman, F.M. Archaeological investigations at Whale Rock Reservoir, Cayucos, California. CDPR-AR 2, 1961.

1499. Riddell, F.A. Archaeological reconnaissance of Whale Rock Dam and Reservoir, San Luis Obispo County, California. California Department of Water Resources, Archaeological Report A-2, Sacramento, 1960.

1500. Saxe, A.W. Observations on shellmounds at Laguna Creek, 6 miles north of Santa Cruz. CAS-P 5:157, 1875.

1501. Tainter, J. Climatic fluctuations and resource procurement in the Santa Ynez Valley. PCAS-Q 7(3), 1971.

1502. Wallace, W.J. Archaeological investigations in the Arroyo Grande Creek watershed, San Luis Obispo County, California. UCLA-AS-AR 4:23-90, 1962.

1503. Wire, M.V.V. Alamo Creek Site, San Luis Obispo County, California. UCLA-AS-AR 3:107-147, 1961.

XXV. SANTA BARBARA COAST AND ISLANDS

1504. Abbott, C.C. Articles in USGS-WCM: Archaeology Vol. 7, 1879. [Chipped implements, pp. 49-69; mortars and pestles, pp. 70-92; steatite vessels, pp. 93-116; objects of wood, pp. 91-92; stone pipes, pp. 125-134; miscellaneous stone objects, pp. 190-217; bone musical instruments, pp. 234-238]

1505. Abbott, C.C. and F.W. Putnam. Implements and weapons made of bone and wood (from Santa Barbara sites). USGS-WCM 7: 222-223, 1879.

1506. Alliot, H. Burial methods of the Southern California Islanders. SCAS-B 15:11-15, 1916. [Reprinted in SM-M 43:125-131, 1969]

1507. Anderson, E.N., Jr. A bibliography of the Chumash and their predecessors. UC-AS-R 61:25-74, 1964.

1508. Anonymous. Californian and Polynesian fish-hooks. American Naturalist 20:833, 1886.

1509. Anonymous. Articles from Southern California donated to the Peabody Museum. Peabody Mus., Ann. Rept. 9:12-17, 1891.

1510. Anonymous. The uses of tar among Indians. Science News. Nov. 18, 1927.

1511. Anonymous. Chumash village site excavated. El Palacio 27:224-226, 1929.

1512. Anonymous. Fish hooks: The Amerind. Archaeological Society of Southern California, Bulletin 5:6, 1937.

1513. Anonymous. Concentration of metates found at Saticoy. ASASC-N 6:6, 1958.

1514. Anonymous. Excavations at Wihachet. ASASC-N 5:10, 1958.

1515. Anonymous. Chumash canoe to be shown. PCAS-S 14:3-4, 1975.

1516. Ascher, R. A prehistoric population estimate using midden analysis and two population models. SWJA 15:168-178, 1959.

1517. Baumhoff, M.A. Preliminary statement on the excavations at the Cachuma Dam site (SBa-477), California, in 1951. SI-RBS (mimeographed), 1951.

1518. Beers, C.D. Toward comparisons in archaeology: The Santa Barbara Coast and the Northern Channel Islands. In Papers on the Chumash. SLOCAS-OP 9:1-18, 1975.

1519. Bennyhoff, J.A. California fish spears and harpoons. UC-AR 9: 294-337, 1950.

1520. Blackburn, T. A manuscript account of the Ventureño Chumash. UCLA-AS-AR 5:138-158, 1963.

1521. Bowers, S. History and antiquities of Santa Rosa Island. SI-AR (1877):316-320, 1878.

1522. _____ Fish-hooks from Southern California. Science 1:575, 1883.
[Reprinted UC-AS-R 59:71-72, 1963]

1523. _____ Relics in Ventura County, California. Science 3: 373-374, 1884.

1524. _____ Relics of the Santa Barbara Indians. The Kansas City Review of Science and Industry 7(12):748-751, 1884.

1525. _____ Relics from an Indian grave. Science 7:35-36, 1886.

1526. _____ Aboriginal fish-hooks. West American Scientist 3: 243-245, 1887.
[Reprinted in UC-AS-R 59:73-75, 1963]

1527. _____ Report on San Nicolas Island, Ventura County, 9th Annual Report of the State Mineralogist, pp. 57-61. California State Mining Bureau, 1890.

1528. Brown, A.K. The aboriginal population of the Santa Barbara Channel. UC-AS-R 69, 1967.

1529. Bryan, B. Excavation at Mishopsnow. Art and Archaeology 31: 176-185, 1931.

1530. _____ The manufacture of stone mortars. SM-M 35:134-139, 1961.

1531. Cambier, R. Antiquités Indiennes de Californie. Bulletin de la Société des Americanistes de Belgique 29:88-96. Brussels, 1939.

1532. Carter, G.F. Archaeological notes on a midden at Point Sal. A. Ant. 6:214-226, 1941.

1533. Clark, R. The thrills of relic hunting. Westways 36(11):10-11, 1944.

1534. Clemmer, J.S. Archaeological notes on a Chumash house floor at Morro Bay. Central California Archaeological Foundation,

Report for Pacific Gas and Electric Co., Sacramento, 1962.

1535. Coggeshall, A.S. Summary of archaeological work on Santa Rosa Island. SBMNH-AR (1949):12-14, 1950.

1536. Cook, S.F. Analysis of refuse midden material from site Ven-62. UC-AS-R 37:40-41, 1957.

1537. Curtis, F. Arroyo Sequit: Archaeological investigations of a Late coastal site in Los Angeles County, California. ASASC-P 4, 1959.

1538. _____ Arroyo Sequit revisited. ASASC-N 7(3):4-7, 1960.

1539. _____ Some Santa Cruz Island artifacts. SM-M 34:62-65, 1960.

1540. _____ Excavations at Arroyo Sequit. SM-M 37:72-75, 1963.

1541. _____ The Glen Annie Canyon site (SBa-142): A case for sedentary village life. UCLA-AS-AR 7:1-18, 1965.

1542. Dimmick, L.N. Account of the native races - contemporaries of the mound-builders. In Jesse D. Mason, History of Santa Barbara County, pp. 17-18, Oakland, 1883.

1543. Duns, ___. Notice of the recent explorations in the kitchen middens of extinct Indian tribes, Santa Barbara, California. Proceedings of the Society of Antiquaries of Scotland 12:557-561, 1874.

1544. Eberhart, H.H. Temporal horizons of the Santa Barbara Coast. ASASC-N 3:7-8, 1956.

1545. _____ The cogged stones of Southern California. A. Ant. 26:361-369, 1961.

1546. Eberhart, H. and A. Babcock. An archaeological survey of Mutau Flat, Ventura County, California. ARA-CCA 5, 1963.

1547. Edwards, H.A. Notes on the archaeology of the Northern Channel Islands. ASASC-N 3:5-6, 1956.

1548. Eisen, G. An account of the Indians of the Santa Barbara Islands in California. Sitzungberichte der Königliche Böhmischen Gesellschaft der Wissenschaften, Klasse II. 1-30, 1904.

1549. Ellison, W.H. History of the Santa Cruz Island grant. Pacific Historical Review 7:270-283, 1937.

1550. Finley, R.S. Sandstone Bowls. SBMNH-MT 30:36-39, 1955.

1551. Finnerty, P., et al. Community structure and trade at Isthmus Cove: A salvage excavation on Catalina Island. PCAS-OP 1, 1970.

1552. Ford, H.C. Notes on excavations made in Indian burial places in Carpinteria. Santa Barbara Society of Natural History, Bulletin 1:11-18, 1887.
[Reprinted in UC-AS-R 50:14-19, 1960]

1553. Fowler, W.S. Stone age methods of woodworking in the Connecticut Valley. Archaeological Society of Connecticut, Bulletin 20:1-32. New Haven, 1946.
[Fig. 20, illustration of 4 wooden hafted flint knives from Santa Cruz Island and Santa Barbara mainland]

1554. Frederick, M.C. Some Indian paintings. Land of Sunshine 15: 223-227, 1901.

1555. Giglioli, E.H. La Collezione Etnografica. Florence, 1911.
[Pt. 2: pp. 130-133: Numbers and brief description of archaeological specimens from Santa Barbara area]

1556. Glassow, M.A. The Conejo Rock Shelter: An Island Chumash site in Ventura County, California. UCLA-AS-AR 7:19-80, 1965.

1557. Grant, C. Chumash artifacts collected in Santa Barbara County, California. UC-AS-R 63:1-44, 1964.

1558. Greenwood, R.S. The Brown site: Early Milling Stone Horizon in Southern California. A. Ant. Memoirs, No. 23, 1969.

1559. Greenwood, R.S. and R.O. Brown. Preliminary survey of the Rancho Cañada Larga, Ventura County, California. UCLA-AS-AR 5:463-497, 1963.

1560. _____A coastal Chumash village: Excavation of Shisholop, Ventura County, California. SCAS-M 8, 1969.

1561. Gruvel, J.A. La pêche dans la préhistoire, dans l'antiquité, et chez les peuples primitifs. Société d'editions geographiques, maritimes, et coloniales. Paris. Pp. 102-103 and figure 87, 1928.
[Curved shell fishhooks from Santa Barbara]

1562. Haldeman, S.S. Beads. USGS-WCM 7:263-271, 1879.

1563. Hamy, E. The French scientific expedition to California, 1877-79. UC-AS-R 12:6-13, 1951.

1564. _____The fishhook industry of the ancient inhabitants of the Archipelago of California. UC-AS-R 59:61-67, 1963.

1565. Hanks, H.F. Piru Creek project. SCA-N 7:12, 1973.

1566. Harrington, J.P. Researches on the archaeology of Southern California. SI-MC 78:106-111, 1927.
[Interim report on the excavation of the Burton Mound]

1567. _____Exploration of the Burton Mound at Santa Barbara, California. BAE-AR 44:23-168, 1928.

1568. _____The Mission Indians of California. In Explorations and fieldwork of the Smithsonian Institution for 1927, pp. 173-178, 1928.
[Los Prietos site near Santa Barbara]

1569. Harrington, M.R. Implements or rejects? SM-M 6:152, 1932.

1570. _____Mysterious ocean waves wash up Indian dagger. Science News Letter, p. 215, October 6, 1934.

1571. _____A remodeled basket. SM-M 16:141-142, 1942.

1572. _____More American elephant-eaters. SM-M 29:206, 1955.

1573. Harrison, W.M. Mikiw: A Coastal Chumash village. UCLA-AS-AR 7:91-178, 1965.

1574. Harrison, W.M. and E.S. Harrison. An archaeological sequence for the hunting people of Santa Barbara, California. UCLA-AS-AR 8:1-89, 1966.

1575. Heizer, R.F. The plank canoe of the Santa Barbara region, California. Etnologiska Studier 7:193-229, 1938.

1576. _____ An inquiry into the status of the Santa Barbara spearthrower. A. Ant. 4:137-141, 1938.

1577. _____ Some Sacramento Valley - Santa Barbara archaeological relationships. SM-M 13:31-35, 1939.

1578. _____ Review of "Prehistoric man of the Santa Barbara Coast" by D.B. Rogers. A. Ant. 6:372-375, 1941.

1579. _____ Curved single-piece fishhooks of shell and bone in California. A. Ant. 15:89-96, 1949.

1580. _____ The frameless plank canoe of the California Coast. Primitive Man 13:80-89, 1949.

1581. _____ Some prehistoric bullroarers from California caves. UC-AS-R 50:5-9, 1960.
[Mountains behind Santa Barbara Coast]

1582. _____ Two ethnographic Chumash stone-weighted digging sticks. SM-M 45:64-68, 1971.

1583. Heizer, R.F. and H. Kelley. Burins and bladelets in the Cessac Collection from Santa Cruz Island, California. Proc. of the Amer. Philos. Society 106:94-105, 1962.

1584. Heizer, R.F. and M.A. Whipple. The California Indians. Berkeley, 1951.
[2nd, revised edition, 1971]

1585. Henshaw, H.W. Perforated stones from California. BAE-B 2, 1887.

1586. Hester, J.A., Jr. Channel Islands archaeology. ASASC-N 3:3-4, 1956.

1587. Hevly, R.H. and J.N. Hill. Pollen from archaeological middens of Santa Cruz Island, California. UCLA-AS-AR 12:104-119, 1970.

1588. Heye, G.G. Certain artifacts from San Miguel Island. MAIHF-INM 7(4), 1921.

1589. _____Chumash objects from a California cave. MAIHF-INM 3:193-198, 1926.

1590. Hodge, F.W. Chumash steatite pipes. SM-M 20:62-64, 1946.

1591. Holder, C.F. The ancient islanders of California. Popular Science Monthly 48:658-662, 1896.

1592. Holland, F.R. Santa Rosa Island: an archaeological and historical study. Journal of the West 1:45-62, 1962.

1593. Holt, W.B. Tomolos rode at anchor. SBMNH-L 12, 1937.
[Discusses alleged stone anchors, Santa Barbara area]

1594. _____Charm stones. SBMNH-L 14:67-68, 1939.

1595. _____The Canalino burial. SBMNH-L 14:99-100, 1939.

1596. Hoover, R.L. Chumash fishing equipment. SDM-ETN 9, 1973.

1597. _____ Aspects of Chumash punctate art. SM-M 48:67-71, 1974.

1598. _____Chumash sunsticks. SM-M 49:105-109, 1975.

1599. Howe, C. Preliminary report of a cave in Simi Valley. ASASC-N 2(1):12, 1954.

1600. Hrdlicka, A. The painting of human bones among the Indians. SI-AR (1904):607-617, 1904.
[Pl. I, p. 615, painted skull from Santa Cruz Island]

1601. Hubbs, C.L. A discussion of the geochronology and archaeology

of the California Islands. Proceedings of the Symposium
on the Biology of the California Islands. Santa Barbara,
1967.

1602. Irwin, M. Are there any more like this? SBMNH-L 21:66-67,
       1946.

1603. _____Canalino fishing tackle. SBMNH-L 21:18-20, 1946.

1604. Johnston, P. El Pueblo de las Canoas. Touring Topics 22:26-
       28,53-54, 1930.

1605. Jones, P.M. (Ed. by R.F. Heizer and A.B. Elsasser). Archaeolo-
       gical Investigations on Santa Rosa Island in 1901. UC-
       AR 17:201-280, 1956.

1606. Jones, P.M. San Nicolas Island archaeology in 1901. SM-M
       43:84-98, 1969.

1607. King, C.D. Chumash inter-village economic exchange. The
       Indian Historian 4(1):31-43, 1971.

1608. Kowta, M. and J.C. Hurst. Site Ven-15: The Triunfo Rockshel-
       ter. UCLA-AS-AR 2:201-230, 1960.

1609. Leonard, N.N. Ven-70 and its place in the Late Period of the
       Western Santa Monica Mountains. UCLA-AS-AR 8:215-241,
       1966.

1610. Leroi-Gourhan, A. Archéologie du Pacifique-Nord. Travaux et
       Memoires de l'Institut d'Ethnologie 47. Paris, 1946.

1611. Mason, J.D. Antiquities of Santa Barbara County. In History
       of Santa Barbara County, pp. 16-17. Oakland, 1883.
       [Quoted information from Rev. S. Bowers, taken from the
       Press (Santa Barbara) of Aug. 7, 1875]

1612. McKusick, M.B., et al. Introduction to Anacapa Island archae-
       ology. UCLA-AS-AR 1:71-104, 1959.

1613. _____Excavations at Goleta. UCLA-AS-AR 3:
       339-453, 1961.

1614. McKusick, M.B. and R.S. Watson. Grinding implements from
       Vaquero Reservoir, San Luis Obispo and Santa Clara Count-
       ies. UCLA-AS-AR 1:11-14, 1959.

1615. Mohr, A. The deep-basined metate of the Southern California
       Coast. A. Ant. 19:394-396, 1954.

1616. Mohr, A. and L.L. Sample. The religious importance of the
       swordfish in the Santa Barbara Channel area and its possi-
       ble implications. SM-M 29:62-68, 1955.

1617. Mohr, A. and L.L. Sample. The sacred bundle complex among the Chumash. American Philosophical Society, Proceedings III: 38-45, 1967.

1618. Nelson, N.C. Notes on the Santa Barbara culture. Kroeber Anniversary Volume:199-209. U.C. Press, Berkeley, 1936.

1619. Olson, R.L. On the island of the dead. California Monthly 21: 166-167,200,202, 1927.

1620. _____Chumash prehistory. UC-PAAE 28:1-21, 1930.

1621. Orr, P.C. The Channel Island survey by the Los Angeles Museum. SBMNH-L 15:58-59, 1940.

1622. _____Exceptional burial in California. Science 94:539-540, 1941.

1623. _____Looking backward. SBMNH-L 16:41-42, 1941.

1624. _____Chumash or Canalino? SBMNH-L 16:78-81, 1941.

1625. _____Hurricane deck diorama. SBMNH-L 17:3-6, 1942.

1626. _____The Ojai expedition. SBMNH-L 17:79-82, 1942.

1627. _____The "Queen" of Mescalitan Island. Scientific Monthly 54:482-484, 1942.

1628. _____Archaeology of Mescalitan Island and customs of the Canalino. SBMNH-OP 5, 1943.

1629. _____The swordfish man. SBMNH-L 19:33-34, 1944.

1630. _____Santa Rosa Island expedition. SBMNH-L 22, 1947.

1631. _____Additional bone artifact types in the Santa Barbara Museum of Natural History. In Gifford, Californian shell artifacts, UC-AR 9:115-132, 1947.

1632. _____Third Santa Rosa Island Expedition. SBMNH-MT 24:109-113, 1949.

1633. _____Island hopping. SBMNH-MT 24:61-68, 1949.

1634. _____(No title). SBMNH-AR (1949):12-14, 1949.
[Photos of Santa Rosa Island burials and house floors]

1635. _____Report from Santa Rosa Island, 1950-51. Santa Barbara Museum of Natural History, 1950.

1636. _____On Santa Rosa Island. SBMNH-MT 25:13-18, 1950.

1637. _____Fourth Santa Rosa Island Expedition. SBMNH-MT 26: 1, 1951.

1638. Orr, P.C. Report from Santa Rosa Island, 1951. Santa Barbara Museum of Natural History, 1951.

1639. _____ Ancient population centers of Santa Rosa Island. A. Ant. 16:221-226, 1951.

1640. _____Cave of the Killer Whales. SBMNH-MT 26:1-2, 1951.

1641. _____Indian caves of Santa Rosa Island and their relation to antiquity. NSS-MRSG 2:41-43, 1952.

1642. _____Fifth Santa Rosa Island expedition. SBMNH-MT 27:1, 1952.

1643. _____Review of Santa Barbara Channel archaeology. SWJA 8:211-226, 1952.

1644. _____Sixth Santa Rosa Island expedition. SBMNH-MT 28:17-20, 1953.

1645. _____Chumash vs. Canalino as cultural name. ASASC-N 2(2): 11-12, 1954.

1646. _____Who painted Painted Cave? ASASC-N 2(2):7-8, 1954.

1647. _____Dwarf mammoths and man on Santa Rosa Island. UU-AP 26:74-81, 1956.

1648. _____Early man on Santa Rosa Island. SBMNH-MT 31:40-44, 1956.

1649. _____Radiocarbon dates from Santa Rosa Island. SBMNH-B 2, 1956.

1650. _____Excavations at Ojai. ASASC-N 5:11-12, 1958.

1651. _____Late Pleistocene marine terraces on Santa Rosa Island, California. GSA-B 71:1113-1120, 1960.

1652. _____Radiocarbon dates from Santa Rosa Island, II. SBMNH-B 3, 1960.

1653. _____The Arlington Springs site, Santa Rosa Island, California. A. Ant. 27:417-419, 1962.

1654. _____Pleistocene chipped stone tool on Santa Rosa Island, California. Science 143:243-244, 1964.

1655. Orr, P.C. and R. Berger. The five areas on Santa Rosa Island, California. Proceedings of the National Academy of Sciences 56:1409-1416, 1966.

1656. Orr, P.C. Geochronology of Santa Rosa Island, California. Proceedings of the Symposium on the Biology of the California Islands. Santa Barbara, 1967.

1657. Orr, P.C. Prehistory of Santa Rosa Island. Santa Barbara
       Museum of Natural History, 1968.

1658. _____The Eleventh Santa Rosa (California) Expedition, 1957.
       Reprinted from National Geographic Society Research Reports,
       1955-1960 Projects, pp. 127-132, 1972.

1659. Owen, R.C. Assertions, assumptions, and Early Horizon (Oak
       Grove) settlement patterns in Southern California: A re-
       joinder. A. Ant. 32:236-241, 1967.

1660. Owen, R.C., F. Curtis, and D.S. Miller. The Glen Annie Canyon
       site, SBa-142. An Early Horizon site of Santa Barbara
       County. UCLA-AS-AR 6:431-520, 1964.

1661. Palmer, F.M. Beginning the Southwest Museum. Southwest Soci-
       ety of the Archaeological Institute of America, Bulletin
       2:16-27, 1905. Repr. from Out West, January 1905.

1662. _____Nucleus of the Southwestern Museum. Out West 22:
       23-34, 1905.

1663. Peck, S.L. An archaeological report on the excavation of a
       prehistoric site at Zuma Creek, Los Angeles County, Calif-
       ornia. ASASC, Publ. 2, 1955.

1664. Pilling, A.R. The British Museum Collection from near Avila,
       California. A. Ant. 18:169-172, 1952.

1665. Putnam, F.W. Perforated stones (from Santa Barbara region).
       USGS-WCM 7:135-189, 1879.

1666. _____Sculptures (in animal form of stone from Santa
       Barbara sites). USGS-WCM 7:218-221, 1879.

1667. _____Textile fabrics, basket-work, etc. USGS-WCM 7:
       239-250, 1879.

1668. _____Ornaments (of shell and red ocher paint from Santa
       Barbara sites). USGS-WCM 7:251-262, 1879.

1669. _____Iron implements and other articles obtained by con-
       tact with Europeans (recovered from Santa Barbara region
       sites). USGS-WCM 7:272-276, 1879.

1670. Rau, C. Prehistoric fishing. SI-CK 25, 1884.

1671. Reichlen, H. and R.F. Heizer. The scientific expedition of
       Léon de Cessac to California, 1877-1879. UC-AS-R 61:5-24,
       1964.

1672. Reinman, F.M. Archaeological investigations at Whale Rock
       Reservoir, Cayucos, California. CDPR-AR, 1961.

1673. Robinson, E. Fishing arrowpoints from Southern California. SM-M 7:149-150, 1933.

1674. _____Shell fishhooks of the California Coast. Occasional Papers of the B.P. Bishop Museum, Honolulu 17:4, 1942.

1675. Rogers, D.B. Prehistoric man of the Santa Barbara coast. Santa Barbara, 1929.

1676. _____ A reconnaissance. A. Ant. 3:184-186, 1937. [Of the Manzana-Sisquoc region of the Santa Barbara hinterland]

1677. Rogers, M.J. California; archaeological field work during 1930. AA 33:465-466, 1931.

1678. Rozaire, C.E. Archaeology in Ventura County. ASASC-N 5:3-4, 1958.

1679. _____Pictographs at Burro Flats. Ventura County Historical Society Quarterly 4(2):2-6, 1959.

1680. Rust, H.N. Archaeological collections from San Miguel Island, California. AA 9:656-657, 1907.

1681. Sanger, A.R. San Miguel Island; the most interesting of all the Channel Islands. Sea, Western Yachting and Boating 15:12-13,33-36, 1951.

1682. Schumacher, P. Some kjökkenmoddings and ancient graves of California. Overland Monthly 13:297-302, 1874.

1683. _____ Some remains of a former people. Overland Monthly 15:374-379, 1875.

1684. _____Die Anfertigung der Angelhaken aus Muschelschalen bei den früheren Bewohnern der Inseln im Santa Barbara Canal. Archiv für Anthropologie 8:223-224, 1875. [Translation: The manufacture of shell fishhooks by the early inhabitants of the Santa Barbara Channel Islands. in UC-AS-R 50, pp. 23-24, 1960]

1685. _____Ancient graves and shell-heaps of California. SI-AR (1874):335-350, 1875.

1686. _____, Etwas über kjökken Möddinge und die Funde in alten Gruben in Sudcalifornien. Archiv für Anthropologie 8:217-221, 1875.

1687. _____Die Inselgruppe im Santa Barbara Kanal in Kalifornien. Aus allen Welttheilen 7:353-355, 1876.

1688. _____ Beobachtungen in den verfallen Dörfern der Ureinwohner an der pacifischen Küste in Nordamerika. Mitt. der

Anthrop. Gesell., Wien 6:287-293. In C. Rau, Prehistoric Fishing. SI-CK 25:250-252, 1884.
[Trans]. Observations made in the ruins of the villages of the original inhabitants of the Pacific Coast of North America. Reprinted UC-AS-R 50:19-23, 1960]

1689. _____Researches in the kjökkenmöddings and graves of a former population of the Santa Barbara Islands and adjacent mainland. USGS-B 3:37-56, 1877.

1690. _____Aboriginal settlements of the Pacific Coast. Popular Science Monthly 10(1), 1877.

1691. _____Die Gräber und Hinterlassenschaft der Urvölker an der Kalifornischen Küste. ZE 10:183-192, 1878.

1692. Smith, J.E. An archaeological survey of Vaquero Reservoir, Santa Maria, California. UCLA-AS-AR 3:161-173, 1961.

1693. Smith, J.E. and J. LaFave. Excavation of site SLO-297, Vaquero Reservoir, San Luis Obispo County, California. UCLA-AS-AR 3:149-159, 1961.

1694. Spanne, L. Excavations at Vandenberg. SCA-N 8:2,6, 1974.

1695. _____Seasonal variability in the population of Barbareño Chumash villages: An explanatory model. In Papers on the Chumash, SLOCAS-OP 9:61-87, 1975.

1696. Stickel, E.G. and A.E. Cooper. The Chumash Revolt of 1824: A case for an archaeological application of feedback theory. UCLA-AS-AR 11:5-22, 1969.

1697. Strong, W.D. Archaeological explorations in the country of the Eastern Chumash. Smithsonian Institution: Exploration and Fieldwork (1934):69-72, 1935.

1698. Susia, M. The Soule Park site (Ven-61). UCLA-AS-AR 4:157-234, 1962.

1699. Swartz, B.K. Evidence for the occupation of Santa Barbara Island, Kiva 26:7-9, 1960.

1700. Tainter, J. Salvage excavation at the Fowler Site: Some aspects of social organization of the Northern Chumash. SLOCAS-OP 3, 1971.

1701. Taylor, A.S. Indian cemeteries - Santa Barbara Channel. California Farmer, May 22, August 28, 1863.

1702. Vaillant, G.C. Indian arts in North America. New York, 1939. [Steatite figurine from San Nicolas Island and a Santa Barbara bowl: pp. 20 & 42, Plate 6]

1703. Walker, E.F. Obsidian used by prehistoric Californians. SM-M 10:15, 1936.

1704. _____ A prehistoric California treasure-box. SM-M 10: 134-136, 1936.

1705. Wallace, W.J. The Little Sycamore site and the Early Milling Stone cultures of Southern California. A. Ant. 20:112-123, 1954.

1706. _____ Archaeology of the Gilmore Ranch site, Ventura County, California. SM-M 29:8-19, 1955.

1707. Wallace, W.J. and E.S. Taylor. The Little Sycamore shellmound. ARA-CCA 2, 1956.

1708. Walters, P. (Ed.). Chumash village site excavated. El Palacio. 27:224-226, 1929.

1709. Wardle, H.W. Stone implements of surgery (?) from San Miguel Island, California. AA 15:656-660, 1913.

1710. Warren, C.N. The Southern California Milling Stone Horizon: some comments. A. Ant. 32:233-236, 1967.

1711. Warren, G.L. Salvage excavations at the Fowler site: skeletal analysis of 4-SLO-406. SLOCAS-OP 4, 1971.

1712. West, J. and R.P. Sekkel. An archaeological survey of the Hearst Ranch (Rancho Piedras Blancas), San Simeon, San Luis Obispo County, California. UCLA-AS-AR 10:262-274, 1968.

1713. Wheeler, G.M. Report on U.S. geographical surveys west of 100th meridian. Archaeology: Vol. 7, 1879. [Cited as USGS-WCM]

1714. Wissler, M. A Canalino site near Deer Canyon, Ventura County, California. SM-M 32:73-87, 1958.

1715. Woodward, A. (Archaeological) Collection from the Channel Islands of California. MAIHF-INM 4:64-67, 1927.

1716. _____ Shell fishhooks of the Chumash. SCAS-B 28:41-46, 1929.

1717. _____ Chumash village site excavated. El Palacio 27: 224-226, 1929.

1718. _____ Shells used by the Indians in the village of Muwu. SCAS-B 29:105-114, 1930.

1719. _____ Los Angeles Museum work at Muwu and Simomo, Ventura County, in 1932. AA 35:490-491, 1933.

1720. Woodward, A. Fluorite beads in California. SCAS-B 36:1-6, 1937.

1721. _____The first ethnologists in California. SM-M 12:141-151, 1938.

1722. Yarrow, H.C. Report on the operations of a special party for making ethnological researches in the vicinity of Santa Barbara, California with an historical account of the region explored. USGS-WCM 7.
[Appeared also in Reprints of Various Papers on California Archaeology, Ethnology, and Indian History. UC-ARF, 1973]

1723. Yates, L.G. Notes on the geology and scenery of the islands forming the southerly line of the Santa Barbara Channel. American Geologist 14:43-52, 1890.
[Pp. 46-47, a description of a freshwater cave on Anacapa Island]

1724. _____Fragments of the history of a lost tribe. AA 4: 373-376, 1891.

1725. _____The deserted homes of a lost people. Overland Monthly, 2nd series, 27:538-544, 1896.

XXVI. GREAT BASIN AND SOUTHERN INTERIOR; COLORADO RIVER AREA

1726. Adams, R.M. Implements from Lake Mohave. A. Ant. 4:154-155, 1938.

1727. Amsden, C.A. A visit to the Serrano-Cahuilla region. SM-M 1:20-25, 1928.

1728. _____The Pinto Basin artifacts. In The Pinto Basin site. SM-P 9, 1935.

1729. Anderson, C. The North Bay No. 1 site (Ora-193). PCAS-Q 5(2), 1969.

1730. Anonymous. War-clubs vs. digging sticks. American Naturalist 20:574, 1886.
[Note on perforated stones from Los Angeles County]

1731. Anonymous. Our first factory; ancient olla industry of California. San Francisco Chronicle, December 6, 1894.

1732. Anonymous. Pot of seeds discovered on Mojave Desert may be ancient civilization sign. Pomona Bulletin, May 2, 1926.

1733. Anonymous. San Nicolas Island exhibit. SDM-B 15, 1931.
[Mention of objects in the collection: "Talc jewelry"]

1734. Anonymous. A human bone from Pinto Basin. SM-M 9:96, 1935.

1735. Anonymous. Early dwellers in Topanga Canyon. Archaeology 12: 271-277, 1959.

1736. Anonymous. New discovery at Newberry Cave. SBCMA-Q 7(2):9, 1959.

1737. Anonymous. Newland Hillside excavation (Orange County Historical Research Project, 1935). PCAS-Q 4(2), 1968.

1738. Anonymous. Report of the excavation of the Griset site at Costa Mesa, Orange County (Anthropological Project, 1938). PCAS-Q 4(2), 1968.

1739. Anonymous. Report of Banning Estate excavation: Norris Property. (Orange County Historical Research Project, 1935). PCAS-Q 4(2), 1968.

1740. Anonymous. Review of the Calico excavation, Yermo, California. SBCMA-Q 19(3), 1972.
[Reprint of various papers by Leakey, Clements, Berger, Witthoft, Simpson, and others]

1741. Babcock, A. Archaeological assemblages of San Bernardino County. ASASC-N 3(2):3-7, 1956.

1742. Baldwin, C.P. Toro Reservation, Indian Wells. SM-M 12:151-153, 1938.

1743. Begole, R.S. Archaeological phenomena in the California deserts. PCAS-Q 10:51-70, 1974.

1744. Belden, L.B. Scientists find cave homes of prehistoric man. San Bernardino Sun-Telegram, June 20, 1954.
[Newberry Cave]

1745. _____ More exploring needed to tell of early man. San Bernardino Sun-Telegram, June 27, 1954.
[Newberry Cave]

1746. _____ Panamint Indian shrines found in rock caves. San Bernardino Sun-Telegram, May 11, 1958.

1747. _____ Historic oasis known to man for 3500 Years. San Bernardino Sun-Telegram, March 12, 1961.

1748. Bell, L. Clues to the tribesmen who lived by the river. Desert Magazine 14(9):5-7, 1951.

1749. Bennyhoff, J.A. The Desert West: A trial correlation of culture and chronology. UC-AS-R 42:98-112, 1958.

1750. Bettinger, R.L. World-views and archaeological investigation in interior Southern California. UCLA-AS-AR 13:185-196, 1971.

1751. Bettinger, R.L. Late prehistoric and historic structures in Owen's Valley, Eastern California. JCA 2(2):198-204, 1975.

1752. Bettinger, R.L. and T.F. King. Interaction and political organization: A theoretical framework for archaeology in Owens Valley, California. UCLA-AS-AR 13:137-152, 1971.

1753. Bock, F. and A.J. Bock. Coso revisited: California hot springs used by Indians and Whites. SM-M 47:4-11, 1973.

1754. Brainerd, G.W. Lake Mohave re-examined. SM-M 25:69, 1951.

1755. Broms, R.S.D. and J.R. Moriarty. The antiquity and inferred use of stone spheroids in Southwestern archaeology. SM-M 41:98-112, 1967.

1756. Campbell, E.W.C. An archaeological survey of the Twenty-Nine Palms region. SM-P 7:1-93, 1931.

1757. _____ Archaeological problems in the Southern California deserts. A. Ant. 1:295-300, 1936.

1758. Campbell, E.W.C., et al. The archaeology of Pleistocene Lake Mohave. SM-P 11, 1937.

1759. Campbell, E.W.C. and C. Amsden. The Eagle Mountain site. SM-M 8:170-173, 1934.
[Pinto Basin]

1760. Campbell, E.W.C. and W.H. Campbell. The Pinto Basin site. SM-P 9:1-51, 1935.

1761. Carter, G.F. Stone circles in the deserts. Anthropological Journal of Canada 2(3):2-6, 1964.

1762. _____ A cross check on the dating of Lake Mohave artifacts. SM-M 41:26-33, 1967.

1763. Childers, W.M. Preliminary report on the Yuha burial, California. Anthro. Journal of Canada 12:2-9, 1974.

1764. Clements, L. Indian artifacts and collecting localities in Death Valley, California. SM-M 25:125-128, 1951.

1765. _____ The Indians of Death Valley. Hollywood: Hollycrofters; 23 pp., 1953.

1766. _____ Death Valley and Panamint Valley. ASASC-N 2(3): 7-8, 1955.

1767. Clements, T. Geology of the Little Lake site. SM-P 17:83-84, 1957.

1768. Clements, T. and L. Clements. Evidence of Pleistocene man in Death Valley, California. GSA-B 64:1189-1204, 1953.

1769. Cooke, R. Desert pavement. Mineral Information Service, Calif. Div. of Mines and Geology 18:197-200, 1965.
[Humanoid figures]

1770. Corle, E. Desert Country. Duel, Sloan & Pierce, N.Y., 1941.
[Pp. 56-65: Mitchell's Caverns]

1771. Cowper, D. Archaeological survey in the Thousand Palms area. ASASC-N 6(1):4-5, 1959.

1772. Davis, E.L. A child burial near Mono Lake. UCLA-AS-AR 1:67-70, 1959.

1773. _____ Hunter-gatherers of Mono Lake. SM-M 36:22-28, 1962.

1774. _____ An archaeological survey of the Mono Lake Basin and excavations of two rockshelters, Mono County, California. UCLA-AS-AR 6:251-392, 1964.

1775. _____ Man and water at Pleistocene Lake Mohave. A. Ant. 32:345-353, 1967.

1776. _____ Archaeology of the North Basin of Panamint Valley, Inyo County, California. Nevada State Museum Anthropological Papers 15:83-142, 1970.

1777. _____ Paleo-Indian land use patterns at China Lake, California. PCAS-Q 10:1-16, 1974.

1778. Davis, E.L. and R. Shutler. Recent discoveries of fluted points in California and Nevada. Nevada State Museum Anthropological Papers 14:154-179, 1969.

1779. Davis, E.L. and S. Winslow. Giant ground figures of the prehistoric deserts. Proceedings of American Philosophical Society 109:8-21, 1965.

1780. Davis, E.L., D. True, and G. Sterud. Notes on two sites in Eastern California: Unusual finds. UCLA-AS-AR 7:323-332, 1965.

1781. Davis, J.T. The Rustler Rockshelter site (SBr-288), A culturally stratified site in the Mohave Desert, California. UC-AS-R 57:25-73, 1962.

1782. Dixon, K.A. A Sandia point from Long Valley, Mono County, California. SM-M 27:97-104, 1953.

1783. Donnan, C. A suggested culture sequence for the Providence Mountains (Eastern Mohave Desert). UCLA-AS-AR 6:1-23, 1964.

1784. Eisen, G. Three full page, illustrated scientific articles in the San Francisco Call, March 18, 19, & 27, 1898.
[About Eisen's archaeological expedition into the Turquoise Mountains and the area to the south between Cima Dome and Soda Lake]

1785. Enfield, R. and G. Enfield. Mammoth Creek Cave, Mono County, California. UCLA-AS-AR 6:393-430, 1964.

1786. Farmer, M.F. and R. deSaussure. Split-twig animal figurines. Plateau 27(4):13-23, 1955.

1787. Fontaine, J.S. A preliminary survey of two palm canyons along the Laguna Salada. PCAS-Q 3(1), 1967.

1788. Gates, P.G. Indian stone constructions near Salton Sea, California. AA 11:322-323, 1909.

1789. Gearheart, P.L. Shoshone Shelter Cave Number Two, Inyo County: A preliminary report. PCAS-Q 10:35-50, 1974.

1790. Glennan, W.S. An unusual steatite pipe from the Tehachapi Mountains, California. SM-M 46:152-156, 1972.

1791. _____The Baker site (SBr-541): An early lithic assemblage from the Mohave Desert. PCAS-Q 10:17-34, 1974.

1792. _____The Manix Lake lithic industry: Early lithic tradition or workshop refuse? UCLA-JNWA 1(7):42-61, 1976.

1793. Goodman, R. and R. Raskoff. The Bernasconi site in Southern California. SM-M 38:17-25, 1964.

1794. Gray, G.E. On the depression of the Colorado Basin. CAS-P 4: 228-230, 1873.
[Indian wells 6-10 feet deep]

1795. Haenszel, A.M. Historic sites in San Bernardino County: A preliminary report. SBCMA-Q 5(2), 1957.

1796. Hamilton, A. Exploring the past: America's oldest housing. Natural History 60:361-364, 1951.
[Stahl site at Little Lake]

1797. Harner, M.J. Lowland Patayan phases in the Lower Colorado River Valley and Colorado Desert. UC-AS-R 42:93-97, 1958.

1798. Harrington, J.P. Researches on the archaeology of Southern California. SI-MC 78(1):106-111, 1927.

1799. Harrington, M.R. A new Pinto site. SM-M 22:116-118, 1948.

1800. _____America's oldest dwelling. SM-M 22:148-152, 1948.
[Iny-182, Stahl site]

1801. Harrington, M.R. A new old house at Little Lake. SM-M 23: 135-136, 1949.

1802. _____ Pinto man at Little Lake. Desert Magazine 13(11):22-27, 1950.

1803. _____ A colossal quarry. SM-M 25:14-18, 1951.

1804. _____ Latest from Little Lake. SM-M 25:188-191, 1951.

1805. _____ The fossil falls site. SM-M 26:191-195, 1952.

1806. _____ A cave near Little Lake. SM-M 27:77-82, 1953.

1807. _____ A Pinto site at Little Lake, California. SM-P 17:1-82, 1957.

1808. Haury, E.W. The stratigraphy and archaeology of Ventana Cave, Arizona. University of New Mexico Press, 1950. [Pp. 192-193, part IV, Passim: A discussion of the relationship of Ventana Cave sequence with the revised sequence for Southern California proposed by M.J. Rogers]

1809. Head, D. Owen's Valley mystery. ASASC-N 3(4):4-10, 1956.

1810. Heizer, R.F. Ancient grooved clubs and modern rabbit-sticks. A. Ant. 8:41-56, 1942.

1811. _____ Environment and culture: The Lake Mohave case. SM-M 44(2):68-76, 1970.

1812. Henderson, R. They guard the caves in the Providence Mountains. Desert Magazine 2:23, 1939.

1813. _____ Palm hunters in the Inkopah wastelands. Desert Magazine, p. 13, July 1946. [Describes several archaeological sites in the Inkopah Mountains, including a petroglyph site at Imp-67, Boundary Palm Springs: maps and photographs]

1814. _____ Old Indian waterhole. Desert Magazine 17(1):10-12, 1954.

1815. Hester, T.R. Great Basin atlatl studies. BP-PAEH 2, 1974.

1816. Heye, G.G. Shaman's cache from Southern California. MAIHF-INM 4:315-323, 1927.

1817. Hicks, F. Archaeological investigations in the Yucaipa Valley. SBCMA-Q 55(3), 1958.

1818. Hidy, L. Harper Dry Lake, California.- A survey and site report. SBCMA-Q 19(2), 1971.

1819. Hillebrand, T.S. Cultural responses to the Neothermal in two
      localities of the basin and range region of Eastern Calif-
      ornia. PCAS-Q 8:45-51, 1972.

1820. Hilton, J. The wells of the ancient Coahuillas. Westways,
      p. 22, March 1936.

1821. Hranicky, W.J. and L.W. Zornes. Surface finds in the Borrego
      Desert of Southern California. The Chesopiean-Journal
      of North American Archaeology 10(5):162-172, 1972.

1822. Hunt, A. Archaeology of the Death Valley Salt Pan, California.
      UU-AP 47, 1960.

1823. Hunt, C.B. Death Valley: Geology, ecology, archaeology. U.C.
      Press, Berkeley, 1976.

1824. Irwin, H.T. Possible eastern connections for the San Jose-Pinto
      Basin Complex. A. Ant. 29:496-497, 1964.

1825. Jackson, G.F. Magnificent desert. CAS-PD 24(6):9-15, 1971.
      [S. California desert archaeology; Joshua tree area]

1826. Jefferson, G.T. A model of adaptive change in late prehistoric
      Southeastern California. UCLA-AS-AR 13:165-172, 1971.

1827. Johnston, F.J. and P.H. Johnston. An Indian trail complex of
      the Central Colorado Desert: A preliminary survey. UC-
      AS-R 37:22-39, 1957.

1828. _____They trod the high mesas.
      Palm Springs Villager 12(5);18-21,45, 1958.

1829. Johnston, F.R. Art gallery of ancient Indians. Desert Maga-
      zine 1(4):20-21, 1938.

1830. Johnston, P. Ancient houses on a hill-top. Touring Topics
      23:26-27,56, 1931.
      [Stone circles in the Black Mts. area, near Randsburg]

1831. _____Crystal caverns of the Mojave. Westways (Touring
      Topics) 28(9):8-9, 1933.
      [Mitchell's Caverns]

1832. _____Maze of mystery. Westways 30(2):10-11, 1938.

1833. King, T.F. Fight to preserve our ancient past. Desert Maga-
      zine 35(6):8-11, 1972.
      [Southern California interior]

1834. _____The trowel and the bulldozer. Westways 65(1):16-19,
      78, 1973.
      [Coachella Valley]

116

1835. King, T.J., Jr. A cache of vessels from Cottonwood Springs
        (Riv-937). JCA 3(1):136-142, 1976.

1836. _____ Archaeological implications of the paleo-botani-
        cal record from Lucerne Valley area of the Mohave Desert.
        SBCMA-Q 23(4), 1976.

1837. Kingman, G. Report on the Campbell lithic collection. SM-M
        40:72-74, 1966.

1838. Kowta, M., et al. Excavations at the Christensen-Webb site,
        Menifee Valley, 1963-64. SBCMA-Q 13(2), 1965.

1839. Lanning, E.P. Archaeology of the Rose Spring site, Iny-372.
        UC-PAAE 49:237-336, 1963.

1840. Lathrap, D.W. and C.W. Meighan. An archaeological reconnaiss-
        ance in the Panamint Mountains. UC-AS-R 11:11-32, 1951.

1841. Lawbaugh, A.L.V. They left their story in the desert sands.
        Desert Magazine 12(11):26-29, 1949.
        [Sites in Coachella Valley, Pushawalla Canyon]

1842. _____ When ancients dwelt on the shores of Old Lake
        Mohave. Desert Magazine 15(9):11-15, 1952.

1843. Lawton, H.W. and L.J. Bean. A preliminary reconstruction of
        aboriginal agricultural technology among the Cahuilla.
        In L.J. Bean and K.S. Saubel, Temelpakh, pp. 197-217,
        Malki Museum Press, Morongo, 1972.

1844. Lawton, H.W., et al. Agriculture among the Paiute of Owens
        Valley. JCA 3(1):13-50, 1976.

1845. Leadabrand, R. Into the past of San Bernardino County. West-
        ways, p. 9, April, 1964.

1846. Lopatin, I. Fossil man in the vicinity of Los Angeles. Proc.
        Sixth Pacific Sci. Cong. 4:177-181, 1939.

1847. Lucas, B.J. Tree-holes at the Stahl site. SM-M 25:191-193,
        1951.

1848. Lytton, A. Archaeological investigations at Laguna Niguel,
        Orange County. UCLA-AS-AR 5:249-294, 1963.

1849. Mahaffey, J. Side trails to adventure. Westways, p. 12, Nov-
        ember 1957.
        [Sites in area of Warner's Ranch and San Felipe]

1850. McCown, B.E. Archaeological survey of [Salton Sea] beach line.
        ASASC-N 1:10-11, 1954.

1851. _____ The avocado jar. ASASC-N 2:7, 1954.

1852. McCown, B.E. Yermo site. ASASC-N 2(1):11-12, 1954.

1853. _____The Lake LeConte beach line survey. SM-M 29:89-92, 1955.

1854. _____The Indio "fish-traps" reexamined. SM-M 30:133-134, 1956.

1855. _____Lake LeConte survey. ASASC-N 4:3-4, 1957.

1856. _____A strange cache in the lava. SM-M 31:24-31, 1957.

1857. _____Collected papers of Benjamin Ernest McCown. ASASC-P 6, 1964.

1858. McKenney, J.W. Ancestral home of the Santa Rosa Cahuilla. Westways, p. 22, April 1937.

1859. Mead, G.R. A unique lithic artifact from Owens Valley. SM-M 41:157-158, 1967.

1860. Mead, G.R. and J. Smith. Microtools from Owens Valley, California. SM-M 42:148-152, 1968.

1861. Meighan, C.W. The Coville rockshelter, Inyo County, California. UC-AR 12:171-224, 1953.

1862. _____Notes on the archaeology of Mono County, California. UC-AS-R 28:6-27, 1955.

1863. _____Archaeological resources of Borrego State Park. UCLA-AS-AR 1:25-44, 1959.

1864. _____The growth of archaeology in the West Coast and the Great Basin, 1935-1960. A. Ant. 27:33-38, 1961.

1865. _____Two views of the Manix Lake lithic industry. UCLA-JNWA 1(7):41, 1976.

1866. Michels, J.W. The Snow Creek rockshelter site. (Riv -210). UCLA-AS-AR 6:85-138, 1964.

1867. Mohr, A. The hunting crook: Its use and distribution in the Southwest. SM-M 25:145-154, 1951.

1868. Moseley, M. and G.A. Smith. Archaeological investigations of the Mohave River drainage. SBCMA-Q 9(3), 1962.

1869. O'Connell, J.F. Recent prehistoric environments in interior Southern California. UCLA-AS-AR 13:173-184, 1971.

1870. O'Connell, J.F., et al. Perris Reservoir archaeology: Late prehistoric change in Southeastern California. CDPR-AR 14, 1974.

1871. O'Neal, L.R. Peculiar piece of desert. Westernlore, Los
      Angeles, p. 32, 1957.
      [Joshua Tree National Monument area]

1872. Ore, H.T. and N. Warren. Late Pleistocene - early Holocene
      geomorphic history of Lake Mohave, California. GSA-B 82:
      2553-2562, 1971.

1873. Patch, R.W. Irrigation in East Central California. A. Ant.
      17:50-52, 1951.

1874. Peck, S.L. Some pottery from the Sand Hills, Imperial County,
      California. ASASC-P 1, 1953.

1875. _____An archaeological report on the excavation of a pre-
      historic site at Zuma Creek, Los Angeles County, Calif-
      ornia. ASASC-P 2, 1955.

1876. Peck, S.L. and G.A. Smith. The archaeology of Seep Spring.
      SBCMA-SS 2:1-31, 1957.

1877. Pepper, J. San Bernardino's archaeologic back yard. Desert
      Magazine, p. 28, May,1967.
      [Includes Black and Inscription Canyons, Newberry Cave,
      and Rodman Mt. sites, in the Barstow-Newberry area]

1878. _____Desert diggings. Desert Magazine 35(6):12-13, 1972.
      [Coachella Valley work of Cabrillo College discussed]

1879. Pourade, R. (Ed.). Ancient hunters of the far west. Copley
      Books, San Diego, 1966.

1880. Prather, B.G. Palm Springs Cahuilla Indians. Notes on archae-
      ological investigation of the Indio area by D.E. and F.
      Schnaar. SBCMA-Q 12(1), 1964.

1881. Price, C. The Phillips site. ASASC-N 2(2):9-10, 1954.

1882. _____Tehachapi camps and cairns. ASASC-N 2:10, 1954.

1883. Quimby, G.M. History of the Potrero Ranch and its neighbors.
      SBCMA-Q 22:1-78, 1975.

1884. Redtfeldt, G. Dig at Hewitt Fault Springs. ASASC-N 7(2):3-4,
      1960.

1885. Reinman, F.M., D.L. True, and C.N. Warren. Archaeological re-
      mains from rockshelters near Coyote Mountain, Imperial
      County. UCLA-AS-AR 2:231-248, 1960.

1886. Riddell, F.A. The Eastern California border: Cultural and
      temporal affinities. UC-AS-R 42:41-48, 1958.

1887. Riddell, H.S. The archaeology of a Paiute village site in

Owens Valley. UC-AS-R 12:14-28, 1951.
[Iny-2]

1888. Riddell, H.S. and F.A. The current status of archaeological
investigations in Owens Valley, California. UC-AS-R 33:
28-33, 1956.

1889. Robertson, D. At the end of a back country trail. Westways,
p. 16, April 1961.
[Sites in Saline Valley, including Iny-406]

1890. _____Three pools in the desert. Desert Magazine, p.
29, February 1965.
[Saline Valley sites]

1891. Rogers, M.J. Report of an archaeological reconnaissance in the
Mohave Sink region. SDM-P 1, 1929.

1892. _____Early lithic industries of the Colorado river and
adjacent desert areas. SDM-P 3, 1939.

1893. _____An outline of Yuman prehistory. SWJA 1:167-198,
1945.

1894. Ruby, J.W. Aboriginal uses of Mount San Jacinto State Park.
UCLA-AS-AR 4:1-10, 1962.

1895. _____Excavations at One Horse Canyon rockshelter (Riv-8),
App. 1:129-138, in J.W. Michels, The Snow Creek rockshelter
site (Riv-210). UCLA-AS-AR 6, 1964.

1896. _____Archaeological investigations of the Big Tujunga site
(LAn-167). UCLA-AS-AR 8:91-150, 1966.

1897. Schnarr, D.E. and J. Schnarr. Notes on archaeological investigation of the Indio area. SBCMA-Q 12(1), 1964.

1898. Schroeder, A.H. A brief survey of the Lower Colorado River from
Davis Dam to the International Border. Boulder City: Bur.
of Reclam., Reprod. Unit, Region Three, 1952.

1899. Shepard, E. Prehistoric cultures along the Amargosa River.
PCAS-Q 1(2), 1965.

1900. Simmons, M.P. Preliminary Report of excavations and survey at
Silva Creek, San Bernardino County, California. SBCMA-Q
13(1):1-31, 1965.

1901. Simpson, R.D. A classic "Folsom" from Lake Mohave. SM-M 21:
24-25, 1947.

1902. _____Tracking the Hohokam. SM-M 24:126-128, 1950.

1903. _____A new discovery of early core and flake tools in
the Mohave Desert. SM-M 26:62-63, 1952.

1904. Simpson, R.D. Archaeological reconnaissance - twentieth century style. SM-M 26:140-141, 1952.

1905. _____The Manix Lake archaeological survey. SM-M 32: 4-10, 1958.

1906. _____Archaeology in Riverside County. ASASC-N 6(1):3, 1959.

1907. _____Archaeological survey of the Eastern Calico Mountains. SM-M 34:25-35, 1960.

1908. _____Coyote gulch. ASASC-P 5, 1961.

1909. _____Owens Valley projectile-point typology. SM-M 35: 99-103, 1961.

1910. _____An archaeological survey of Troy Lake, San Bernardino County. SBCMA-Q 12(3):1-47, 1965.

1911. _____A commentary on W. Glennan's (Manix Lake lithic industry) article. UCLA-JNWA 1(7):63-66, 1976.

1912. Simpson, R.D., et al. Rock Camp: San Bernardino Mountain archaeological excavation. SBCMA-Q 20(1), 1972.

1913. Smith, G.A. Circular pits of Summit Valley [San Bernardino County], California. SM-M 13:169-171, 1939.

1914. _____Traces of early man at Bloomington, California. SM-M 16:124-127, 1942.

1915. _____More about split-twig figurines. SM-M 23:153-158, 1949.

1916. _____Prehistoric man of San Bernardino Valley. San Bernardino County Historical Society, 1950.

1917. _____Rancheria Amuscopiabit. SM-M 27:123-127, 1953.

1918. _____Black-paint stones. SM-M 28:187-190, 1954.

1919. _____A preliminary report of the archaeological survey of the Deep Creek site in San Bernardino County, California. SBCMA-Q 2(2), 1955.

1920. _____Preliminary report of the Schuiling Cave, Newberry, California. SBCMA-Q 3(2), 1955.

1921. _____Split-twig animal figurines. ASASC-N 3(2):7, 1956.

1922. _____The archaeology of Newberry Cave, San Bernardino County, Newberry, California. SBCMA-Q 4(3), 1957.

1923. Smith, G.A. Archaeological investigations of the Mojave River drainage, Part I. SBCMA-Q 9(2), 1962.

1924. _____Split-twig figurines from San Bernardino County, California. SM-M 37:86-90, 1963.

1925. _____Archaeological survey of the Mohave River area and adjacent regions. San Bernardino Museum Association, San Bernardino, California, 1963.

1926. _____Agua Mansa, home of prehistoric Indians. SBCMA-Q 21:21-28, 1973.

1927. Smith, G.A., R. Sexton, and E.J. Koch. Juan Antonio, Cahuilla Indian chief and friend of the Whites. SBCMA-Q 8:1, 1960.

1928. Smitn, G.A., et al. The archaeology of Newberry Cave, San Bernardino County, Newberry, California. SBCMA-SS 1, 1957.

1929. Stephenson, R.L. Thoughts on the Calico Mountain site. Note-book, University of South Carolina 3:1-9, 1971.

1930. Steward, J.H. Archaeology, Appendix 5 in Ethnography of the Owens Valley Paiute, UC-PAAE 33:334-335, 1933.

1931. Stewart, K.M. Mohave Indian agriculture. SM-M 40:5-15, 1966.

1932. _____The aboriginal territory of the Mohave Indians. Ethnohistory 16:257-276, 1969.

1933. Taylor, A.S. Curious aboriginal paintings, graves, and pottery in the Coso Indian country of Owen's Lake. In The Indian-ology of California. Second Series: California Farmer 14(17), December 21, 1860.
[Owens Lake area]

1934. Thomas, D.H. Regional sampling in archaeology: a pilot Great Basin research design. UCLA-AS-AR 11:87-100, 1969.

1935. _____Artiodactyls and man in the prehistoric Great Basin. In Papers on California and Great Basin prehist-ory. CARD Pub. No. 2, 1970.

1936. Townsend, J.B. Two rock shelters and a village site in Bor-rego State Park. UCLA-AS-AR 2:249-276, 1960.

1937. Treganza, A.E. An archaeological reconnaissance of Northeast-ern Baja California and Southeastern California. A. Ant. 8:152-163, 1942.

1938. _____The "ancient stone fish traps" of the Coachella Valley, Southern California. A. Ant. 10:285-294, 1945.

122

1939. True, D.L., E.L. Davis, and E.L. Sterud. Archaeological surveys in the New York Mountains region, San Bernardino
County, California. UCLA-AS-AR 8:243-278, 1966.

1940. _____An archaeological sur-
vey at Indian Ranch, Panamint Valley, California. UCLA-
AS-AR 9:1-24, 1967.

1941. Turner, W.G. Rock house mystery in Anza-Borrego. Desert
Magazine, p. 12, January, 1968.
[A Letter to Editor in Desert Magazine, February, 1968,
identifies the Cahuilla residents of 2 of the houses,
as given in Reed, Old Time Cattlemen]

1942. Valore, M. Indian reminders of the past. Desert Magazine,
p. 29, March, 1968.

1943. Walker, E.F. Finding an old Paiute mush basket. SM-M 15:10-
12, 1941.

1944. Wallace, W.J. A basket-weaver's kit from Death Valley. SM-M
28:216-221, 1954.

1945. _____ A rockshelter excavation in Death Valley National
Monument. SM-M 31:144-154, 1957.

1946. _____ Archaeological investigations in Death Valley
National Monument. 1952-1957. UC-AS-R 42:7-22, 1958.

1947. _____ Archaeological explorations in the southern section of Anza-Borrego Desert State Park. CDPR-AR 5, 1962.

1948. _____ Prehistoric cultural developments in the Southern
California deserts. A. Ant. 28:172-180, 1962.

1949. _____ Two basalt quarries in Death Valley. Archaeology
15:46-49, 1962.

1950. _____ The archaeology of the Sheep Pass district,
Joshua Tree National Monument. Journal of the West 3(1):
90-101, 1964.

1951. _____ A cache of unfired clay objects from Death Valley
California. A. Ant. 30:434-441, 1965.

1952. _____ An archaeological survey of the Southern California Edison Company electric distribution line in Death
Valley National Monument. ARA-CCA 6, 1968.

1953. Wallace, W.J. and R. Desautels. An excavation at the Squaw
Tank site, Joshua Tree National Monument, California.
ARA-CCA 4(2), 1960.

1954. Wallace, W.J., A.P. Hunt, and J.P. Redwine. An investigation of some stone mounds in Death Valley National Monument, California. ARA-CCA 3(1), 1959.

1955. Wallace, W.J. and E.S. Taylor. Archaeology of Wildrose Canyon, Death Valley National Monument. A. Ant. 20:355-367, 1955.

1956. _____The surface archaeology of Butte Valley, Death Valley National Monument. AP^ ·CCA 1, 1956.

1957. _____An archaeological reconnaissance in Bow Willow Canyon, Anza-Borrego State Park. SM-M 32: 155-166, 1958.

1958. _____A preceramic site at Saratoga Springs, Death Valley National Monument. ARA-CCA 3(2): 1-13, 1959.

1959. _____An archaeological survey of the Deep Tank-Squaw Tank District, Joshua Tree National Monument, California. ARA-CCA 4(1), 1960.

1960. _____The surface archaeology of Indian Hill. SM-M 34:4-18, 1960.

1961. _____Indian Hill rockshelter, preliminary investigations. SM-M 34:66-82, 1960.

1962. Warren, C.N. The Southern California Milling Stone Horizon: some comments. A. Ant. 32:233-236, 1967.

1963. _____Time and topography: The prehistory of the California deserts. SM-M 44:5-14, 1970.

1964. _____Comments on "Man and environment in the late prehistory of Southeast California." UCLA-AS-AR 13:197-199, 1971.

1965. Wedel, W. Archaeological investigations at Buena Vista Lake, Kern County, California. BAE-B 130, 1941.

1966. Weide, D.L. The Altithermal as an archaeological "non-problem" in the Great Basin. In Holocene environmental change in the Great Basin. Nevada Archaeological Survey Research Paper 6:174-184, 1976.

1967. Weight, H.O. Rockhound trail to Indian Pass. Desert Magazine 12(4):16-21, 1949.
[Trail and petroglyph in the Chocolate Mountains]

1968. Wheeler, S.M. Prehistoric miniatures. SM-M 11:181, 1937.

1969. Wilke, P.J. Late prehistoric change in land-use patterns at Perris Reservoir. UCLA-AS-AR 13:153-164, 1971.

1970. Wilke, P.J. Background to prehistory of the Yuha Desert region. BP-PA:5, 1976.
[Reports by D.L. Weide, M.L. Weide, J.P. Barker and H.W. Lawton]

1971. Wilke, P.J. and D. Fain. An archaeological cucurbit from Coachella Valley, California. Archaeological Research Unit, Department of Anthropology, University of California, Riverside, 1972.

1972. Woodward, A. Good luck shrines of the desert. Desert Magazine, p. 22, January, 1941.
[Bee Rock Mesa, Riv-51, 53, & 54]

1973. Zelenka, F. and N. Mitchell's Caverns, Mojave Desert, California. Pacific Pathways 2(6):4-8, 1947.

XXVII. SOUTHWESTERN COAST AND ISLANDS

1974. Anonymous. Putuiden [near San Juan Capistrano] found? PCAS-S 13:8, 1974.

1975. Anonymous. Museum dig continues. [San Clemente Island and La Jolla] SCA-N 9:214, 1975.

1976. Anonymous. Santa Ana site explored. PCAS-S 14:2, 1975.

1977. Ashby, G.E. and J.W. Winterbourne. A study of primitive man in Orange County and some of its coastal areas. PCAS-Q 2(1), 1966.
[Reprint of the WPA Anthropological Report of 1939]

1978. Banks, T.J. A late Mountain Diegueño site. PCAS-Q 8:47-59, 1972.

1979. Bates, E.H. Los Altos (LAn-270): A Late Horizon site in Long Beach, California. PCAS-Q 8(2), 1972.

1980. Bowden, A.O. and I.A. Lopatin. Pleistocene man in Southern California. El Palacio 41:121-123, 1936.

1981. _____ Fossil man in Southern California. GSA-B 52:1995, 1941.

1982. Bowers, S. Relics in a cave. Pacific Science Monthly 1:45-47, 1885.
[Collection from a cave in the San Martin Mountains, Los Angeles County, now in US National Museum and in Peabody Museum, Harvard University]

1983. Brainerd, G.W. Topanga Canyon archaeology. SM-M 22:195, 1948.

1984. Brindamour, B.G. Trade and subsistence at Mulholland: A site report on LAn-246. UCLA-AS-AR 12:120-162, 1970.

1985. Brooks, S.T., B.L. Conrey, and K.A. Dixon. A deeply buried
       skull and recent stratigraphy at the present mouth of the
       San Gabriel River, Seal Beach, California. SCAS-B 64,
       1965.

1986. Bryan, B. Collecting Indian relics on a desert island. Museum
       Graphic I:145-150, Los Angeles, 1927.

1987. _____San Nicolas Island, treasure house of the ancients.
       Art and Archaeology 29:147-156 (part 1); 29:215-223 (part
       VII), 1930.

1988. _____A treasure island of the Pacific. Discovery 11:240-
       244, London, 1930.

1989. _____Southwest Museum excavations on San Clemente Island.
       SM-M 37:44-49, 1963.

1990. _____An unusual bowl from San Clemente Island. SM-M 38:
       138-139, 1964.

1991. _____Archaeological explorations on San Nicolas Island.
       SM-P 22, 1970.

1992. Burnett, E.K. Inlaid stone and bone artifacts from Southern
       California. MAIHF-C 1, 1944.

1993. Butler, W.B. The San Pedro Harbor site: a primary subsistence
       village on the Southern California coast. PCAS-Q 10:1-79,
       1974.

1994. Carrico, R.L. and P.W. Ainsworth. The Bancroft ranch house:
       A preliminary report. In Two papers on the archaeology
       of San Diego County, pp. 1-32. San Diego County Archaeol-
       ogical Society, Publication 1, 1974.

1995. Carter, G.F. Evidence for Pleistocene Man at La Jolla, Calif-
       ornia. Transactions of the New York Academy of Sciences
       11(7), 1949.

1996. _____Ecology - geography - ethnobotany. Scientific
       Monthly 70:73-80, 1950.
       [La Jolla site]

1997. _____Evidence of Pleistocene Man in Southern California.
       Geographical Review 40:84-102, 1950.

1998. _____Interglacial artifacts from the San Diego area.
       SWJA 8:444-456, 1952.

1999. _____An Interglacial site at San Diego, California.
       SM-M 28:165-174, 1954.

2000. _____On submarine archaeology about San Diego. SM-M
       29:21-27, 1955.

2001. Cessac, M.L. de. Observations sur des fétiches de pierre sculptés en forme d'animaux découverts a l'Île de San Nicolas (Californie). Revue d'Ethnographie 1:30-40, 1882.
[Republished in English in UC-AS-R 12:6-13, 1951]

2002. Chace, P.G. An ethnographic approach to the archaeology of the Luiseño Indians. SBCMA-Q 12(2), 1964.

2003. _____A history of archaeology in Orange County. PCAS-Q 1(3), 1965.

2004. _____A spoon-shaped steatite artifact from San Nicolas Island. PCAS-Q 1(4), 1965.

2005. _____An archaeological survey in the Northwestern San Joaquin Hills, Orange County, California. PCAS-Q 2(2), 1966.

2006. _____A review of the 1939 Sunny Hills site No. 1 report. PCAS-Q 2(4), 1966.

2007. _____Biological archaeology of some coastal middens, Orange County, California. PCAS-Q 5(2), 1969.

2008. _____Redating the Buck Gully [Orange County] site, with implications for settlement patterns. PCAS-Q 10:99-113, 1974.

2009. Chace, P.G., G.R. Mead, and A. McKinney. The Bonita Mesa IV site (Ora-134) near Newport Bay, Orange County, California. PCAS-Q 3(4), 1967.

2010. Chartkoff, J.L. and K.K. Chertkoff. Archaeological research potential in urban Los Angeles. PCAS-Q 8:57-66, 1972.

2011. Crabtree, R.H., C.N. Warren, and D.L. True. Archaeological investigations at Batiquitos Lagoon, San Diego County, California. UCLA-AS-AR 5:319-406, 1963.

2012. Creutz, E. and J. Moriarty. Inferences on the use position of San Dieguito percussion-flaked artifacts. A. Ant. 29: 82-89, 1963.

2013. Curtis, F. The European reaction to American "paleoliths." SM-M 30:140-145, 1956.

2014. _____Arroyo Sequit. ASASC-P 4, 1959.

2015. _____Arroyo Sequit: Archaeological investigations in Leo Carillo Beach State Park, Los Angeles County, California. CDPR-AR 9, 1963.

2016. Davis, J.R. An incised stone bowl associated with the Goff Island site. PCAS-Q 3(4), 1967.

2017. Decker, D.A. Early archaeology of Catalina Island: Potential and problems. UCLA-AS-AR 11:69-86, 1969.

2018. Desautels, R.J. An unusual cogged stone from LAn-283. PCAS-Q 4(3), 1968.

2019. Dixon, K.A. Cogged stones and other ceremonial cache artifacts in stratigraphic context at Ora-58, a site in the lower Santa Ana River drainage, Orange County. PCAS-Q 3(3), 1968.

2020. _____Reviving Puvunga: An archaeological project at Rancho Los Alamitos. SM-M 46(3):84-92, 1972.

2021. Dougan, M. The memorial ceremony of the Luiseño Indians. SM-M 38:140-149, 1964.

2022. Drover, C.E. and J.N. Spain. An early, articulated inhumation from 4-Ora-64. PCAS-Q 8:35-44, 1972.

2023. Dunn, H.H. The prehistoric painter of Poway. Touring Topics, pp. 36-38,56, May, 1930.

2024. Eberhart, H. Mesarica: A San Gabriel Valley site. SM-M 36: 69-76, 1962.

2025. _____The Milling Stone Complex: Genuine or spurious. A. Ant. 30:352-353, 1965.

2026. Eberhart, H. and W. Wasson. The Sassone site (LAn-339): A Milling Stone Horizon station in the San Gabriel Valley, California. California Anthropologist 5:9-45, 1975.

2027. Eisenbud, J. A recently found carving as a breast symbol. AA 66:141-147, 1964.

2028. Ezell, P.H. The archaeological survey of the Fallbrook and De Luz Reservoir sites, Santa Margarita project. PCAS-Q 8: 27-37, 1972.

2029. Farmer, M.F. Southern California discoidals. SM-M 27:177-183, 1953.

2030. _____ An Indian camp-site in Tuna Canyon. ASASC-N 5(2): 15, 1958.

2031. Finnerty, W.P., et al. Community structure and trade at Isthmus Cove: a salvage excavation on Catalina Island. PCAS-OP 1, 1970.

2032. Forbes, J.D. The TongVa of Tujunga to 1801. UCLA-AS-AR 8: 137-151, 1966.

2033. Fritz, K. The Los Pinos site (Ora-35). PCAS-Q 7(3), 1971.

2034. Glennan, W.S. An asphaltum repaired cogged stone from Southern California. SM-M 47(3):112-113, 1973.

2035. Greenwood, R.S. Early dwellers in Topanga Canyon. Archaeology 12:271-277, 1959.

2036. Greenwood, R.S. and R.O. Brown. Preliminary survey of the Rancho Canada Larga, Ventura County, California. UCLA-AS-AR 5:462-514, 1963.

2037. Hafner, D.H. An archaeological survey of two Upper Newport Bay sites, Orange County, California. PCAS-Q 2(2), 1966.

2038. Hafner, D.H., et al. The Buck Gully No. 2 site (Ora-189): The archaeology of a Late Horizon coastal site in Orange County, California. PCAS-Q 7(4), 1971.

2039. Hamilton, A. Rancho to rocketry. Westways, pp. 5-7, Dec., 1965.
[Potrero area south of Beaumont; contains some material on Indian sites]

2040. Harding, M. La Jollan culture. El Museo 1:10-11,31-38, 1951.

2041. Harrington, J.H. [Glass] arrowheads from the San Fernando Mission area. SM-M 7:81-82, 1933.

2042. Harrington, M.R. Once in a lifetime - perhaps! SM-M 8:177-178, 1934.
[Discovery of a wooden-handled flint knife near Long Beach]

2043. _____A real link with the past. SM-M 26:134-135, 1952.

2044. Hayden, J.D. Restoration of the San Dieguito type site to its proper place in the San Dieguito sequence. A. Ant. 31: 439-440, 1966.

2045. Hayes, S. and P.V. Long, Jr. Stone artifacts from Ora-196. PCAS-Q 5(3), 1969.

2046. Hedges, K. A rabbitskin blanket from San Diego County. SDM-ETN 10, 1973.

2047. Heizer, R.F. A steatite whale figurine from San Nicolas Island. UC-AS-R 38:10, 1957.

2048. _____A San Nicolas Island twined basketry water bottle. UC-AS-R 50:1-3, 1961.

2049. _____Some prehistoric wooden objects from San Nicolas Island. UC-AR-R 50:4-5, 1960.

2050. Heizer, R.F. and E.M. Lemert. Observations on archaeological
          sites in Topanga Canyon, California. UC-PAAE 44:237-258,
          1947.

2051. Henshaw, H.W. Perforated stones from California. BAE-B 2,
          1887.

2052. Herring, A.K. Surface collections from Ora-83, a cogged stone
          site at Bolsa Chica, Orange County, California. PCAS-Q
          4(3), 1968.

2053. Heye, G.G. Certain aboriginal pottery from Southern Calif-
          ornia. MAIHF-INM 7(1), 1919.

2054. _____Shaman's cache from Southern California. MAIHF-INM
          4(4), 1927.

2055. Hicks, F. Archaeological investigations in the Yucaipa Valley.
          SBCMA-SS 1(3), 1958.

2056. Holder, C.F. The Channel Islands of California. Chicago:
          A.C. McClurg and Co., 1910.

2057. Hollenbach, M. Islands of adventure. Los Angeles Museum
          Quarterly 1:21-24, 1941.
          [San Clemente Island cave archaeology]

2058. Hoffman, W.J. Notes appended to Hugo Reid's "Account of the
          Indians of Los Angeles County, California." Bulletin of
          the Essex Institute 17:1-33, Salem, Mass., 1885.

2059. Hoover, R.L. Incised steatite tablet from the Catalina Museum.
          SM-M 47:106-109, 1973.

2060. Hudson, D.T. The archaeological investigations during 1935
          and 1937 at Ora-237, Ora-238, and Ora-239, Santiago Can-
          yon, Orange County, California. PCAS-Q 5(1), 1969.

2061. _____Proto-Gabrielino patterns of territorial organiza-
          tion in South Coastal California. PCAS-Q 7(2), 1971.

2062. Iovin, J. A summary description of Luiseño material culture.
          UCLA-AS-AR 5:79-130, 1963.

2063. Iribarren Ch., J. Correlations between Archaic cultures of
          Southern California and Coquimbo, Chile. A. Ant. 27:
          424-425, 1962.

2064. Johnson, K.L. Site LAn-2: A late manifestation of the Topanga
          Complex in Southern California prehistory. UC-AR 23,
          1966.

2065. Johnston, B.E. The Gabrielino Indians of Southern California,
          Parts I-XIV. SM-M 29-32, 1955-1958.

2066. King, C.D.   Excavations at Parker Mesa (LAn-215).   UCLA-AS-AR
      4:91-256, 1962.

2067. _____The Sweetwater Mesa site (LAn-267) and its place in
      Southern California prehistory.   UCLA-AS-AR 9:25-76, 1967.

2068. _____Research results.   [La Jollan site, San Elijo Lagoon]
      SCA-N 9:3-4, 1975.

2069. King, C.D., T. Blackburn, and E. Chandonet.   The archaeological
      investigation of three sites on the Century Ranch, Western
      Los Angeles County, California.   UCLA-AS-AR 10:12-107,
      1968.

2070. King, L.   The Medea Creek cemetery (LAn-243):   An investiga-
      tion of social organization from mortuary practices.
      UCLA-AS-AR 11:23-68, 1969.

2071. Kowta, M.   The Sayles Complex-A Late Milling Stone Assemblage
      from Cajon Pass and the ecological implications of its
      scraper planes.   UC-PA 6, 1969.

2072. Leonard, N.N.   Ven-70 and its place in the late period of the
      Western Santa Monica Mountains.   UCLA-AS-AR 8:215-242,
      1966.

2073. _____Natural and social environments of the Santa
      Monica Mountains (6000 B.C. to 1800 A.D.).   UCLA-AS-AR
      13:93-136, 1971.

2074. _____Summer fieldwork [LAn-264 - Malibu].   SCA-N 6:6,
      1972.

2075. Long, P.V. and R.V. May.   An archaeological survey of Rancho
      de San Felipe.   PCAS-Q 6(4), 1970.

2076. Lounsberry, N.   Indian stone artifacts: Six year's study by
      S.C. Evans.   Sports and Hobbies: A Monthly Magazine for
      Swappers, Collectors, and Outdoor Sportsmen, June, 1930.
      [Cogged stones]

2077. Lytton, A.C.   Archaeological investigations at Laguna Niguel,
      Orange County.   UCLA-AS-AR 5:245-294, 1963.

2078. Maguire, J. and Savio, L.   Ora-82.   PCAS-S 13:3, 1974.

2079. Martz, P.   The Vandenburg Air Force Base project: A correla-
      tion of relative dates with radiocarbon dates.   UCLA-
      JNWA 1(7):1-40, 1976.

2080. May, R.V.   Suggestive evidence of prehistoric culture contact
      between the Southwest and the Far Southwest: Two crema-
      tions exposed in the Laguna Mountains of San Diego County,
      California.   In Two papers on the archaeology of San

Diego County, pp. 33-61. San Diego County Archaeological Society Publication 1, 1974.

2081. McCown, B.E. An archaeological survey of San Vicente Lake Bed, San Diego County, California. A. Ant. 10:255-264, 1945.

2082. _____Report of excavation site No. 7, Fallbrook Area. Archaeological Survey Association of Southern California, Los Angeles, 1950.

2083. _____Temeku: A page from the history of the Luiseño Indians. ASASC-P 3, 1955.

2084. McKinney, A. A report on the Burroughs site, Upper Newport Bay, Orange County, California. PCAS-Q 2(2), 1966.

2085. _____Cogged stones in private collections. PCAS-Q 4(3), 1968.

2086. _____Two mortuary urns from San Diego County. PCAS-Q 8:38-46, 1972.

2087. McKinney, A., et al. A report on the China Ranch area. PCAS-Q 7(2), 1971.

2088. McKusick, M.B. Three cultural complexes on San Clemente Island, California. SM-M 33:22-25, 1959.

2089. McKusick, M.B., C.N. Warren, et al. Introduction to San Clemente Island archaeology. UCLA-AS-AR 1:105-184, 1959.

2090. Mead, G.R. Redigging the WPA, The Bonita Corral site. PCAS-Q 5(4), 1969.

2091. Mead, J.R. Archaeology of Catalina Island. Transaction of the Kansas Academy of Science for 1899-1900, 17:215-216, 1901.

2092. Meighan, C.W. The Nicoleño. CAS-PD 7(1):23-27, 1954.

2093. _____A Late complex in Southern California prehistory. SWJA 10:215-227, 1954.

2094. _____The Little Harbor site, Catalina Island: An example of ecological interpretation in archaeology. A. Ant. 24:383-405, 1959.

2095. _____A ritual cave in Topanga, California. SM-M 43: 112-117, 1969.

2096. Meighan, C.W. and H. Eberhart. Archaeological resources of San Nicolas Island, California. A. Ant. 19:109-125, 1953.

2097. Meighan, C.W. and S. Rootenberg. A prehistoric miner's camp on Catalina Island. SM-M 31:176-184, 1958.

2098. Miller, F.H., Jr. Astro II: A pre-Spanish Diegueño site in Poway, California. San Diego Science Foundation, Occasional Paper No. 1. San Diego, 1962.

2099. Minshall, H.W. The broken stones. Copley Books, San Diego, 1976.

2100. Moriarty, J.R. A tanged side scraper from San Diego County. SM-M 36:149-152, 1962.

2101. _____Evidence of mat weaving from an early La Jolla site. SM-M 40:44-53, 1966.

2102. _____Culture phase divisions suggested by typological change coordinated with stratigraphically controlled radiocarbon dating at San Diego. Anthropological Journal of Canada 4(4):20-30, Ottawa, 1966.

2103. Moriarty, J.R. and H. Minshall. A new pre-desert site discovered near Texas Street. Anthropological Journal of Canada 10:10-13, 1972.

2104. Moriarty, J.R., G. Shumway, and C.N. Warren. Scripps Estates site 1 (SDi-525): A preliminary report on an early site on the San Diego coast. UCLA-AS-AR 1:185-216, 1959.

2105. Moriarty, J.R. and W.R. Weyland. Excavations at San Diego Mission. SM-M 45:124-137, 1971.

2106. Mykrantz, J.W. Indian burials from Southern California. MAIHF-INM 4:154-163, 1927.

2107. Nance, C.R. Cultural evidence for the Altithermal in Texas and Mexico. SWJA 28:169-192, 1972.
[P. 182: short discussion about the correlation of the Milling Stone Horizon and the Altithermal. Malaga Cove site cited in discussion]

2108. Norris, R.M. Desert San Nicolas and the last Nicoleño. CAS-PD 13(3):10-13, 1960.

2109. Orr, P.C. Return to San Nicolas. SBMNH-L 20(7):75-79, 1945.

2110. Palmer, F.M. Researches at Redondo Beach, California. AJA 10:21-26, 1906.

2111. Payne, W.O. A summary of the excavation of the "Santa Ysabel" site, Ora-168, Upper Newport Bay, Orange County, California. PCAS-Q 2(2), 1966.

2112. Peck, S.L. An archaeological report on the excavation of a prehistoric site at Zuma Creek. ASASC-P 2, 1955.

2113. Pond, G.P. Steatite tablets from Malaga Cove. SM-M 42:124-133, 1968.

2114. Putnam, F.W. The former Indians of Southern California, as bearing on the origins of the red man in America. Bull. of the Essex Institute 12:4-6, 1881.

2115. Redtfeldt, G. Excavations at the Ledge site [San Clemente Island]. SM-M 38:8-10, 1964.

2116. Reinman, F.M. New sites on San Nicolas Island, California. UCLA-AS-AR 4:11-22, 1962.

2117. _____Maritime adaptation on San Nicolas Island, California. UCLA-AS-AR 6:47-77, 1964.

2118. Reinman, F.M. and S.J. Townsend. Six burial sites on San Nicolas Island. UCLA-AS-AR 2:1-13, 1960.

2119. Robinson, E. Fishing arrowpoints from Southern California. SM-M 7:147-150, 1933.

2120. Rogers, M.J. The stone art of the San Dieguito Plateau. AA 31:454-467, 1929.

2121. _____California archaeological horizons. AA 42:178, 1940.

2122. _____San Dieguito implements from the terraces of the Rincon-Patano and Rillito drainage system. Kiva 24:1-23, 1958.

2123. Roosa, W.B. and S.L. Peckham. Notes on the Third Interglacial artifacts. A. Ant. 19:280-281, 1954.

2124. Ross, L.A. 4-Ora-190: A descriptive site report of a late prehistoric horizon site in Orange County, California. PCAS-Q 6(2 and 3), 1970.

2125. Rozaire, C.E. Archaeology in Los Angeles County. ASASC-N 5(2):3-6, 1958.

2126. _____Preliminary report on excavations at Chilao Flats. ASASC-N 5(2):13-14, 1958.

2127. _____Archaeology in Orange County. ASASC-N 5(3):3-4, 1958.

2128. _____Preliminary report on the Los Pinos Site, Orange County. ASASC-N 5(3):9-11, 1958.

2129. _____Excavation work on San Nicolas Island. ASASC-N 6(2):3-4, 1959.

2130. Rozaire, C.E. Archaeological investigations at two sites on San Nicolas Island, California. SM-M 33:129-152, 1959.

2131. _____The archaeology at Encino, California. UCLA-AS-AR 2:307-355, 1960.

2132. _____A complete Serrano arrow. SM-M 36:8-14, 1962.

2133. _____ A burial from San Clemente Island. SM-M 36:84-86, 1962.

2134. _____Some coastal sites in Baja California. SM-M 38:11-16, 1964.

2135. _____Archaeological considerations regarding the Southern California Islands. In R.N. Philbrick (Ed.), Proceedings of the symposium on the biology of the California Islands, Santa Barbara (pp. 327-336), 1967.

2136. Rozaire, C.E. and G. Kritzman. A petroglyph cave on San Nicolas Island. SM-M 34:147-151, 1960.

2137. Ruby, J.W. Surface collections from two coastal sites, Los Angeles County. UCLA-AS-AR 3:175-188, 1961.

2138. _____ Excavations at Zuma Mesa (LAn-40). UCLA-AS-AR 3:190-232, 1961.

2139. Rust, H.N. A cache of stone bowls in San Fernando, California. AA 8:686-687, 1906.

2140. Sawyer, E.O. Remarkable relics of aborigines found at Redondo. ASASC-N 6(4):5-7, 1959.

2141. Sayles, R. Flores site. ASASC-N 2:12-14, 1955.

2142. Schumacher, P. Something about kitchen middens and discoveries in old graves in Southern California. Zeitschrift für Anthropologie 8:217-221, 1875.

2143. _____Method of manufacture of several articles by the former inhabitants of Southern California. Eleventh Ann. Rept. of the Peabody Museum (Harvard) 8:258-268, 1875.

2144. _____Ancient olla manufactory on Santa Catalina Island, California. UC-AS-R 59:83, 1963.
       [Repr. from The American Naturalist 12(9):629, 1878]

2145. Shiner, J.L. A Fernandeño site in Simi Valley, California. SM-M 23:79-81, 1919.

2146. Shumway, G, C.L. Hubbs, and J.R. Moriarty. Scripps Estate site, San Diego, California: A La Jolla site dated 5460 to 7370 years before the present. Annals of the New York Academy of Sciences 93:37-132, 1961.

2147. Simpson, R.D. Shoshonean burial ground excavated. SM-M 27: 69, 1953.

2148. Singer, C.A. and R.O. Gibson. The Medea Creek Village site (LAn-4-243v): A functional lithic analysis. UCLA-AS-AR 12:184-204, 1970.

2149. Smith, W.S.T. The geology of Santa Catalina Island. CAS-P 1:1-71, 1897.

2150. Stephenson, T.E. Shadows of Old Saddleback. Santa Ana, 1931. [Descriptions of a number of archaeological sites in the canyons of the Santa Ana Mountains]

2151. Stickel, E.G. Status differentiations at the Rincon Site. UCLA-AS-AR 10:209-261, 1968.

2152. _____ Villa Pacifica (Ca-LAn-271): Theory and method applied to the salvage excavation of a site in Long Beach, California. UCLA-JNWA 1(4):36-63, 1976.

2153. Tenny, W.A. The hermit of San Nicolas Island. Pacific Monthly 18:23-30, Portland, 1907.

2154. Thomas, D.B. and J. Beaton. The Trancas Canyon cemetery site (4-LAn-197): An analysis of mortuary customs. UCLA-AS-AR 10:162-174, 1968.

2155. Townsend, S.J. Some comments on the archaeology of San Clemente Island, California. A. Ant. 28:554-555, 1963.

2156. Treganza, A.E. Notes on the San Dieguito lithic industry of Southern California and Northern Baja California. UC-PAAE 44:253-255, 1947.

2157. Treganza, A.E. and A. Bierman. The Topanga Culture: Final report on excavations, 1948. UC-AR 20(2):45-86, 1958.

2158. Treganza, A.E. and C.G. Malamud. The Topanga culture: First season's excavation of the Tank site, 1947. UC-AR 12: 129-155, 1950.

2159. True, D.L. An early complex in San Diego County, California. A. Ant. 23:255-263, 1958.

2160. _____ Investigation of a late prehistoric complex in Cuyamaca Rancho State Park, San Diego, California. Archaeological Survey Monograph, UCLA, 1970.

2161. True, D.L., C.W. Meighan, and H. Crew. Archaeological investigations at Molpa, San Diego County, California. UC-PA 11, 1974.

136

2162. Walker, E.F. A ceremonial site at Porter Ranch, San Fernando. SM-M 10:98-104, 1936.

2163. _____Sequence of prehistoric material culture at Malaga Cove, California. SM-M 11:210-214, 1937.

2164. _____A cemetery of prehistoric Indians in Pasadena. SM-M 13:5-8, 1939.

2165. _____Prehistoric mortuary cairns at Chatsworth, California. SM-M 13:131-135, 1939.

2166. _____Indians of Southern California. SM-M 17:201-216, 1943.

2167. _____The dig at Big Tujunga Wash. SM-M 19:188-193, 1945.

2168. _____Five prehistoric archaeological sites in Los Angeles County, California. Southwest Museum Publications, F.W. Hodge Anniversary Fund, No. 6, 1952.

2169. Wallace, E.T. and G. Kritzman. A shell encrusted artifact. ASASC-N 3:11-12, 1956.

2170. Wallace, W.J. The Little Sycamore site and the early Milling Stone cultures of Southern California. A. Ant. 20:112-123, 1954.

2171. _____ A suggested chronology for Southern California coastal archaeology. SWJA 11:214-230, 1955.

2172. _____ Archaeology of the Gilmore Ranch Site, Ventura County, California. SM-M 29:8-20, 1955.

2173. _____The Little Sycamore shellmound, Ventura County. ARA-CCA 2, 1956.

2174. _____Archaeological resources of the Buena Vista watershed, San Diego County, California. UCLA-AS-AR 2: 277-306, 1960.

2175. _____Hollywood Riviera: An early Milling Stone Horizon site in Los Angeles County, California. A. Ant. 31: 422-427, 1966.

2176. _____Prehistoric seasonal campsites in Southern California. SM-M 42:134-141, 1968.

2177. Warren, C.N. Further comments on the archaeology of San Clemente Island, California: A reply. A. Ant. 29:393-395, 1964.

2178. _____The San Dieguito Complex: A review and hypothesis. A. Ant. 32:168-185, 1967.

2179. Warren, C.N. (Ed.). A stratified San Dieguito site: Malcom Rogers' 1938 excavation in the San Dieguito River Valley. SDM-P 5, 1966.

2180. Warren, C.N. and H.P. Thompson. Test excavations at the Del Mar site (SDi-191). UCLA-AS-AR 1:217-233, 1959.

2181. Warren, C.N. and D.L. True. The San Dieguito complex and its place in California prehistory. UCLA-AS-AR 3:246-337, 1961.

2182. Warren, C.N., D.L. True, and A.A. Eudey. Early gathering complexes of Western San Diego County. UCLA-AS-AR 3:1-105, 1961.

2183. Warren, C.N., E.V. Warren, and E. Chandonet. Archaeology. California Highways and Public Works, pp. 45-51, May-June, 1961.
      [Batiquitos Lagoon, San Diego County]

2184. Weide, M.L. Seasonality of Pismo clam collecting at Ora-82. UCLA-AS-AR 11:127-142, 1969.

2185. Wheeler, S.M. A site at Descanso, California. SM-M 12:192-194, 1938.

2186. Williamson, M.B. Catalogue of Indian relics found on Santa Catalina Island in the museums of Los Angeles Chamber of Commerce, the Smithsonian Institution, and Peabody Museum of Archaeology and Ethnology, Harvard University, Cambridge, Massachusetts. SCAS-B 3:38-41,60-63,149-152, 1904.

2187. Windle, E. Does Catalina history date back 3000 years? Avalon Catalina Islander, August 18, 1926.

2188. Winterbourne, J.W. The 1935 Adams-Fairview excavation, Orange County Historical Research Project. PCAS-Q 2(3), 1966.

2189. _____Report of the Goff's Island site excavation, May 1, 1939 to January 22, 1940. PCAS-Q 3(2 and 3), 1967.

2190. Woodward, A. Atlatl dart foreshafts from the LaBrea pits. SCAS-B 36:41-60, 1937.

2191. _____ Domestic fowl as ceremonial offerings. (Recovered from caves on San Clemente Island) SAA-N 2:43-44, 1942.

2192. Zahn, C. Strange saga of San Nicolas Island. National Motorist 25(4):6-7,23, San Francisco, 1949.

2193. Allen, H. Crania from the mounds of the St. John's River, Florida: A study made in connection with crania from other parts of North America. Journal of the Academy of Natural Sciences, Philadelphia 10:367-448, 1896.

2194. Angel, J.L. Tranquillity skeletons: Early man in California (Abstract). AJPA 21:422-423, 1963.

2195. Anonymous. Dental surgery practiced by primitive Americans. Popular Mechanics, September, p. 379, 1916.
[Ocean Park, Los Angeles County: Tooth-pulling, and filling with mastic of pulverized stone and asphaltum]

2196. Bard, C.L. Medicine and surgery among the first Californians. Touring Topics, p. 20, January 1930.
[Includes medical and health practices among California Indians]

2197. Birdsell, J.B. The racial origin of the extinct Tasmanians. Records of the Queen Victoria Museum 2:105-122, 1949.
[P. 118: mention of parasagittal grooving of crania from Santa Cruz and Santa Catalina Islands]

2198. _____The problem of the early peopling of the Americas as viewed from Asia. Papers on Physical Anthropology of American Indians; Viking Fund Publications in Anthropology; pp. 36-47, 1951.
["Amurian" characteristics among Cahuilla and other Southern California Indians]

2199. Boas, F. Zur Anthropologie der nordamerikanischen Indianer. ZE 27:366-411, 1895.

2200. _____Anthropometrical observations on the Mission Indians of Southern California. Proceedings of the American Association for the Advancement of Science 44:261-269, 1895.

2201. _____Anthropometry of Shoshonean tribes. AA 1:751-758, 1899.

2202. _____Anthropometry of Central California. AMNH-B 17(4): 347-380, 1905.

2203. Bonin, G.V. and G.M. Morant. Indian races in the United States. A survey of previously published cranial measurements. Biometrika 30:94-129, 1938.

2204. Brabender, I. Die Palaobiologische Rekonstruktion zweier Prähistorischer Bevölkerungen aus Kalifornien. Mainz, 1965.

2205. _____Beitrag zur paläobiologischen Rekonstruktion prä-

historischen Kalifornischen Populationen. Homo: Zeitschrift für die vergleichende Forschung am Menschen 16:
200-233, Göttingen, 1965.

2206. Brooks, S.T. Skeletal age at death: The reliability of cran-
ial and pubic age indicators. AJPA 13:567 ff., 1956.
[California Indian skeletons in Anthropology Museum at
Berkeley included]

2207. Brooks, S.T., B.L. Conrey, and K.A. Dixon. A deeply buried
human skull and recent stratigraphy at the present mouth
of the San Gabriel River, Seal Beach, California. SCAS-
B 64:229-241, 1965.

2208. Carr, L. Observations on the crania from the Santa Barbara
Islands, California. Special Publication of Peabody
Museum, Harvard University, 1877.
[Also in USGS-WCM 7:277-292, 1879]

2209. _____Measurements of crania from California. PM-R 12:497-
505, 1880.

2210. Cook, S.F. The extent and significance of disease among the
Indians of Baja California, 1697-1773. UC-IA 12:1-39,
1937.

2211. _____Survivorship in aboriginal populations. Human Biology 19:83-89, 1947.
[Age at death as indicated in some California Indian
skeletal materials]

2212. Count, E.W. The "Australoid" in California. Zeitschrift für
Rassenkunde 8:62-95, 1938.

2213. _____Primitive Amerinds and the Australo-Melanesians.
Revista del Instituto de Antropología de la Universidad
Nacional de Tucuman, Vol. 1, 1939.
[Among others, California Indians' cranial morphology
compared to Australo-Melanesians']

2214. Courville, C.B. Prehistoric California head injuries. Bulletin of the Los Angeles Neurological Society, 1952.

2215. D'Amico, A. The canine teeth: Normal functional relations of
the natural teeth in man. Journal of the Southern California State Dental Association 26(1, 2, 4-7), 1958.

2216. Gifford, E.W. California anthropometry. UC-PAAE 22:217-390,
1926.

2217. _____Californian Indian types. Natural History 26:
50-60, 1926.

2218. Gladwin, H.S. A history of the ancient Southwest. Portland,
Maine. Bond Wheelwright Co., 1957.

2219. Haney, P.J. Atlatl elbow in Central California prehistoric cultures. CARD Publ. No. 4:31-34, 1974.

2220. Harris, E.F. and C.G. Turner, Dental morphology and its bearing on the "dihybrid theory". UC-C-ARF 22:1-46, 1974.

2221. Heizer, R.F. and T.D. McCown. The Stanford Skull, a probable early man from Santa Clara County, California. UC-AS-R 6, 1950.

2222. Heizer, R.F. and C. Treanor. Observations on physical strength of some western Indians and "Old American" Whites. UC-C-ARF 22:47-57, 1974.

2223. Hohenthal, W.D. and S.T. Brooks. An archaeological scaphocephal from California. AJPA 18(1):59-65, 1960.

2224. Hooton, E.A. The Indians of Pecos Pueblo. Phillips Academy, Papers of the Southwestern Expedition 4:236-238, 1930. [Measurements of Santa Barbara Channel Island crania and comparisons with Pecos skulls]

2225. Hrdlička, A. Contribution to the physical anthropology of California. UC-PAAE 4:49-64, 1906.

2226. _____ Skeletal remains suggesting or attributed to early man in North America. BAE-B 33:21-28, 1907. [Calaveras skull and others]

2227. _____ Stature of the Indians of the Southwest and of Northern Mexico. Putnam Anniv. Vol. 405-426. N.Y., 1909. [Stature measurements for Colorado River Yumans]

2228. _____ Recent discoveries attributed to early man in America. BAE-B 66:17-22, 1918. [LaBrea]

2229. _____ Catalogue of human crania in the U.S. National Museum collections. The Algonkin and related Iroquois; Siouan, Caddoan, Salish, and Sahaptin, Shoshonean, and Californian Indians. USNM-P 69:1-127, ca. 1930.

2230. Hulse, F.S. Ripples on a gene pool: The shifting frequencies of the blood-type alleles among the Indians of the Hupa Reservation. AJPA 18(2):141-152, 1960.

2231. Jarcho, S. (Ed.). Human paleopathology. Yale Univ. Press, 1966. [Chapter on California Indian specimens by J.G. Roney]

2232. Kennedy, K.A.R. The dentition of Indian crania of the early and late archaeological horizons in Central California. UC-AS-R 50:41-50, 1960.

2233. Klimek, S. The structure of California Indian culture, culture element distributions: I. UC-PAAE 37:31-33, 1935.

2234. LeConte, J.L. On the distinctive characters of the Indians of California. Proceedings of the American Association for the Advancement of Science, Sixth Meeting, N.Y., G.P. Putnam, 1852.

2235. Leigh, R.W. Dental pathology of aboriginal California. UC-PAAE 23:399-440, 1928.

2236. Littlewood, R.A. Analysis of skeletal material from the Zuma Creek site (LAn-174). UCLA-AS-AR 2:135-154, 1960.

2237. Matiegka, H. Über Schädel und Skelette von Santa Rosa (Santa Barbara - Archipel bei Californien). Sitzungsberichte der königlichen Böhmischen Gesellschaft der Wissenschaften, Mathematisch 2:1-123, 1905.

2238. McCown, T.D. Summary of T.D. McCown, "The sequence of physical types in California," a paper given at the 4th Summer Seminar in Physical Anthropology, Viking Fund, Inc. In Yearbook of Physical Anthropology 1948:33-34 (Ed. by G.W. Lasker and F.P. Thieme) New York, 1949.

2239. McHenry, H. Transverse lines in long bones of prehistoric California. AJPA 29:1-18, 1968.

2240. McKern, T.W. Anthropometric and morphological analysis of a prehistoric skeletal population from Santa Cruz Island, California. Archives of Archaeology 10, Society for American Archaeology and University of Wisconsin Press, 1960.

2241. Molner, S. Sex, age, and tooth positions as factors in the production of tooth wear. A. Ant. 36:182-188, 1971.

2242. _____ Human tooth wear, tooth function, and cultural variability. AJPA 34:175-190, 1971.

2243. Moodie, R.L. Deafness among ancient Californian Indians. SCAS-B 28:46-49, 1929.

2244. Morton, S.G. Physical type of the American Indians. In Schoolcraft, Indian Tribes II:320,335, pl. 68, 1852.

2245. Neumann, G.K. Archaeology and race in the American Indian. In Griffin, J.B. (Ed.), Archaeology of the Eastern United States, Chicago, 1952.
[P. 29, Hupa physical type]

2246. Newman, R.W. Preliminary report on the skeletal remains (of the Early Central California culture). In R.F. Heizer, the archaeology of Central California, I: The Early Horizon, App. II, UC-AR 12:49-50, 1949.

2247. Newman, R.W.   Abstract of "Cranial changes in a sequential skeleton series."   AJPA 9:225-260, 1951.

2248. _____ A comparative analysis of prehistoric skeletal remains from lower Sacramento Valley. (abstract). KASP 14:102-103, 1956.
[Statistical evidence for population replacement in succeeding archaeological horizons]

2249. _____ A comparative analysis of prehistoric skeletal remains from the lower Sacramento Valley. UC-AS-R 39, 1957.

2250. Oetteking, B. Morphological and metrical variation in skulls from San Miguel Island, California. I: The sutura nasofrontalis. MAIHF-INM 7:51-85, 1920.

2251. _____ The Santa Barbara crania. MAIHF-INM 1:76-83, 1924.
[Burton Mound]

2252. _____ Declination of the pars basilaris in normal and artifically deformed skulls. MAIHF-INM (Ms) 27:1-25, 1924.

2253. _____ Skeletal remains from Santa Barbara, California. I: Craniology. MAIHF-INM (Ms) 39:1-168, 1925.

2254. _____ Morphology and metrical variation in skulls from San Miguel Island: II. MAIHF-INM (Ms) 45:1-54, 1928.

2255. _____ An extreme case of arthritis deformans from San Nicolas Island. MAIHF-IN 7:52-56, 1930.

2256. Otis, G. Check list of preparations and objects in the Section of Human Anatomy of the U.S. Army Medical Museum for use during the International Exhibition of 1876 in connection with the representation of the Medical department, U.S. Army; No. 8. Washington, D.C., 1876.

2257. _____ List of the specimens in the Anatomical Section of the U.S. Army Medical Museum. Washington, D.C., 1880.

2258. Pantin, A.M. and R. Kallsen. The blood groups of the Diegueño Indians. AJPA 11:91-96, 1953.

2259. Pepper, O.H.P., and E.P. Pendergrass. Hereditary occurrence of enlarged parietal foramina. American Journal of Roentgenology and Radium Therapy 35:1-8, 1936.

2260. Pocock, W.I. Crania from shell-bearing sand-hills near San Francisco, now in the Cambridge Museum. Man 5:148-152, 1905.

2261. Putnam, F.W. The former Indians of Southern California, as bearing on the origin of the red man in America. Bulletin of the Essex Institute 12:4-6, 1880.

2262. Remondino, P.C. Mediterranean shores of America. F.A. Davis of Philadelphia Publication, pp. 14-15, 1892.
[Physician reports first-hand information from two army doctors stationed at Fort Yuma in 1853 and early 1870's about the climate and the food and customs of Indians, on prevalence of pneumonia, tuberculosis, rheumatism, and syphilis among them]

2263. Rogers, S.L. The physical characteristics of the aboriginal La Jollan population of Southern California. SDM-P 4, 1963.

2264. _____ An ancient human skeleton found at Del Mar, California. SDM-P 7, 1974.

2265. Roney, J.G., Jr. Palaeopathology of a California archaeological site. Bulletin of the History of Medicine 33(2):97-109, 1959.

2266. Schoolcraft, H.R. Cranial measurements of American Indians. Archives of Aboriginal Knowledge II:335, 1860.
[15 crania "altered by art"; Oregon and California not distinguished]

2267. Sera, G.L. Residui di popolazioni mongoloidi nelle Isoli di California. Archivio per l'antropologia e l'etnologia 44:28-38,143-147, 1914.

2268. Smith, J. and L. Carr. Measurements of the crania received during the year. PM-R 11:221-223, 1880.
[Table of measurements of 50 crania from San Clemente and Santa Catalina Islands]

2269. Stewart, T.D. Skeletal remains from the Buena Vista sites, California. BAE-B 130:172-188, 1941.

2270. Sussman, R. Skeletal analysis for the archaeologist. UCLA-AS-AR 7:333-362, 1965.

2271. Ten Kate, H.F.C. Somatological observations of Indians of the Southwest. Jour. Amer. Ethnol. and Archaeol. 3:134, 1892.
[Measurements of Mohave Indians]

2272. Virchow, R. Beitrage zur Craniologie der Insulaner von der Westküste Nordamerikas. Verhandlungen der Berliner Gesellscheft für Anthropologie, Ethnologie, und Urgeschichte pp. 382-403, 1889.

2273. Warren, G.L. Salvage excavations at the Fowler site: Skeletal analysis of 4-SLO-406. SLOCAS-OP 4, 1971.

2274. **Yates, L.G.** Calaveras skull controversy. Report of the recording secretary of the Natural History Society of Santa Barbara, 1885.

XXIX. UNDERWATER ARCHAEOLOGY

2275. **Breede, W.** Skin diver finds old stone bowl. Santa Barbara News-Press, pp. A-11, October 4, 1959.

2276. Carter, G.F. On submarine archaeology about San Diego. SM-M 29:21-27, 1955.

2277. Harrington, M.R. Mysterious ocean waves wash up Indian dagger. Science News Letter, p. 215, October 6, 1934.

2278. Hudson, D.T. Marine archaeology along the Southern California coast. SDM-P 9, 1976.

2279. Marshall, N.F. and J.R. Moriarty. Principles of underwater archaeology. CAS-PD 17:18-25, 1964.

2280. Rozaire, C.E. Underwater finds at Dana Point. SM-M 36:77-78, 1962.

2281. Shepard, F.P: Sea level changes in the past 6000 years: possible archaeological significance. Science 143:574-576, 1964.

2282. Shepard, F.P., J.R. Curray, et al. Submarine geology by diving saucer. Science 145:1042-1045, 1964.

2283. Tuthill, C. and A. Allanson. Ocean-bottom artifacts. SM-M 28:222-232, 1954.

2284. Wallace, E. and E. Bates. Two additional underwater mortars. Archaeological Research Association, Bull. 7. Los Angeles, 1962.

2285. Wallace, E. and G. Kritzman. A shell-encrusted artifact. ASASC-N 3(2):11-12, 1956.

2286. Walters, K.R. An underwater artifact. SM-M 43:72-74, 1969.

2287. _____ Another underwater artifact. PCAS-Q 8:53-58, 1972.
[Also in SM-M 46:112-115, 1972]

Map 2

California Indian Tribes and Territories

PART II: INDIAN HISTORY

I A1: PERIOD OF NATIVE HISTORY (? B.C.-1542 A.D.):
       PREHISTORIC ARCHAEOLOGY

There is a very large literature on California archaeology as consultation of Heizer and Elsasser (1970) will demonstrate. Persons wishing to determine what kind of research has been conducted in specific areas will find the systematic listings in Baumhoff and Elsasser (1956) and Eberhard (1970) useful. For broad surveys of the cultural sequence and chronology of California archaeology see Heizer (1963), Meighan (1965) and Willey (1966), each of which contains abundant references to published reports.

Archaeological Survey Annual Report (UCLA-AS-AR), No. 1 (1958-1959) - No. 12 (1970). Department of Anthropology, University of California, Los Angeles.
[Mainly, but not wholly, archaeology]

2288. Bada, J.L., R.A. Schroeder and G.F. Carter. New evidence for the antiquity of man in North America deduced from aspartic acid racemization. Science 184: 791-793, 1974.
[Results of a new method of archaeological dating. Ages of up to 40,000 years for California are proposed. Most archaeologists are doubtful of the accuracy of these results]

2289. Baumhoff, M.A. and A.B. Elsasser. Summary of archaeological survey and excavation in California. UC-AS-R 33: 1-27, 1956.
[Review of work done up to 1956]

2290. Beardsley, R.K. Temporal and areal relationships in Central California archaeology. Parts I, II. UC-AS-R 24,25, 1954.
[General survey of Central California prehistory]

2291. Eberhard, H. Published archaeological sites and surveys in Southern California. ASASC-N 17:4-21, 1970.

2292. Grant, C. The rock painting of the Chumash: a study of a California Indian culture. University of California Press, 1965.

2293. Heizer, R.F. The western coast of North America. In J. Jennings and E. Norbeck (eds.), Prehistoric Man in the New World. (pp. 117-148), 1963. University of Chicago Press.
[General review of California cultures and chronology]

2294. Heizer, R.F. and M.A. Baumhoff. California settlement patterns. In Prehistoric Settlement Patterns in the New World. Viking Fund Publications in Anthropology 23:32-44, 1956.
[Mainly from the perspective of archaeology]

149

2295. Heizer, R.F. and C.W. Clewlow Jr. Prehistoric rock art of
California. 2 Vols. Ballena Press. Ramona, California,
1974.
[General survey of petroglyphs and pictographs of
California]

2296. Heizer,R.F. and A.B. Elsasser. A bibliography of California
archaeology. UC-C-ARF 6, 1970.
[References to publication on archaeological sites
and subjects; includes physical anthropology]

2297. Meighan, C. Pacific coast archaeology. In H.E. Wright
and D.G. Frey (eds.),The Quaternary of the United
States. Princeton University Press, (pp. 709-719), 1965.
[General survey of California archaeology]

2298. Reichlen, H. and R.F. Heizer. La Mission de Leon de Cessac
en Californie, 1877-1879. Objets et Mondes 3:17-34,
1963. English translation in Reports of the University
of California Archaeological Survey 61:9-23, 1964.
[Archaeology and ethnology in the Chumash area]

2299. University of California Archaeological Survey. Reports, No.
1 (1948)-No. 75 (1972). Department of Anthropology,
University of California, Berkeley.
[Mainly contains papers on archaeology. Report No.
75 contains a check list and index of Reports 1-75]

2300. Willey, G.R. An introduction to American archaeology. Vol. 1,
North and MIddle America. Prentice-Hall. New York,
1966.
[Ch. 6, pp. 361-379, deals with California archaeology]

I A2: PERIOD OF NATIVE HISTORY (? B.C.-1542 A.D.):
HISTORIC ARCHAEOLOGY

Investigations by archaeologists of Franciscan
mission sites or native village sites occupied in the
historic period are referred to here. No adequate summary
of historic archaeology has been published and such a
collection of data would be a welcome addition to the
literature.

2301. Bennyhoff, J.A. and A.B. Elsasser. Sonoma Mission: an
historical and archaeological study of primary constructions, 1823-1913. UC-AS-R 27, 1954.

2302. Chartkoff, J.L. and K.K. Chartkoff. Late period settlement of the middle Klamath river of Northwest
California. A Ant 40:172-179, 1975.

2303. Deetz, J.J.F. Archaeological investigations at La Purisima
Mission. UCLA-AS-AR for 1962-1963: 161-244, 1963.

2304. Heizer, R.F. The direct historical approach in Central
California archaeology. A Ant 7:98-122, 1941.
[Attempts to link late period archaeology with
ethnographic cultures in northcentral California]

2305. _____ Archaeological evidence of Sebastian Rodriguez
Cermeno's California visit in 1595. California Historical
Society Quarterly 20:315-328, 1941.
[Recovery of portions of the cargo and remains of
Cermeno's ship in archaeological sites at Drake's Bay]

2306. _____ Observations on historic sites and archaeology
in California. UC-AS-R 9:1-5, 1950.
[A survey of work done up to 1950]

2307. _____ California's oldest historical relic? Robert
H. Lowie Museum of Anthropology, University of
California, 1972.
[Possible gravestone of Cabrillo who died and was
buried on one of the Channel Islands in January,
1543]

2308. Heizer, R.F. and J.E. Mills. The four ages of Tsurai.
University of California Press, 1952.
[Ethnohistory and archaeology of a Yurok Village
at Trinidad Bay. Covers the period from 1776 to
1918]

2309. Humphrey, R.V. The La Purisima Mission cemetery, UCLA-AS-AR
for 1965, Vol. 7:179-192. 1965, Los Angeles.

2310. Jones, P.M. Archaeological investigations on Santa Rosa Island
in 1901. UC-AR 17:201-280, 1956.
[Jones reports some historic materials, probably dating
from the mission period]

2311. Kessler, D.E. The restoration of Ramona's marriage place.
Pacific Monthly, June 1910. pp. 585-588.

2312. Meighan, C.W. and R.F. Heizer. Archaeological exploration of
16th century Indian mounds at Drake's Bay. California
Historical Quarterly 31:99-106, 1952.
[Recovery of porcelain and iron spikes attributed to
Cermeno, 1595]

2313. Schuyler, R.L. Indian-Euroamerican interaction in California:
Archaeological Evidence From Non-Indian Sites. To
appear in Vol. VIII, Handbok of North American
Indians. Smithsonian Institution, 1977.

2314. Soto, A. Mission San Luis Rey, California: Excavations in
the Sunken Garden. Kiva 26:34-43, 1960/61.

2315. Treganza, A.E. Fort Ross: a case study in historical
        archaeology. UC-AS-R 23, 1954.

2316. _____ Sonoma Mission: an archaeological recon-
        struction of the Mission San Francisco de Solano
        Quadrangle. KASP 14:1-8, 1956.

I B: PERIOD OF NATIVE HISTORY (? B.C.-1542 A.D.):
       LINGUISTICS

        No attempt is made here to list the abundance of
publications on native languages. Non-specialists who
wish to find word lists can consult Gatschet (1876), Powell
(1891) and Powers (1877). An excellent bibliography of
such word lists is by Bright (1964, pp. 217-235). Modern
linguistic studies (grammars and texts) are available for
many languages in the University of California Publications
in Linguistics (1943 et seq.). Tribal distribution maps which
are also maps of languages can be found in Heizer (1966).

2317. Bright, W. Animals of acculturation in the California Indian
        languages. UC-PL 4:215-246, 1960.
        [Names of domestic animals in California native
        languages]

2318. _____ A field guide to Southern California Indian
        languages. UCLA-AS-AR 1965:403-406, 1965.

2319. _____ Studies in Californian linguistics. UC-PL 34,
        1964.
        [Collection of papers by several linguists--an
        important work. At end of volume is a complete
        listing of linguistic publications]

2320. Bright, W. and E. Spanish words in Patwin. Romance
        Philology 13:161-164, 1959.
        [A lunguistic acculturation study]

2321. Callaghan, C. Lake Miwok dictionary. UC-PL 39, 1965.

2322. _____ Bodega Miwok dictionary. UC-PL 7, 1970.
        [Concerns the Coast Miwok]

2323. Dixon, R.B. The Chimariko Indians and language. UC-PAAE
        5: 293-380, 1910.

2324. Dixon, R.B. and A.L. Kroeber. Linguistic families of
        California. UC-PAAE 16 (3), 1919.
        [A basic work. Terminology and classification have
        been somewhat changed since 1919]

2325. Fowler, C.S. Some Northern Paiute native categories.
        Ethnology 6:381-404, 1967.

2326. Freeland, L.A. and S.M. Broadbent. Central Sierra Miwok dictionary with texts. UC-PL 23, 1960.

2327. Gatschet, A.S. Analytical report upon Indian dialects spoken in Southern California. U.S. Geographical Surveys West of the 100th Meridian. Annual Report [of the Chief of Engineers] for 1876, Appendix jj, pp. 550-563, 1876. Washington, D.C. [Numerous word lists]

2328. Goddard, P.E. Kato texts. UC-PAAE 5:65-238, 1909.

2329. Heizer, R.F. Alexander S. Taylor's map of California Indian tribes, 1864. California Historical Society Quarterly 20:171-180, 1941. [With reproduction of Taylor's map which was the first to be attempted for California]

2330. _____ Languages, territories and names of California Indian tribes. University of California Press, 1966. [Survey of the history of study and classification of California Indian languages; linguistic classification of A.L. Kroeber with a detailed map of tribal territories; linguistic classification of C. Hart Merriam with a detailed map of tribal territories; list of published maps showing areas occupied by individual tribes, pp. 31-34]

2331. Henshaw, H.W. California Indian linguistic records: the mission Indian vocabularies of H.W. Henshaw. Edited, with ethnographic notes, by R.F. Heizer. UC-AR 15 (2), 1955. [Languages of the Costanoan and Chumash tribes based on work done in California in 1884]

2332. Hyde, V. An introduction to the Luiseno language. Malki Museum Press, Banning, 1971. [Language text prepared by a tribal member]

2333. Joel, J. Classification of the Yuman languages. UC-PL 34: 99-105, 1964.

2334. Kroeber, A.L. The languages of the coast of California south of San Francisco Bay. UC-PAAE 2 (2), 1904. [A basic work on linguistic relationships]

2335. _____ The languages of the coast of California north of San Francisco Bay. UC-PAAE 9 (3), 1911. [Like the preceding for the area to the north]

2336. Kroeber, A.L. and G.W. Grace. The Sparkman grammer of Luiseno. UC-PL 16, 1959.

2337. Lamb, S.M. The classification of the Uto-Aztekan languages: an historical survey. UC-PL Vol. 34:106-125, 1964.

2338. Langdon, M. A grammer of Diegueno, the Mesa Grande dialect. UC-PL Vol. 66, 1970.

2339. Levy, R.L. Costanoan internal relationships. UC-ARF, 1976.
        [A linguistic study. Includes map showing distribution of Costanoan languges and tribelet centers]

2340. Newman, S.S. Yokuts language in California. Viking Fund Publications in Anthropology No. 2: 1-247, 1944.

2341. Olmsted, D.L. Achumawi dictionary. UC-PL 45, 1966.

2342. Oswalt, R.L. Russian loanwords in Southwestern Pomo. International Journal of American Linguistics 24:245-247, 1958.
        [Linguistic acculturation]

2343. _____ The internal relationship of the Pomo family of languages. Actas y Memorias, XXXV Congresso Internacional de Americanistas (Mexico) 2:413-427, 1964.

2344. Pinart, A. California Indian linguistic records; the mission Indian vocabularies of Alphonse Pinart. Edited by R.F. Heizer. UC-AR 15 (1), 1952.
        [Languages of the Costanoans, Chumash, Salinan and Esselen tribes, recorqded in 1878]

2345. Powell, J.W. Indian linguistic families of America north of Mexico. BAE-AR 7:1-142, 1891.
        [The first adequate attempt at a continent-wide classification; California is considered. Now outdated]

2346. Powers, S. Tribes of California. Contributions to North American Ethnology, Vol. III. Washington, 1877.
        [Numerous word lists edited by J.W. Powell. 1976. Vocabularies not printed in reprint by University of California Press]

2347. Robins, R.H. The Yurok language. UC-PL 15, 1958.

2348. Sapir, E. and M. Swadesh. Yana dictionary. UC-PL 22, 1960.

2349. Sawyer, J.O. Wappo words from Spanish. UC-PL 34:163-169, 1964.
        [Linguistic acculturation study]

2350. Sawyer, J.O. English-Wappo vocabulary. UC-PL Vol. 43, 1965.

2351. Shirley, W.F. Spanish elements in the indigenous languages of Central California. Romance Philology 16:1-21, 1962.

2352. Shirley, W.F. Maidu grammar. UC-PL 41, 1964.

2353. _____ Maidu texts and dictionary. UC-PL 33, 1964.

2354. _____ California [Indian linguistic studies]. In Current Trends in Linguistics 10:1046-1078, 1974. Mouton.
[Historical review of linguistic recording and efforts at classification]

2355. Teeter, K.V. The Wiyot language. UC-PL 37, 1964.

2356. Uldall, H.J. and W. Shipley. Nisenan texts and dictionary. UC-PL 46, 1966.

2357. University of California Publications in American Archaeology and Ethnology. (UC-PAAE) University of California. 1903-1964. Berkeley.
[Includes numerous linguistic studies]

2358. University of California Publications in Linguistics. University of California. 1943-date. Berkeley.
[Grammars and dictionaries of California Indian languages done by modern methods]

2359. Voegelin, C.F. Tubatulabal texts. UC-PAAE 34:191-246, 1935.

2360. Weber, F.J. Versatile Franciscan linguist. SM-M 42:153-156, 1968.
[Work and writings on California Indian languages of Fr. Felipe Arroyo de la Cuesta, 1780-1840]

I C: PERIOD OF NATIVE HISTORY (? B.C.-1542 A.D.):
PHYSICAL ANTHROPOLOGY: DEMOGRAPHY

Anthropologists have long been interested in how many Indians occupied California at the beginning of the historic period, the dateline usually being 1769 which marks the first overland exploration and founding of the first Franciscan mission (San Diego). Merriam (1905) suggested 260,000; Kroeber (1921, 1925) said 133,000. Cook (1943) raised the total to 150,000, but on the basis of a more detailed survey Cook (1955, 1956, 1957 reports this in part) raised his estimate to about 275,000 (Cook 1964). In a final assessment Cook (1976) concludes that the aboriginal population of California was about 300,000.

Genetic persistence of "Indian blood" is considered in Kroeber and Heizer (1970), and Cook (1976). Causes of population decline are considered by Cook (1943, 1955). The study of the physical characteristics of California Indians by Gifford (1926) has not been improved on, except that more

155

detailed analyses of the anthropometry of prehistoric (sketetal) populations have since been carried out.

2361. Aginsky, B.W. Population control among the Shanel Pomo. American Sociological Review 4 (2), 1939.

2362. Baumhoff, M.A. Ecological determinants of aboriginal California populations. UC-PAAE 49 (2), 1963.
[New approach to determining population density and numbers]

2363. Boas, F. Anthropometry of Central California. AMNH-B XVII (4), 1905. New York.
[Physical measurements of living Indians]

2364. Bright, W. A field guide to Southern California Indian languages. UCLA-AS-AR 1965:403-406, 1965.

2365. Brown, A. The aboriginal population of the Santa Barbara Channel. UC-AR-R 69, 1967. Berkeley.
[Demographic survey of the Chumash based largely on explorers' and mission records]

2366. Cook, S.F. The conflict between the California Indian and White civilization: II. Ibero-Americana 22, 1943.
[Table 1, Indian population from the end of Mission times to the modern period; a basic work but now substantially revised upward by Cook's later work, cited below]

2367. _____ The aboriginal population of the San Joaquin Valley, California. UC-AR 16:31-80, 1955.
[The basic work on these valley populations, mainly Yokuts]

2368. _____ The epidemic of 1830-1833 in California and Oregon. UC-PAAE 43:303-326, 1955. Berkeley.
[Pandemic identified as malaria introduced from the Columbia River by Hudson Bay Company fur trappers]

2369. _____ The aboriginal population of the north coast of California. UC-AR 16:81-130, 1956.
[Deals with this section of the state--the most complete study ever done]

2370. _____ The aboriginal population of Alameda and Contra Costa Counties, California. UC-AR 16 (4), 1957.
[Numbers and distribution of native groups]

2371. _____ The aboriginal population of Upper California. Actas y Memorias del XXXV Congreso Internacional de Americanistas, Mexico, 1962, Vol. 2:397-403, 1964.
[Reprinted in Heizer and Whipple 1971:66-72, cited in I D1]

2372. Cook,S.F. The population of the California Indians, 1769-1770. University of California Press, 1976.
[The most complete survey of the subject ever attempted. Cook concludes that just before Spanish settlement in 1769 the native population numbered 310,000. The volume has essays on age distribution, vital statistics, degree of blood, and urban-rural distribution]

2373. Day, S. Census of our Indian population. Overland Monthly 2:465-472, 1883.
[Includes California]

2374. Gifford, E.W. Californian anthropometry. UC-PAAE 26 (2), 1926.

2375. Harvey, H.R. Population of the Cahuilla Indians: Decline and Its Causes. Eugenics Quarterly 14:185-198, 1967.
[Detailed demographic study of this tribe]

2376. Hoffman, J.M. and L. Brunker. Studies in California paleo-pathology. UC-ARF 30, 1976.

2377. Kelsey, C.E. Census of non-reservation California Indians, 1905-1906. UC-ARF, 1971.
[Detailed census giving names of persons and location of over 13,000 landless Indians, mainly in Northern California]

2378. Kroeber, A.L. The aboriginal population of California. Science 54:162-163, 1921.
[Concludes that 1770 population was 133,000]

2379. _____ Handbook of the Indians of California. BAE-B 78, 1925.
[pp. 880-891, aboriginal population; maintains conclusion reached in 1921 paper]

2380. Kroeber, A.L. and R.F. Heizer. Continuity of Indian population in California from 1770/1845 to 1955. UC-C-ARF 9: 1-22.
[Summary of tribal "blood survivorship" based on the California Roll of 1928]

2381. Kroeber, T. and R.F. Heizer. Almost ancestors: the first Californians. Sierra Club. San Francisco, 1968.
[In part a volume of facial portraits of California Indians]

2382. McKern, T.W. An anthropometric and morphological analysis of a prehistoric skeletal population from Santa Cruz Island, California. Archives of Anthropology, Society for American Archaeology, No. 10, 1960.

2383. Merriam, C.H. The Indian population of California. AA 7:
594-606, 1905.
[Based on mission records Merriam concludes native
precontact population was 260,000]

2384. Moodie, R.L. Deafness among ancient California Indians.
Bulletin of the Southern California Academy of
Sciences 28:46-49, 1929.

2385. Newman, R.S. A comparative analysis of prehistoric skeletal
remains from the lower Sacramento Valley. UC-AS-R 39:
1-66, 1957.

2286. Pantin, A.N. and R. Kallsen. The blood groups of the
Diegueno Indians. AJPA 11:91-96, 1953.

2387. Powers, S. Tribes of California. Contributions to North
American Ethnology, Vol. III, 1877.
[Estimates Indians population of California at 705,000
at time of first European contact. All later students
believe this is too high a figure]

2388. Roney, J.G. Paleopathology of a California archaeological site.
Bulletin of the History of Medicine 33:97-109, 1959.
[Interesting study of disease and injuries as evi-
denced in a prehistoric village at Bodega Bay, Marin
County]

2389. Whitehead, J.M. The physical anthropology of the Yuki
Indians. Ph.D. dissertation. University of
California, Berkeley, 1968.

I D1: PERIOD OF NATIVE HISTORY (? B.C.-1542 A.D.):
TRIBAL ETHNOGRAPHIES: GENERAL SURVEYS

General ethnographic surveys of California Indian
cultures by Forbes (1969), Kroeber (1925, 1962), Merriam (1966)
and Powers (1877) are adequate to supply the reader with an
overall view. Powers' work is reliable except for a certain
degree of literary exuberance and his lack of anthropological
training, the result being a lively account but with certain
misinterpretations. The standard survey is Kroeber (1925);
Heizer and Whipple (1971) is a source book which tries for a
general coverage through selected articles from which the
bibliographic references have been omitted. One or two basic
works dealing with nearly every tribe of California have been
cited.

2390. Aginsky, B.W. Culture element distributions XXIV: Central
Sierra. UC-AR 8:393-468, 1943.
[Regional coverage]

2391. Andrews, D. and V. Brown. The Pomo Indians of California and their neighbors. Naturegraph Publishers. Healdsburg, California, 1969.
[Barrett's and Loeb's Pomo reports are more full and better]

2392. Angulo, J. de and L.S. Freeland. Notes on the Northern Paiute of California. Journal de la Societe des Americanistes 21:313-335, 1929.

2393. Anonymous. Indians of California. Bureau of Indian Affairs Government Printing Office, 1968.
[Classic example of Bureau of Indian Affairs misunderstanding of the people they are supposed to know]

2394. Bancroft, H.H. The native races of the Pacific states of North America. 1, Wild Tribes. D. Appleton and Company. New York, 1875.
[Abundant citations to native cultures from the published literature, mainly travellers' accounts]

2395. Bard, C.L. Medicine and surgery among the first Californians. Touring Topics 22:20-30, 1930.

2396. Barnett, H.G. Culture element distributions VII: Oregon Coast. UC-AR 1:155-204, 1937.
[Includes tribes of northwestern California]

2397. Barrett, S.A. The Ethno-geography of the Pomo and neighboring Indians. UC-PAAE 6:1-245, 1908.

2398. _____ The Washo Indians. Bulletin of the Public Museum of the City of Milwaukee 2:1-52, 1917.

2399. Baumhoff, M.A. California Athabascan groups. UC-AR 16: 157-237, 1958.
[Ethnographic notes and ethnogeography of the several Athabascan tribes south of the Hupa]

2400. Beals, R.L. Ethnology of the Nisenan. UC-PAAE 31:335-410, 1933.

2401. Beals, R.L. and J.A. Hester. A new ecological typology of the California Indians. In Man and Cultures. A. Wallace, ed., pp. 411-419, 1960. Philadelphia.
[Classification based on basic environmental adaptations rather than culture areas]

2402. Bean, L. and H. Lawton. The Cahuilla Indians of Southern California. Malki Museum Brochure No. 1 Banning, 1965.
[Brief review of history and culture of this tribe]

159

2403. Beattie, H.P. Indians of San Bernardino County. Historical
Society of Southern California 35:239-264, 1953.
[Deals with the Cahuilla tribe]

2404. Benedict, R. A brief sketch of Serrano culture. AA 26:366-
392, 1924.

2405. Bingaman, John W. The Ahwahneechees: a story of the Yosemite
Indians. End-Kian Publishing Company.

2406. Bleeker, S. The Mission Indians of California. William
Morrow and Company. New York, 1956.

2407. Bursa, B.W. Salinan Indians of California and their
neighbors. Naturegraph Publishers: Healdsburg,
California, 1975.

2408. Coville, F.V. The Panamint Indians of California. AA5:351-
361, 1892.

2409. Curtis, E.S. The North American Indian. Norwood, Mass.,
1907-1930.
[Vols. 2, 13, 14, 15 deal with California tribes]

2410. Davis, E.L. An ethnography of the Kuzedika Paiute of Mono
Lake, Mono County, California. In Miscellaneous
Collected Papers 8-10, pp. 1-55. UU-AP No. 75, 1965.

2411. D'Azevedo, W.L. (ed). The Washo Indians of California and
Nevada. UU-AP No. 67, 1963.

2412. Dixon, R.B. The Northern Maidu. AMNH-B 17: 119-346, 1905.

2413. _____ The Shasta. AMNH-B 17:381-498, 1907.

2414. Dixon, R.B. and A.L. Kroeber. Numeral systems of the languages
of California. AA 9:663-690.
[Statewide survey. Could be improved on and enlarged
with data available since 1907]

2415. Driver, H.E. Wappo ethnography. UC-PAAE 36:179-220, 1936.

2416. _____ Culture element distributions VI: Southern
Sierra Nevada. UC-AR 1:53-154, 1937.

2417. _____ Culture element distributions X: Northwest
California. 1:297-433, 1939.

2418. Drucker, P. Culture element distributions V: Southern
California. UC-AR 1:1-52, 1937.

2419. _____ The Tolowa and their southwest Oregon kin.
UC-PAAE 36:221-300, 1937.

2420. DuBois, C. Wintu ethnography. UC-PAAE 36:1-148, 1935.

2421. Elsasser, A.B. Indians of Sequoia and Kings Canyon National Parks. Sequoia Natural History Association. Three Rivers, California, 1972.

2422. _____ The History of Culture Classification in California. UC-AS-R 49:1-10, 1960. Berkeley.
[A survey of various attempts to identify regional types of native culture]

2423. Essene, F. Culture element distributions XXI: Round Valley. UC-AR 8:1-177, 1942.
[Covers the Yuki and neighboring groups]

2424. Forbes, J.D. Native Americans of California and Nevada. Naturegraph Publishers. Healdsburg, California, 1969.
[Wide-ranging survey of native cultures and leading up to the modern period]

2425. _____ Warriors of the Colorado. University of Oklahoma Press, 1965.

2426. Forde, C.D. Ethnography of the Yuma Indians. UC-PAAE 28: 83-278, 1931.

2427. Foster, G.M. A summary of Yuki culture. UC-AR 5:155-244, 1944.

2428. Garth, T.R. Atsugewi ethnography. UC-AR 14:123-212, 1945.

2429. Gayton, A.H. Northern Foothill Yokuts and Western Mono. UC-AR 10:143-302, 1948.
[The most detailed study of these tribes]

2430. _____ Tulare Lake, Southern Valley and Central Foothills Yokuts. UC-AR 10:1-140, 1948.
[Detailed record of tribal cultures of lower San Joaquin Valley area]

2431. Gifford, E.W. The Kamia of Imperial Valley. BAE-B 97, 1931.

2432. _____ The Coast Yuki. Anthropos 34:292-375, 1939.
[The main study of this group]

2433. Gifford, E.W. and S. Klimek. Culture element distributions II: Yana. UC-PAAE 37:71-100, 1936.

2434. Gifford, E.W. and A.L. Kroeber. Culture element distributions IV: Pomo. UC-PAAE 37:117-254, 1937.

2435. Goldschmidt, W.R. Social organization in native California and the origin of clans. AA 50:444-456, 1948.
[Includes summary of social organization of tribes throughout the state]

2436. Goldschmidt, W.R. Nomlaki ethnography. UC-PAAE 42:303-443, 1951.

2437. Gould, R.A. Aboriginal California burial and cremation practices. UC-AS-R 60:144-168, 1963. Berkeley. [An updating of Kroeber's 1925 information on methods of disposing of the dead]

2438. Gudde, E.G. California place names. University of California Press, 1949. [Includes place names of Indian origin]

2439. Harrington, J.P. Culture element distributions XIX: Central California Coast. UC-AR 7:1-46, 1942.

2440. Heizer, R.F. Village shifts and tribal spreads in California prehistory. SM-M 36:60-67, 1962. [Survey of reasons why Indian village locations were moved; tribal territory shifts in the protohistoric and historic periods]

2441. _____ The California Indians: archaeology, varieties of culture, arts of life. California Historical Quarterly 41:1-28, 1962. [A brief general survey]

2442. Heizer, R.D. (ed) The archaeology of the Napa region. UC-AR 12:225-358, 1953. [Includes ethnographic and historical summaries of Wappo culture]

2443. Holt, C. Shasta ethnography. UC-AR 3:299-349, 1946.

2444. Hooper, L. The Cahuilla Indians. UC-PAAE 16:316-380, 1920.

2445. James, H.C. The Cahuilla Indians. Westernlore Press, Los Angeles, 1960.

2446. Johnston, B.E. California's Gabrielino Indians. Southwest Museum, 1962. [Thorough review of the culture and history of this tribe]

2447. Kelly, I.T. Ethnography of the Surprise Valley Paiute. UC-PAAE 31:67-210, 1932.

2448. Kniffen, F.B. Achomawi geography. UC-PAAE 23:297-332, 1928. [Ethnogeography, tribelets, economy and environmental adjustment]

2449. Kroeber, A.L. Types of Indian culture in California. UC-PAAE 2 (3), 1904. [General survey of California Indian culture]

2450. Kroeber, A.L. Games of the Indians of California. AA 22:272-277, 1920.
        [A survey]

2451. _____ The history of native culture in California. UC-PAAE 20:125-142, 1923.
        [An attempt to reconstruct the development of California Indian culture]

2452. _____ Handbook of the Indians of California. BAE-B 78, 1925.
        [The basic work on California Indians as a whole]

2453. _____ The Patwin and their neighbors. UC-PAAE 29:253-423, 1932.

2454. _____ Culture element distributions: III, area and climax. UC-PAAE 37:101-116, 1936.
        [Important article in which the several culture areas and hearth tribes of native California are specified]

2455. _____ Cultural and natural areas of native North America. UC-PAAE 38, 1939.
        [California Indians from the ecological viewpoint]

2456. _____ Recent ethnic spreads. UC-PAAE 47:259-281, 1958.
        [Evidence of territorial readjustments in late pre-historic times as evidenced by language similarities]

2457. _____ Two papers on the aboriginal ethnography of California. UC-AS-R 56, 1962.
        [Two important general perspectives by Kroeber. One is a general review of California anthropology written in 1908 and evaluated in 1962 by D.W. Hymes and R.G. Heizer. The other is a survey of the nature of land-holding groups in native California]

2458. Landberg, L.C.W. The Chumash Indians of Southern California. SM-P No. 18, 1965. Los Angeles.

2459. Latta, F.F. Handbook of Yokuts Indians. Oildale, California, 1949.
        [Contains much information not to be found elsewhere]

2460. Loud, L.L. Ethnogeography and archaeology of the Wiyot territory. UC-PAAE 14:221-436, 1918.
        The major study of this tribe]

2461. Loeb, E.M. Pomo folkways. UC-PAAE 19:149-405, 1926.

2462. Lowie, R.H. Ethnographic notes on the Washo. UC-PAAE 36:301-352, 1939.

2463. McKern, W.C. Functional families among the Patwin. UC-PAAE 13:235-258, 1922.
[Emphasizes craft specialization in families]

2464. Mason, J.A. The ethnology of the Salinan Indians. UC-PAAE 10:97-240, 1912.

2465. Merriam, C.H. The classification and distribution of the Pit River Indian tribes. S1-MC 78:1-52, 1927.

2466. _____ Studies of California Indians. University of California Press, 1955.
[Reprinted without change, 1962]
[Original field data collected by Merriam 1903-1935]

2467. _____ Ethnographic notes on California Indian tribes. Compiled and edited by R.F. Heizer. UC-AS-R 68, Parts I-III, 1966.
[Large collection of original field data on various subjects; deals with tribes of northern, central and southern California]

2468. _____ Contributions to native California ethnology from the C. Hart Merriam Collection. No. 1, Ethnogeographic and ethnosynonymic data from northern California tribes. Ed. by R.F. Heizer. UC-ARF, 1976.
[Extended listing of village names of tribes in northern California]

2469. _____ Contributions to native California ethnology from the C. Hart Merriam Collection, No. 2: Ethnogeographic and ethnosynonymic data from northern California tribes. Ed. by R.F. Heizer.
[Extended listing of village place names and locations and names of tribes]

2470. Miller, R.D. and P.J. Miller. The Chemehuevi Indians of southern California. Malki Museum Brochure No. 3, 1967.

2471. Nomland, G.A. Sinkyone notes. UC-PAAE 36:149-178, 1935.

2472. _____ Bear River ethnography. UC-AR 2:91-123, 1938.

2473. O'Neal, L.R. The History of Ramona, California and environs. Ballena Press: Ramona, California, 1975.
[Includes information on the Cupeno and Cahuilla]

2474. Parker, H. The early Indians of Temecula. Librito No. 1. Paisano Press, Balboa Island, California, 1965.

2475. Powers, S. Tribes of California. S1-CNAE 3. U.S. Department of the Interior. Washington, D.C., 1877.
[The first general study of California Indians; Southern California is not considered. This important

work was reprinted in 1976 by the University of California Press]

2476. Powers, S. The Northern California Indians. R.F. Heizer, ed. UC-ARF-C No. 25, 1975.
[Reprinting of 19 articles originally published 1872-1877. These are the basis of his Tribes of California, 1877]

2477. Ray, V.F. Primitive pragmatists: the Modoc Indians of Northern California. University of Washington Press, 1963.

2478. Reid, H. The Indians of Los Angeles County: Hugo Reid's letters of 1852. Edited and annotated by R.F. Heizer. SM-P No. 21, 1968.
[Detailed account of culture of the Gabrielino Indians by a Scotsman who was married to a member of the tribe]

2479. Riddell, F.A. Honey Lake Paiute ethnography. Nevada State Museum Anthropological Papers, No.4, 1960. Carson City.

2480. Sapir, E. and L. Spier. Notes on the culture of the Yana. UC-AR 3:239-297.

2481. Sherwin, J. Face and body painting practices among California Indians. UC-AS-R 60:81-148, 1963.
[General survey]

2482. Sparkman, P.S. The culture of the Luiseno Indians. UC-PAAE 8:187-234, 1908.

2483. Spier, L. Southern Diegueno customs. UC-PAAE 20:297-358, 1923.

2484. _____ Mohave culture items. Museum of Northern Arizona Bulletin 28, 1955.
[Excellent survey, including a definitive study of calendar systems in western North America]

2485. Steward, J.H. Ethnography of the Owens Valley Paiute. UC-PAAE 33:233-350, 1933.

2486. _____ Basin-Plateau aboriginal sociopolitical groups. BAE-B 120, 1938.
[Includes tribes of the arid eastern border of California]

2487. Strong, W.D. Aboriginal society in Southern California. UP-PAAE 26:1-358, 1929.
[Deals with the Serrano, Cahuilla, Cupeno and Luiseno]

2488. Swezey, S.L. and R.F. Heizer. Ritual management of salmonid fish resources in California. To appear in Vol 4 (1) of JCA, 1977.

2489. Taylor, H.C. and L.L. Hoaglin. The "intermittent fever" epidemic of the 1830's on the Lower Columbia. Ethnohistory 9:160-178, 1962.
[Same disease that devastated Central California, 1830-1833, as described by S.F. Cook, 1955]

2490. University of California Anthropological Records, Vols. 1 (1937) - 27 (1972).
[This and the series cited above constitute the largest single body of ethnographic data on California Indians. This series includes the Culture Element Distribution studies in 26 separate numbers]

2491. University of California Publications in American Archaeology and Ethnology, Vols. 1 (1903) - 50 (1964).
[The oldest series dealing with California Indians. Includes studies of general ethnography, archaeology, linguistics, folklore]

2492. University of California Publications in Anthropology, Vol.1 (1964) - Vol. 10 (1973).
[Continuation, under shortened title, of the last-cited series]

2493. Voegelin, E.W. Tubatulabal ethnography. UC-AR 2:1-84, 1938.

2494. _____ Culture element distributions XX: Northeast California. UC-AR 7:47-251, 1942.
[Regional coverage]

2495. Waterman, T.T. The Yana Indians. UC-PAAE 13:35-70, 1918.

2496. _____ Yurok geography. UC-PAAE 16:174-314, 1920.
[Ethnogeography and Yurok culture facts]

2497. Whitehead, R.S. and R.L. Hoover. Ethnohistoric Chumash place-names. San Luis Obispo County Archaeological Society, Occasional Paper No. 9, 1975.

2498. Wuertele, E. Bibliographical history of California anthropological research, 1850-1917. UC-ARF-C No. 26, 1975.

I D2: PERIOD OF NATIVE HISTORY (?B.C.-1542 A.D.):
ETHNOGRAPHY: SOCIAL-POLITICAL ORGANIZATION: NATIVE WARFARE

There is no one work which covers native social and political organizations of California tribes. Kroeber's Handbook of California Indians contains more than any single source; wide coverage is also provided by Gifford (1926), Goldschmidt (1948) and Kroeber (1962), the latter addressing itself specifically to the nature of the tribelet which was the basic land-owning unit. Some life crises rites, or their traces, are treated by Driver (1941) and Gould (1963).

How native Californians divided responsibilities between men and women is fully treated by Willoughby (1963).

2499. Bean, L.J. and T.C. Blackburn. Native Californians: a theoretical perspective. Ballena Press, Ramona, California, 1976.

2500. Dobyns, H.F., et.al. Thematic changes in Yuman warfare. In Cultural Stability and Cultural Change, V.F. Ray, ed., pp. 46-71, 1957. Seattle.
[Ethnohistoric data on warfare of Colorado River tribes]

2501. Driver, H.E. Girl's puberty rites in Western North America. UC-AR 6:21-90, 1941.
[Detailed survey of this life crisis rite]

2502. Fathauer, G.H. The structure and causation of Mohave warfare. SWJA 10:97-118, 1954.

2503. Gayton, A.H. Yokuts-Mono chiefs and shamans. UC-PAAE 24: 361-420, 1930.
[How chiefs and shamans cooperated to exercise social control]

2504. Gifford, E.W. Clans and moieties in Southern California. UC-PAAE 14 (2), 1918.

2505. _____ Miwok lineages and the political unit in California. AA 28:389-401, 1926.
[Concludes the lineage was basic to society]

2506. Goldschmidt, W.R. Social organization in native California and the origin of clans. AA 50:444-456, 1948.
[A compact summary of what is known of descent and residence; contains good bibliography on the subject]

2507. Gould, R.A. Aboriginal California burial and cremation practices. UC-AS-R 60:149-168, 1963.

2508. _____ The wealth quest among the Tolowa Indians of Northwestern California. Proceedings of the American Philosophical Society 110 (1):67-89, 1966.

2509. James, S. and S. Graziani. California Indian warfare. UC-ARF-C 23:47-109, 1975.

2510. Kroeber, A.L. The nature of land-holding groups in aboriginal California. UC-AS-R 56:19-58, 1962.
[Also published in Ethnohistory 2:303-314. Important in defining the nature and number of tribelets]

2511. Kroeber, A.L. and C.B. Kroeber. A Mohave war reminiscence, 1854-1880. UC-PA 10, 1973.

2512. Kunkel, P.H. The Pomo kin group and the political unit in aboriginal California. JCA 1 (1):7-18, 1974.

2513. Nelson, K. Marriage and divorce practices in native California. UC-ARF, 1975.
[P. 36: post-contact changes in marriage patterns]

2514. Sherer, L.M. Great chieftains of the Mohave Indians. Southern California Quarterly 48:1-35, 1966.

2515. Stewart, K.M. Mohave warfare. SWJA 3:257-278, 1947.

2516. Wallace, W.J. Hupa warfare. Southwest Museum Leaflets 23, 1949.

2517. White, R.C. Luiseno social organization. UC-PAAE 48 (2), 1963.

2518. Willoughby, N.C. Division of labor among the Indians of California. UC-AS-R 60:1-80, 1963. Berkeley.
[Roles of men and women in aboriginal society]

I D3: PERIOD OF NATIVE HISTORY (? B.C.-1542 A.D.):
ETHNOGRAPHY: RELIGION

Except for the rather brief summaries of the subject by Kroeber (1907, 1925), we lack general consideration of the topic. Regional treatment of cult systems has been done --by Loeb (1932, 1933) and Kroeber (1932) for the north central California Kuksu Cult; by Kroeber and Gifford (1949) for the northwestern World Renewal Cult; and by DuBois (1908) and Strong (1929) for the Chinigchinich Cult of southern California. The Ghost Dance is cited in Section IV B.

2519. Applegate, R. The Datura cult among the Chumash. JCA 2:7-17, 1975.
[Describes a religious cult centering around the taking of a narcotic plant]

2520. Baldwin, C. The Palm Springs medicine man. SM-M 11:159-160, 1937.

2521. Barrett, S.A. The Wintun Hesi ceremony. UC-PAAE 14:4,1919.
[Part of the Kuksu Cult system]

2522. Bourke, J.G. Notes on the cosmogony and theogony of the Mohave Indians of the Rio Colorado, Arizona. JAFL 2:169-189, 1889.
[General survey of Mohave culture]

2523. Downs, J.F. Washo religion. UC-AR 16 (1), 1961.

2524. Drucker, P. A Karuk World-Renewal ceremony at Panaminik.
       UC-PAAE 35:3, 1936.
       [Ritual renewing of the world for another year]

2525. DuBois, C.G. Religious ceremonies of the Mission Indians.
       AA 7:620-629, 1905.

2526. _____ The religion of the Luiseno Indians of Southern
       California. UC-PAAE 8 (3), 1908.
       [Basic to the region; Chinigchinich Cult]

2527. Gifford, E.W. Miwok cults. UC-PAAE 18 (3), 1926.

2528. _____ Yuma dreams and omens. JAFL 39:58-69, 1926.

2529. _____ Central Miwok ceremonies. UC-AR 14 (4), 1955.
       [Elaboration of article by Gifford, 1926]

2530. Goldschmidt, W.R. and H.E. Driver. The Hupa White Deerskin
       dance. UC-PAAE 35:103-142, 1940.
       [The dance as witnessed in 1935 and 1937]

2531. Heizer, R.F. A note on Boscana's posthumous Relacion.
       SM-M 50:99-102, 1976.
       [Discusses the several versions of Boscana's
       Chinigchinich manuscript. Cf. Reichlen and Reichlen
       1971]

2532. Knudtson, P.M. Flora shaman of the Wintu. Natural History
       84(5): 6-17, 1975.
       [Contemporary curing and shamanistic beliefs and
       practices]

2533. Kroeber, A.L. The religion of the Indians of California.
       UC-PAAE 4 (6), 1907.
       [An early attempt to cover shamanism and cult systems]

2534. _____ Handbook of the Indians of California. BAE-B
       78, 1925.
       [Ch. 56, pp. 851-879, summarizes native religions]

2535. _____ The Patwin and their neighbors. UC-PAAE
       29 (4), 1932.
       [Pg. 391-419, summary of California Kuksu cult system]

2536. Kroeber, A.L. and E.W. Gifford. World Renewal: a cult
       system of native Northwest California. UC-AR 13 (1),
       1949.
       [Detailed account of all aspects of the religious system
       of northwestern California; concentrates on Yurok,
       Karok and Hupa]

2537. Loeb, E.M. The Western Kuksu Cult. UC-PAAE 35:1-137, 1932.
       [The Kuksu Cult among the coast range tribes north
       of San Francisco Bay]

2538. Loeb, E.M. The Eastern Kuksu Cult. UC-PAAE 19 (2), 1933.
[Deals with the Maidu and Patwin]

2539. Merriam, C.H. Transmigration in California. JAFL 22: 433-434, 1909.
[Cites native beliefs that souls of Indians after death were transmuted into animals]

2540. Reichlen,H. and P. Reichlen. Le manuscrit Boscana de la Bibliotheque Nationale de Paris. Journal de la Societe des Americanistes 60:233-273, 1971.
[Discussion of how many versions of Boscana's account of the native religion of the Indians of San Juan Capistrano Mission. Full translation of the copy in France]

2541. Stewart, K.M. Mojave Indians shamanism. SM-M 44:15-29, 1970.

2542. Strong, W.D. Aboriginal society in Southern California. UC-PAAE 26, 1929.
[The most comprehensive study of social and religious practices of tribes for this area ever attempted]

2543. Swezey, S. and F.R. Heizer. Ritual management of Salmonid fish resources in California. To appear in JCA 4 (1), 1977.

I D4: PERIOD OF NATIVE HISTORY (? B.C.-1542 A.D.):
ETHNOGRAPHY: MATERIAL CULTURE

Satisfactory referencing is almost impossible for this topic. Kroeber (1925) is still the best one volume treatment both as regards description and illustrations. Most titles in this section do not require explanation.

2544. Barrett, S.A. Pomo Indians basketry. UC-PAAE 7 (3), 1908. Berkeley.
[Detailed study of this art]

2545. _____ The material culture of the Klamath Lake and Modoc Indians of Northeastern California and Southern Oregon. UC-PAAE 5:239-292, 1910.

2546. _____ Pomo buildings. Holmes Anniversary Volume, pp. 1-17, 1916. Washington, D.C.
[Survey of the subject]

2547. _____ Material aspects of Pomo culture. Bulletin of the Public Museum of the City of Milwaukee 20, Parts 1 and 2, 1952.
[Thorough review of all aspects of Pomo technology except for basketry]

2548. Barrett, S.A. and E.W. Gifford. Miwok material culture. Bulleton of Milwaukee Public Museum 2 (4), 1933. [Reprinted by Yosemite National History Association, Inc.]

2549. Blackburn, T. Ethnohistoric descriptions of Gabrielino material culture. UCLA-AS-AR 1962/63: 1-49.

2550. Cody, B.P. California Indian baby cradles. Southwest Museum Leaflets No. 12, n.d. [Forms and distributions]

2551. Dixon, R.B. Basketry designs of the Maidu Indians of California. AA 2:266-276, 1900.

2552. _____ Basketry designs of the Indians of Northern California. AMNH-B 17:1-32, 1902. [Thorough study of names and meaning of designs for over a dozen tribes. The Maidu are emphasized]

2553. Gayton, A.H. Yokuts and Western Mono pottery making. UC-PAAE 24 (3), 1929. Berkeley.

2554. Heizer, R.F. and W.C. Massey. Aboriginal navigation off the coasts of Upper and Baja California. BAE-B 151: 285-311, 1953. [General study of Californian native watercraft]

2555. Heizer, R.F. and A.E. Treganza. Mines and quarries of the Indians of California. California Journal of Mines and Geology 40:291-359, 1944. Reprinted 1972 by Ballena Press, Ramona, California. [Statewide survey of Indian mining and use of geologic resources]

2556. Iovin, J. A summary description of Luiseno material culture. UCLA-AS-AR 1962/63:79-130.

2557. Kelly, I.T. The carver's art of the Indians of Northwestern California. UC-PAAE 24 (7), 1930. [Reprinted 1972 by Ballena Press]

2558. Kroeber, A.L. Basket designs of the Indians of Northwestern California. UC-PAAE 2 (4), 1905.

2559. _____ California basketry and the Pomo. AA 11:233-249, 1905. [Compares Pomo with other California basketry]

2560. _____ Basket designs of the Mission Indians of California. AMNH-AP 20 (2), 1922. [Reprinted 1973 by Ballena Press, Ramona, California with additional illustrations of Chumash baskets]

2561. McKern, W.C. Patwin houses. UC-PAAE 20:159-171, 1923. Berkeley.

2562. Mason, O.T. Aboriginal american basketry. USNM-AR for 1902: 171-248, 1904.
[The basic work on the subject; California is amply treated]

2563. Merrill, R.E. Plants used in basketry by the California Indians. UC-PAAE 20:215-242, 1923.
[A specialized ethnobotanical study]

2564. O'Neale, L.M. Yurok-Karok basket weavers. UC-PAAE 32 (1), 1932.
[Study of contemporary Yurok and Karok basket weaving; designs and meanings]

2565. Pope, S.T. Yahi archery. UC-PAAE 13 (3), 1918.
[Bow and arrow making and use by Ishi]

2566. Purdy, C. Pomo Indians baskets and their makers. Out West 15: 438-449; 16:8-19, 151-158, 262-273, 1901-1902.
[Amateurish in most ways, but written from direct observation. Barrett, 1908, is a much more authoritative treatment of the subject]

2567. Rogers, M.J. Yuman pottery making. SDM-P 2, 1936.

2568. Squier, R.J. The manufacture of flint implements by the Indians of Northern and Central California. UC-AS-R 19:15-44, 1953.
[Collection of eyewitness descriptions of how California Indians chipped stone to produce implements]

2569. Waterman, T.T. and A.L. Kroeber. The Kepel fishdam. UC-PAAE 35 (6), 1938.
[Ritual-economic practices of the Yurok on the Klamath River]

I D5: PERIOD OF NATIVE HISTORY (? B.C. - 1542 A.D.):
ETHNOGRAPHY: ECONOMY

The food quest is considered in statewide perspective by Kroeber (1925); the relation between food resources and population numbers is treated by Baumhoff (1963). Ethnobotany has been treated for all tribes in Mead (1972); for particular topics or tribes see Schenck and Gifford (1952), Barrows (1900), Chesnut (1902), Bean and Saubel (1968) and Merriam (1918). Trade in raw materials, manufactures and foods and trails (i.e., trade routes) are summarized by Davis (1961).

2570. Barrows, D.P. Ethnobotany of the Coahuilla Indians of Southern California. University of Chicago, 1900.
[Reprinted in part in Heizer and Whipple 1971,

2571. Baumhoff, M.A. Ecological determinants of aboriginal California
       populations. UC-PAAE 49(2), 1963.
       [Relationship of numbers and economy to the environment]

2572. Bean, L.J. and H.W. Lawton. Some explanations for the rise
       of cultural complexity in native California with
       comments on proto-agriculture and agriculture.
       BP-PA 1:1-xlvii, 1973.
       [Exploration of the question why California Indians
       were not farmers]

2573. Bean, L.J. and K.S. Saubel. Temalpakh. Malki Museum Press.
       Banning, California, 1968.
       [Ethnobotany of the Cahuilla which supersedes Barrows'
       earlier work]

2574. Castetter, E.F. and W.H. Bell. Yuman Indian agriculture.
       University of New Mexico Press, 1951.
       [Thorough reporting of the river flood plain farming
       of the Yuman tribes on the Colorado River]

2575. Chesnut, V.K. Plants used by the Indians of Mendocino
       County, California. Contributions of the U.S. National
       Herbarium 7 (3), 1902. Washington, D.C.
       [An early study in native botanical knowledge and uses
       of plants. Reprinted 1974 by Mendocino County
       Historical Society under author's name as V.K. Chestnut]

2576. Curtin, L.S.M. Some plants used by the Yuki Indians of
       Round Valley, Northern California, SM-M 31:40-48,
       85-94, 1957.

2577. Davis, J. Trade routes and economic exchange among the
       Indians of California. UC-AS-R 54, 1961.
       [Reprinted in BP-PAEH No. 3, 1974. The most complete
       survey done on this subject. Contains map showing
       trade routes and trails]

2578. Gifford, E.W. Californian balanophagy. In Essays in
       Anthropology Presented to A.L. Kroeber. pp. 87-98.
       University of California Press, 1936.
       [Thorough study of California Indian methods of pre-
       paring acorns for food]

2579. Greengo, R.E. Shellfish foods of the California Indians.
       KAS-P 7:63-114, 1952.
       [Survey of archaeological and ethnological data on
       molluscan food resources]

2580. Hewes, G.W. Economic and geographical relations of
       aboriginal fishing in Northern California. California
       Fish and Game 28:103-110, 1942.

2581. Kroeber, A.L. Handbook of the Indians of California.
       BAE-B 78, 1925.
       [Pg. 523-526, the food problem in California]

2582. Kroeber, A.L. and S.A. Barrett. Fishing among the Indians
       of Northwestern California. UC-AR 21:1, 1960.
       [Intensive study of fishing methods and implements;
       contains a number of distribution maps]

2583. Landberg, L.C.W. Fishing effort in the aboriginal fisheries
       of the Santa Barbara region, California. In Maritime
       Adaptations of the Pacific, R. Casteel and G. Quimby,
       eds., pp. 145-170. Mouton, 1975.

2584. Lewis, H.T. Patterns of Indians burning in California:
       ecology and ethnohistory. BP-PA 1, 1973. Ramona,
       California.
       [Survey of the native practice of Indian burning.
       Falls short of being a thorough ethnographic-
       ethnohistorical survey of the data]

2585. Mayer, P.J. Miwok balanophagy: implications for the
       cultural development of some California acorn-eaters.
       UC-ARF, 1976.

2586. Merriam, C.H. The acorn, a possibly neglected source of
       food. National Geographic Magazine 34:129-137,
       1918.
       [Argues that acorns are good food and could be used
       today]

2587. Mead, G.R. The ethnobotany of the California Indians.
       University of Northern Colorado Occasional Publications
       in Anthropology. Ethnology series No. 30, 1972.

2588. Powers, S. Tribes of California. SI-CNAE, 1877.
       [Chap. 38 is titled Aboriginal botany. It deals with
       the Nisenan. This volume was reprinted in facsimile
       by University of California Press, 1976]

2589. Romero, J.B. The botanical lore of the California Indians.
       New York, 1954.
       [Could be much improved on]

2590. Schenck, S.M. and E.W. Gifford. Karok ethnobotany. UC-AR
       13:377-392, 1952.
       [Details of the botanical knowledge and uses of
       plants by this Klamath River tribe]

2591. Stewart, K.M. Mohave Indian agriculture. SM-M 40:5-15,
       1966.

2592. Swezey, S.L. The energetics of subsistence-assurance ritual
       in native California. UC-ARF-C 23:1-46, 1975.
       [Shows how ritual was connected with guaranteeing
       continuation of food supply]

2593. Ziegler, A.C. Quasi-agriculture in North-central California
       and its effects on aboriginal social structure. KAS-P
       38:52-67, 1968.
       [Native social structure and economy in central
       California]

I D6: PERIOD OF NATIVE HISTORY (? B.C.-1542 A.D.):
       ETHNOGRAPHY: WORLD VIEW

       No cultural anthropologist or native Californian has
attempted to outline world view for particular tribes or
California Indians as a whole. Some published articles
contributing to this subject are cited here. Every aspect
of native culture, of course, is a reflection of world view.
Native cosmological ideas as represented in world maps,
whether mental or actually drawn among the Yurok (Waterman
1920) or in the Luiseno and Diegueno sand paintings (Kroeber
1925:663--cited in I D5) are part of this world view. So
also are place names, a subject largely neglected since
Kroeber's (1916) initial effort.

2594. Aginsky, B.W. The socio-psychological significance of death
       among the Pomo Indians. American Imago 1:1-18,
       1940.

2595. Aginsky, B. and E. Deep valley. Stein and Day Publishers,
       1967.
       [A sensitively written account of Pomo life done in
       a literary way rather than a straight ethnographic
       account. Names and places are fictional, but the
       whole work is ethnographically correct]

2596. Almstedt, R.F. Multiple world view in a Diegueno community.
       A.M. Thesis (unpublished), San Diego State University,
       1970.

2597. Bean, L.J. Mukat's people: the Cahuilla Indians of
       Southern California. University of California Press,
       1972.
       [Analysis of Cahuilla culture, changes in the
       historic period, world view]

2598. Devereux, G. Mohave culture and personality. Character and
       Personality 8:91-109, 1939.

2599. _____ Education and discipline in Mohave society.
       Primitive Man 23:85-102, 1950.

2600. _____ Dream learning and individual ritual difference
       in Mohave shamanism. AA 59:1036-1045, 1957.

2601. _____ Mohave ethnopsychiatry and suicide. BAE-B 175,
       1961.

2602. Erikson, E.H. Observations on the Yurok: childhood and world image. UC-PAAE 35 (10), 1943. Berkeley.
[Analysis of Yurok culture and personality in Freudian terms. Interesting but not wholly convincing]

2603. Garth, T.R. Emphasis on industriousness among the Atsugewi. AA 47:554-566, 1945.
[Shows in detail how the work ethic dominates people's actions and aims]

2604. Goldschmidt, W. Ethics and the structure of society. AA 53: 506-524, 1951.
[Compares Yurok society with emerging European capitalism and the Protestant ethic]

2605. Gudde, E.G. California place names. University of California Press, 1949.
[Indian place names are included]

2606. King, A.R. The dream biography of a Mountain Maidu. Character and Personality 11:227-234, 1943.

2607. Kroeber, C.B. The Mohave as nationalist. Proceedings of the American Philosophical Society 109:173-180, 1965.

2608. Kroeber, A.L. California place names of Indian origin. UC-PAAE 12:31-69, 1916.
[Could be considerably expanded but excellent as far as it goes]

2609. _____ Yurok national character. UC-PAAE 47 (3): 236-240, 1959.

2610. _____ Yurok speech usages. In Culture and History: Essays in Honor of Paul Radin, pp. 994-999. Columbia University Press, 1960.
[Study of the sensitivity of speech practices of persons and situations]

2611. Lee, D. Demetracopoulou. Categories of the generic and the particular in Wintu. AA 46 (3):362-369, 1944.

2612. _____ Notes on the concept of self among the Wintu Indians. Journal of Abnormal and Social Psychology 45:538-543, 1951.

2613. Sanchez, N.V. Spanish and Indian place names of California. San Francisco, 1922.

2614. Toffelmeier, G. and K. Luomela. Dreams and dream interpretation of the Diegueno Indians. Psychoanalytic Quarterly 5:195-225, 1936.

2615. Valory, D. Yurok doctors and devils: a study in identity anxiety and deviance. Unpublished Ph.D. dissertation. University of California, Berkeley, 1970.

2616. Wagner, E. The oldest Californian. Land of Sunshine 5: 234-235, 1896.
[Story of Old Gabriel, "Tulare" Indian chief who died at age of 151 years]

2617. Wallace, W.J. Personality variation in a primitive society. Journal of Personality 15:321-328, 1947.
[Analysis of Hupa personality]

2618. _____ The role of humor in the Hupa Indian tribe. JAFL 66:135-141, 1953.

2619. Waterman, T.T. Diegueno identification of color in the cardinal points. JAFL 21:40-42, 1908.

2620. _____ Yurok geography. UC-PAAE 16:177-314, 1920. Berkeley.
[Pg. 189-200, Yurok world map, geographical concepts, place names]

I E: PERIOD OF NATIVE HISTORY (? B.C.-1542 A.D.):
         ETHNOGRAPHY: FOLKLORE; MUSIC

The tremendous literature on native Californian folklore is not cited here. Extensive bibliographic citations can be found in Gayton (1935) which is an ultra-condensed presentation of myth plots and useful as a guide.

Popular books which retell recorded Indian myths are ignored here because they are invariably poorly done and aimed at commercial gain for the editor.

Indian myths are important in constituting the native version of creation and explaining how the world and the animals and plants resident there came into being acquired their special characteristics and act in their particular ways.

For records or tapes of California Indian music see Section VII C.

2621. White, R.C. The Luiseno theory of "knowledge". AA 59:1-19, 1957.

2622. de Angulo, J. Pomo creation myth. 48:203-262, 1935.

2623. Barrett, S.A. Myths of the Southern Sierra Miwok. UC-PAAE 16 (1), 1919.
[Numerous myths]

2624. Barrett, S.A. Pomo myths. Bulletin of the Public Museum, City of Milwaukee, Vol. 15, 1933.
[Monumental collection]

2625. Barrows, D.P. Some Coahuia songs and dances. Land of Sunshine 4:38-41, 1895.

2626. Curtin, J. Creation myths of primitive America. Boston, 1898.
[Includes Wintun and Yana tales]

2627. Demetracopoulou, D. and C. DuBois. A study of Wintu mythology. JAFL 45:373-500, 1932.
[Large collection; introduction by authors important in discussing literary aspects and the place of myths in the culture]

2628. Densmore, F. Yuman and Yaqui music. BAE-B 110, 1932.
[Music of the Colorado River Yuman tribes]

2629. _____ Music of the Maidu. Frederick Webb Hodge Anniversary Publications Fund, Publication 7. Southwest Museum, 1958.

2630. DuBois, C. and D. Demetracopoulou. Wintu myths. UC-PAAE 28 (5), 1931.

2631. Gatschet, A.S. Songs of the Modoc Indians. AA 7:26-31, 1894.

2632. Gayton, A.H. Areal affiliations of California folktales. AA 37 (4):582-599, 1935.
[Abundant references to publications containing origin myths]

2633. Gayton, A.H. and S.S. Newman. Yokuts and Western Mono myths. UC-AR 5 (1), 1940.

2634. Gifford, E.W. and G.H. Block. Californian Indian nights entertainment. A.H. Clark Co., Glendale, 1930.
[Collection drawn from tribes over the state and recast in simple literary style]

2635. Goddard, P.E. Hupa texts. UC-PAAE 1:91-378, 1904.
[Extensive body of texts in Hupa language with translations]

2636. _____ Kato texts. UC-PAAE 5:65-238, 1909.
[Large series of texts in Kato language with English translations]

2637. _____ Wailaki texts, ISAL 2:77-135, 1923.

2638. Harrington, J.P. Yuma account of origins. JAFL 21:324-348, 1908.

2639. _____ Karuk Indians myths. BAE-B 107, 1932.

2640. Hatch, J. Tachi Yokuts music. KAS-P 19:47-66, 1958.

2641. Herzog, G. The Yuman musical style. JAFL 41:183-231, 1928.
        [Musical style of the Colorado River Yuman tribes]

2642. Kroeber, A.L. Origin tradition of the Chemehuevi Indians.
        JAFL 21:240-242, 1908.

2643. _____ Seven Mohave myths. UC-AR 11 (1), 1948.

2644. _____ A Mohave historical epic. UC-AR 11:71-176, 1951.

2645. _____ Yurok myths. University of California
        Press, 1976.
        [Large collection of folktales. Included are
        personality sketches of informants]

2646. Loeb, E.M. The creator concept among the Indians of North
        Central California. AA 28:467-493, 1926.

2647. Lowie, R.H. Ethnographic notes on the Washo. UC-PAAE 36(5),1939.
        [Myths and tales, pp. 333-351]

2648. Merriam, A. and W.L. D'Azevedo. Washo peyote songs.
        AA 59:615-641, 1957.

2649. Nettl, B. The songs of Ishi: musical style of the Yahi
        Indians. The Musical Quarterly 51:469-477, 1965.

2650. Reichard, G.A. Wiyot grammar and texts. UC-PAAE 22:1-215,
        1925.
        [Myths of the people around Humboldt Bay]

2651. Roberts, H.H. Form in primitive music. New York, 1933.
        [Barielino songs]

2652. Robins, R.H. and M. McLeod. Five Yurok songs: a musical
        and textual analysis. Bulletin of the School of
        Oriental and African Studies, University of
        London 18:592-609, 1956.

2653. Sapir, E. Yana texts. UC-PAAE 9:1-235, 1910.
        [Large collections of myths of the people of Tehema
        County]

2654. Spott, R. and A.L. Kroeber. Yurok narratives. UC-PAAE
        35 (9), 1942.
        [Spott was a Yurok and these are stories recited by him]

2655. Warburton, A.D. and J.F.Eudert. Indian lore of the northern
California coast. Pacific Pueblo Press, Santa Clara,
1966.

2656. Waterman, T.T. Analysis of the Mission Indian creation story.
AA 11:41-55, 1909.

2657. Wey, A. The Captain's song. Land of Sunshine 6:3-8, 1898.
[Song of the last Capitana of Mission San Gabriel,
Luisa Serrano, a neophyte]

II A: PERIOD OF SPANISH AND MEXICAN CONTACT (1542-1846):
EXPLORATION

Listed here are some of the more important accounts
of discovery and early exploration of California by Whites.
Bolton (1926-1931), Coues (1900),Priestley (1937) and
Wagner (1929) cover the early Spanish discovery voyages and
overland expeditions. Francis Drake's summer visit in
1579 with the Coast Miwok is duscussed in Heizer (1947,
1975).

For a more complete listing of exploration accounts
see Cowan and Cowan (1964) cited below in Section VII E.

These explorers' accounts are important becuase they
describe the Indians encountered at the time of the first
meeting of the native residents and the white occupiers
of the land.

2658. Anza, Juan Bautista de. Anza's California expeditions.
5 vols. Translated by H.E. Bolton. University of
California Press, 1930.
[Expedition of 1775-1776 to found Monterey and San
Francisco. Much on Indians. Font's diary covers
the same trip]

2659. Bean, L.J. and W. Mason. The Romero expeditions in California
and Arizona, 1823-1826. Palm Springs Desert Museum.
Palm Springs, California, 1962.
[Translation of reports of Spanish expeditions to
the Colorado River in 1823-1827. Not much on
native culture was recorded]

2660. Beechey, F.W. Narrative of a voyage to the Pacific and
Beering's Strait, 1825-1826. London, 1831.
[Observations of Costanoan Indians]

2661. Bolton, H.E., ed. Historical memoirs of New California by
Fr. Francisco Palou. University of California Press,
1926.

2662. Bolton, H.E., ed. Fray Juan Crespi, missionary explorer on the Pacific Coast. University of California Press, 1927.

2663. _____ Anza's California expeditions. Vols. I-IV. University of California Press, 1930.

2664. _____ Font's complete diary. University of California Press, 1931.

2665. Broadbent, S.M. The Rumsen of Monterey, an ethnography from historical sources. UC-ARF-C 14:45-94, 1972.
[One of the few ethnohistoric studies for California]

2666. Brown, A.K. The various journals of Juan Crespi. The Americas 21:375-398, 1965.

2667. _____ Pomponio's world. Argonaut, No. 6, May 1975. 1975.
[Thorough history of a Coast Miwok neophyte whose origin was Bolinas Bay and who became an outlaw. Born ca. 1800, died 1824]

2668. Castillo, E. History of the impact of Euro-American exploration and settlement on the Indians of California. Manuscript to be published in Vol. VIII, Handbook of North American Indians, Smithsonian Institution, 1977.

2669. Coues, E. On the trail of a Spanish pioneer: the diary and itinerary of Francisco Garces, 1775-1776. Vols. I-II. New York, 1900.
[More recent edition translated and edited by John Galvin, A Record of Travels in Arizona and California. John Howell, San Francisco, 1965]

2670. Eastwood, A. (ed.) Archibald Menzies' journal of the Vancouver expedition. California Historical Society Quarterly 2:265-340, 1924.
[Menzies was the naturalist on the Vancouver expedition which visited San Francisco, Monterey, and Santa Barbara in 1792. Contains good description of Indians at each mission]

2671. Gayton, A. Estudillo among the Yokuts: 1819. In Essays in Anthropology Presented to A.L. Kroeber, pp. 67-85. University of California Press, 1936.

2672. Heizer, R.F. Francis Drake and the California Indians, 1579. UC-PAAE 42 (3), 1947.
Reprinted, with added discussion, under title of Elizabethan California. Ballena Press, Ramona, CA, 1975
[Contains reprint of Fletcher's World Encompassed account of the Coast Miwok Indians among whom Drake

stayed in June 1579; ethnographic analysis of the
description of native customs recorded in Fletcher's
account]

2673. Keller, A.S., O.J. Lissitzyn and F.J. Mann. Creation of rights
through symbolic acts, 1400-1800. Columbia University
Press, 1938.

2674. Maloney, A.B. Fur brigade to the Bonaventura: John Work's
California expedition, 1832-1833, for the Hudson's
Bay Company. California Historical Society Special
Publication No. 19, 1945.
[Much on Indians in Sacramento Valley; observations on
the malaria (?) pandemic of 1833]

2675. Ordaz, Blas. La ultima exploracion espanol en America.
Revista de Indias 18 (72) April-June, 1958.
[Diary of 1821 expedition of Arguello]

2676. Priestley, H. I. A historical, political and natural
description of California, by Pedro Fages. University
of California Press, 1937.
[Much on Indians of southern California seen by
Fages]

2677. Serrin, M. The act of sovereignty in the Age of Discovery.
Unpublished Ph.D. dissertation in History, University
of Southern California, 1959.

2678. Shur, L.A. and J.R. Gibson. Russian travel notes and journals
as sources for the history of California, 1800-1850.
California Historical Quarterly 52:37-63, 1973.
[Indians are included in these accounts]

2679. Simpson, L.B. California in 1792: the expedition of Jose
Longinos Martinez. The Huntington Library, San Marino,
1938.

2680. Stanger, F.M. and A.K. Brown. Who discovered the Golden Gate:
the explorer's own accounts. San Mateo County
Historical Association, San Mateo, 1969.
[Verbatim accounts which contain much on Indians
seen, 1769-1776]

2681. Wagner, H.R. Spanish Voyages to the Northwest Coast of
America in the Sixteenth Century. California
Historical Society, Special Publication No. 4, 1929.
[Journals of Cabrillo, Cermeno, and Vizcaino in
1542, 1595, and 1602]

II. B: PERIOD OF SPANISH AND MEXICAN CONTACT (1542-1846): SETTLEMENT

The Indian experience in the Franciscan missions is described first-hand by Beechey (1831), an English ship captain, whose account is cited here as only one of many (Weber 1968). Borah (1970) and Cook (1943) also treat this subject from the documentary records. Numbers of Indians residing at each mission from 1769 to 1834 have been compiled by Bowman (1958).

Names of villages and numbers of natives drawn from them into the missions are given in Merriam (1955, 1968, 1970). No full and complete listing of villages recorded in the mission baptismal records has ever been compiled. Alexander S. Taylor in 1860-1863 published a vast miscellany of information on native California under the title "Indianology of California" in a weekly newspaper The California Farmer and Journal of Useful Arts. These articles are replete with erros, among which are the rendering of many names of villages from which neophytes were drawn into the missions. These misspellings are repeated in F.W. Hodge's Handbook of North American Indians (2 vols., Bureau of American Ethnology Bulletin 30, 1907-1910).

A valuable source of information, never brought together in a single work, is the replies from each California mission to the official Interrogatorio of 1812. An abstract of these was published by Kroeber (1908), and five replies from Costanoan missions are reprinted in Heizer (1974).

Secularization of the twenty-one missions in 1834 and the release of the neophytes from the power of the church is discussed by Geary (1934), Hutchinson (1969) and Servin (1965).

The history of the Russian settlement at Fort Ross in Mendocino County is described by Essig, et.al. (1933), but local Indians (Southwestern Pomo) are slighted in this work.

Bancroft's History of California, Vols. I-III (not cited here), has much useful information on this subject.

2682. Adam, J. A defense of the missionary establishments of Alta California. Historical Society of Southern California 3:35-39, 1896.

2683. Baer, K.E. and G. von Helmersen. Beitrage zur Kentniss des Russischen Reiches. St. Petersburg, 1839. [Observations on the Pomo by the Russians at Fort Ross, Mendocino County. Published in English

translation under the title: Ethnographic Obser-
vations on the Coast Miwok and Pomo by Contre-Admiral
F.P. von Wrangell and P. Kostromitonov of the Russian
Colony Ross, 1839. ARF, 1974]

2684. Beattie, G.W. Spanish plans for an inland chain of missions
in California. Historical Society of Southern
California 24: 243-264, 1928.

2685. Beechey, F.W. Narrative of a voyage to the Pacific and
Bering Strait, to cooperate with the Polar expeditions.
2 vols. London, 1831.
[Objective reporting of Indian conditions in the
California missions in the 1830's]

2686. Beeler, M.S. Noptinte Yokuts. In Studies in American
Indian languages, J. Sawyer ed. UC-PL 65:1-76, 1971.
[Although primarily a linguistic study, the introduction
sketches the activities in California of Padre
Felipe Arroyo de la Cuesta between 1808-1840. Arroyo
was one of the few missionaries who bothered to record
ethnographic data]

2687. Bennyhoff, J.A. Ethnogeography of the Plains Miwok. Center
for Archaeological Research at Davis, Publication No. 5,
1977.

2688. Bleeker, S. The Mission Indians of California. New York,
1956.

2689. Borah, W.W. The California Mission. In Ethnic Conflict in
California History, pp. 1-22, C. Wollenberg, ed.,
Tinnon-Brown, Inc. Los Angeles, 1970.

2690. Bowman, J.N. The resident neophytes (Existentes) of the
California Missions. Historical Society of Southern
California Quarterly 40:138-148, 1958.
[Neophyte populations in the California missions,
1769-1834, listed annually for each mission]

2691. _____ California Indians baptised during the Mission
period. Historical Society of Southern California
Quarterly 42:273-277, 1960.

2692. _____ The names of the California Missions. The
Americas 21:363-374, 1965.
[Useful collection of variant names used for the
21 Franciscan missions in California]

2693. Campbell, W.B. and J.R. Moriarty. The struggle over
secularization of the Missions on the Alta California
frontier. Journal of San Diego History 15:3-16, 1969.

2694. Caughey, J.W. (ed.). The Indians of Southern California in
      1852. Huntington Library, San Marino, 1952.
      [Reprint of B.D. Wilson's report on Indians conditions]

2695. Colley, C.C. The missionization of the Coast Miwok Indians
      in California. California Historical Society Quarterly
      49:143-162, 1970.
      [Useful but leaves much to be desired]

2696. Cook, S.F. The conflict between the California Indian and
      White Civilization: I, The Indian Versus the Spanish
      Mission. Ibero-Americana 21:1-194, 1943.
      [The best work yet written on the Indians and the
      mission system, 1769-1834. Reprinted 1976 by University
      of California Press]

2697. Egenhoff, E.L. Fabricas: a collection of pictures and state-
      ments of the mineral materials used in building in
      California prior to 1850. Supplement to California
      Journal of Mines and Geology, for April, 1952.
      [Includes verbatim descriptions of California missions
      by explorers, missionaries, and travellers]

2698. Engelhardt, Z. The missions and missionaries of California.
      Vol. II, Upper California. Santa Barbara, 1930.
      [Spirited defense of the mission system written in
      part to offset the influence of H.H. Bancroft who is
      labelled as "selfish", "mendacious", and "commercialistic"]

2699. Essig, E.O., A. Ogden, and C.J. DuFour. The Russians in
      California. California Historical Society Special
      Publication No. 7, 1933.
      [Reprinted from Quarterly of the California Historical
      Society XII (3). Fort Ross was in Pomo territory]

2700. Gayton, A.H. Estudillo among the Yokuts: 1819. In Essays in
      Anthropology, pp. 67-85. University of California
      Press, 1936.

2701. Geary, G.J. The secularization of the California Indian
      missions. Catholic University of America, Studies in
      American Church History 17, 1934.
      [Important study--not all of his conclusions are
      supported by other analyses]

2702. Guest, F.F. The Indian policy under Fermin Francisco de
      Lasuen, California's Second Father President.
      California Historical Society Quarterly 45:195-224,
      1966.

2703. _____ Fermin Francisco de Lasuen, 1736-1803. Academy
      of American Franciscan History, 1973.
      [Chap. 17 treats in detail the 1798 inquiry into
      living conditions, food and work regime of the mission
      neophytes]

2704. Harrington, M.R. An old inventory of San Fernando Mission.
SM-M 24:197-200, 1950.
[Detailed list of storehouse items, furnishing, shop
equipment, etc. for 1843]

2705. Heizer, R.F. The Indians of Los Angeles County: Hugo Reid's
letters of 1852. Southwest Museum, 1968.
[These 22 letters have been printed several times. One
version, although not complete and not annotated is
in S.B. Dakin, A Scotch Paisano. University of
California Press, 1939]

2706. _____ The Costanoan Indians. DeAnza College, California
History Center, Local History Studies, Vol. 18, 1974.
Cupertino.
[A collection of historical and ethnographical in-
formation]

2707. Hewes, M. and G. Hewes. Indian life and customs at Mission
San Luis Rey. The Americas 9:87-106, 1952.
[Mission life as described by P. Tac--see Section VI]

2708. Hutchinson, C.A. The Mexican government and the Mission
Indians of Upper California. The Americas 21:335-
362, 1965.
[Relations of Mexicans and Indians after Mexican
independence; secularization process]

2709. _____ Frontier settlement in Mexican California.
Yale University Press. New Haven, 1969.
[Similar to the last, but more detailed]

2710. von Kotzebue, O. Voyage of discovery into the South Sea
and Bering's Strait, 1815-1818. 2 vols. London,
1821.
[Observations on conditions of Indians of the missions
of Carmel and San Francisco]

2711. Kroeber, A.L. A Mission record of the California Indians.
UC-PAAE 8:1-27, 1908.
[Abstracts and replies sent from 16 of the California
missions to the Interrogatorio of 1811. A copy in
Bancroft Library was made in 1877 by E.F. Murray from
the earlier copy in the archives of Santa Barbara
Mission. The Bancroft Library version is in Archives
of Mission Santa Barbara, Miscellaneous Papers, Vol.
VII:112ff.]

2712. Mason, W.M. Fages' code of conduct toward Indians, 1787.
JCA 2:90-100, 1975.

2713. Merriam, C.H. California mission baptismal records. In
Studies of California Indians. University of California

Press, 1955.
[Pp. 191-225, Santa Barbara, San Luis Obispo, San Miguel, Santa Clara, San Jose missions]

2714. Merriam, C.H. Village names in twelve California Indian mission records. R.F. Heizer, (ed.). UC-AS-R 74, 1968.
[Missions: San Rafael, San Francisco, San Carlos, Santa Cruz, Le Soledad, San Antonio, La Purisma Concepcion, San Diego]

2715. _____ Indian rancheria names in four mission records. UC-ARF-C 9:29-58, 1970.
[La Purisima, San Buenaventura, San Francisco, Santa Ynez missions]

2716. Mills, E.T. Old Indian paintings at Los Angeles. Overland Monthly 37:766-771, 1901.
[Paintings in San Fernando Mission done by neophytes]

2717. Peatfield, J.J. Mission music and musicians: The padres and their wards. Out West 28:277-286, 1895.

2718. Piette, M. An unpublished diary of Fray Juan Crespi, O.F.M. (1770). Academy of Franciscan History 3:102-114, 1946.

2719. Servin, M.P. The secularization of the California Missions: a reappraisal. Southern California Quarterly 47:133-149, 1965.

2720. Villegas, I. San Fernando mission, 1797-1825. Southwest Museum Masterkey 20:5-10, 1946.
[Life in the mission through observations of F. Mellus from 1838-1847]

2721. Weber, F.J. The California missions and their visitors. The Americas 24:319-336, 1968.
[Useful roster of visitors, many of whom left accounts of their observations]

2722. Willard, C.D. The padres and the Indians. Land of Sunshine 1:73-75, 1894.
[Relations of missionaries and Indians in the missions]

2723. Zalvidea, J.M. Mission San Gabriel in 1814. Transl. and ed. by M. Geiger. Southern California Quarterly 53: 235-250, 1971.

II. C: PERIOD OF SPANISH AND MEXICAN CONTACT (1952-1846):
THE INDIAN RESPONSE

Indian response, whether it be the passive one of
suffering from introduced diseases (Cook 1939) or the requirement to serve as peons after secularization (Cook 1943), or
the active reaction in the form of revolt (Bancroft 1886,
Holterman 1970, Stickel and Cooper 1969) was varied.

The tale of a woman marooned alone on San Nicolas
Island for eighteen years can be read as a response to contact
with western civilization (Heizer and Elsasser 1961), as
also was the abortive messianic movement of 1801 among the
Chumash (Heizer 1941).

Much needed is the energy of some scholar to bring
together the scattered information on how the California
Indians reacted to the missionization process and post-
secularization Mexican domination. Some direct information
on this will be found in Section VI.

2724. Bancroft, H.H. History of California. Vol. 1, 1952-1800.
San Francisco, 1886.
[Pg. 249-255, San Diego Mission revolt of 1775,
pp. 362-371, Colorado River Mission revolt 1781]

2725. _____ California pastoral. San Francisco. The
History Company, 1888.
[Pg. 585, ff., legal proceedings involving Indians
in the Mexican period]

2726. Blackburn, T. The Chumash revolt of 1824: a native account.
JCA 2:223-227, 1975.

2727. Broadbent, S.M. The Rumsen of Monterey: an ethnography
from historical sources. UC-ARF-C14:45-93, 1972.
Department of Anthropology, University of California,
Berkeley.

2728. _____ Conflict at Monterey: Indian horse raiding,
1820-1850. JCA 1:86-101, 1974.

2729. Cook, S.F. Smallpox in Spanish and Mexican California,
1770-1845. Bulletin of the History of Medicine
7:153-191, 1939.

2730. _____ The conflict between the California Indian and
White civilization: II, the physical and demographic
reaction of the nonmission Indians in Colonial and
Provincial California. Ibero-Americana 22:1-55,
1943.
[The California Indians after independence of Mexico ·
up to the American invasion in 1846]

2731. Cook, S.F. Colonial expeditions to the interior of California: Central Velley, 1800-1820. UC-AR 16:239-292, 1960. [Translations of Spanish accounts of expeditions]

2732. _____ Expeditions to the interior of California: Central Valley, 1820-1840. UC-AR 20:151-214, 1962. [Spanish-Mexican expeditions against Indians]

2733. Dobyns, H.F., P.H. Ezell and G.S. Ezell. Death of a society: The Halchidhomas. Ethnohistory 10:105-161, 1963.

2734. Forbes, J. Warriors of the Colorado: The Yumas of the Quechan nation and their neighbors. University of Oklahoma Press, 1965.

2735. _____ The Native American experience in California history. California Historical Quarterly 50:234-242, 1971. [A perceptive analysis of the Indian viewpoint]

2736. Geiger, M. Fray Antonio Ripoli's description of the Chumash revolt at Santa Barbara in 1824. Southern California Quarterly 52:345-364, 1970. [See also Stickel and Cooper 1969]

2737. Heizer, R.F. A Californian messianic movement of 1801 among the Chumash. AA 43:128-129, 1941. [What little is known of this abortive attempt]

2738. Heizer, R.F. and A.B. Elsasser. Original accounts of the lone woman of San Nicolas Island. UC-AS-R 55,1961. [Reprinted 1972 by Ballena Press, Ramona, California] [Collection of primary accounts of Juana Maria, the woman marooned alone for 18 years, 1835-1853. Like Ishi, she was a last survivor, but she lived only about six months after her rescue and removal to Santa Barbara]

2739. Holterman, T. The revolt of Estanislao. The Indian Historian 3 (1): 43-55, 1970. [One Indian leader's response to European domination]

2740. _____ The revolt of Yozcalo: Indian warrior and the fight for freedom. The Indian Historian 3 (2):19-25, 1970. [Another of the same]

2741. Hudson, M.F. The Pauma massacre. Publications of the Historical Society of Southern California 7:13-21, 1907.

2742. Kroeber, A.L. Problems on Boscana. Ethnographic Interpretations 7-11. UC-PAAE 47 (3):282-293, 1959. Berkeley. [P. 293 suggests possibility that the Chinigchinich cult of Southern California was inspired by Christianity. Boscana's manuscript Chinigchinich was written at Mission

San Juan Capistrano among the Juaneno tribe]

2743. Staniford, E.F. The California Indians: a critique of their treatment by historians. Ethnohistory 18:119-125, 1971.

2744. Stewart, K.M. The Mohave Indians and the fur trappers. Plateau 39:73-79, 1966.

2745. _____ The Mohave Indians in Hispanic times. The Kiva 32:25-36, 1966.

2746. Stickel, E.G. and A.E. Cooper. The Chumash revolt of 1824: a case for an archaeological application of feedback theory. UCLA-AS-AR 11:5-22, 1969. Los Angeles. [An attempt to analyze the Chumash revolt of 1824]

2747. Temple, T.W. Toypurina the Witch and the Indian uprising at San Gabriel. SM-M 32:136-152, 1958. [Revolt of neophytes at Mission San Gabriel in 1785]

2748. De Thoma, F. The first martyr: a chapter in the history of San Diego. Land of Sunshine 10:126-130, 1899. [The Indian revolt at San Diego Mission]

2749. Weber, F.J. Toypurina the witch. SM-M 43:75-76, 1969.

III A: PERIOD OF ANGLO CONQUEST (1846-1873): LEGAL STATUS OF INDIANS

References to this subject are in short supply, mainly because Indians had so few legal rights under American rule that they may be said to have been non-existent. Section IV E continues with this subject after 1873.

2750. Bailey, H.C. Indians of the Sacramento Valley in 1852. San Bernardino County Museum Quarterly 7(1), 1959.

2751. California Statutes 1863. [P. 69: Prohibits Indians "or persons having one-half or more Indian blood, or Mongolian or Chinese" from giving testimony in favor of or against any white person]

2752. Fernandez, F. Except a California Indian: a study in legal discrimination. Historical Society of Southern California Quarterly 50:161-176, 1968. [Excellent summary]

2753. Gibbs, G. Observations on the Indians of the Klamath River and Humboldt Bay, accompanying vocabularies of their languages. UC-ARF, 1973. [Manuscript, not before published, reporting observations on Yurok and Wiyot people in 1852]

2754. Goodrich, C.S. The legal status of the California Indian. California Law Review 14:83-100, 157-187, 1926. [Basic survey up to date of publication]

2755. Hastings, J.R. California ethnohistory: anglo-world view and the Indian laws, 1850-1863. MA thesis in Anthropology, California State University, Sacramento, 1971.

2756. Heizer, R.F. Civil rights in California in the 1850's--a case history. KAS-P 31:129-137, 1965. [Interesting legal case revolving around prohibition of Indians giving testimony for or against whites]

2757. Heizer, R.F. and A.J. Almquist. The other Californians. University of California Press, 1971. [Chs. II-V treats with Indians and American law]

2758. Hutchinson, C.A. Frontier Settlement in Mexican California. Yale University Press. New Haven, 1969. [Indian legal status under Mexico, 1821-1846]

2759. California Statutes 1850. Act for the government and protection of Indians, April 22, 1850. Statutes of California, 1850. Ch. 133; amended April 18, 1860 in Statutes of California, Ch. 231. [Act legalizing what can only be called Indian slavery in California. Act and amendments reprinted in Heizer and Almquist 1971: 212-217--cited in III B. Examples of Indian indenturing discussed in Heizer and Almquist 1971: 40-58. Legalization of the indenturing of Indian children repealed in California Statutes 1863, Chap. 475, par. 1 in conformity with Lincoln's emancipation proclamation. Balance of the Act repealed in California Statutes 1937, Chap. 369]

2760. California Statutes 1850, Chap. 143, par. 1. [Indians exempted from military service. Also in California Political Code of 1872, par. 1895. This exemption was removed in California Statutes 1933, Chap. 975, par. 32]

2761. California Statutes, 1850. Act to regulate elections. California Statutes, 1850, Chap. 38. [Voters limited to "white male citizens of the United States and white male citizens of Mexico who shall have elected to become a citizen of the United States" under the Treaty of Guadalupe Hidalgo, 1848. California Indians entitled to vote in California Constitution of 1879, Art. II, Pt. 1]

2762. California Statutes 1850, Chap. 125, par. 14. [No Indian, black or mulatto, could give testimony against a white person in a criminal case. Indians were defined as having one-half Indian blood]

2763. California Statutes 1851, Chap. 123, par. 394.
[No Indian or negro could be witness in a civil case
where a white person was a party. Indians were defined
here as having one-quarter Indian blood. This last
provision was amended in California Statutes 1854,
Chap. 3, par. 42 to define Indians as having one-half
Indian blood. In the Codes of 1872 all of these
definitions were removed by omission]

2764. California Statutes 1854. Act prohibiting transfer of arms
or ammunition to Indians of either sec. California
Statutes 1854, Chap. 12.
[Repealed in California Statutes, 1913, Chap. 56,
p. 57]

2765. California Statutes 1860, Chap. 329, par. 8.
[Indians excluded from public schools]

2766. California Statutes, 1864. Right of Indians to attend public
schools. California Statutes, 1864, Chap. 209, Sec.
68, p. 213.
[See also California Statutes, 1866, Chap. 342,
Secs. 56-58, p. 398; California Statutes, 1869-1870,
Chap. 556; Amended Statutes, 1873-1874, Sec. 26:
Amended Statutes, 1880, pp. 38, 47; California
Statutes, 1902, Chap. 77; California Statutes, 1909,
Chap. 594, Sec. 3]
[In 1921 the State Legislature revised Sec. 1662 of
the Political Code and permitted Indians to attend
public schools]

2767. California Statutes 1865-1866, Chap. 342, par. 56.
[Half-breed Indian children, Indian children living
with white families, or Indian children living under
white guardianship to be admitted to public schools
after approval of the Board of Trustees]

2768. California Statutes 1873-1874, Chap. 543, par. 26.
[Education of Indian children in white schools
permitted if no separate school was provided]

2769. United States vs. Ritchie, 58 U.S. (17 How.), 1855.
[Supreme Court declared California Indians to be
Mexican citizens and therefore liable to provisions
of the Treaty of Guadalupe Hidalgo. Despite this,
California Indians were not treated as citizens]

2770. Wozencraft, O.M. Proclamation to the people living and
trading among the Indians in the State of California
with an act to regulate trade and Indian tribes,
and to preserve peace...32nd Congress, 1st Session,
Senate Executive Document No. 1, Part 3:490-493,
1851.
[No attention whatsoever was paid by the gold miners
to this notice]

III B: PERIOD OF ANGLO CONQUEST (1846-1873): GOLD RUSH;
RELATIONS OF INDIANS AND MINERS

For affairs involving Indians and gold miners see
Cook (1943) and Heizer and Almquist (1971). As an example
of how Indians were hunted down by state militia see
Kibbe (1860).

There are hundreds of diaries of white gold miners
of the 1850's and Bruff (1949) is only one of these. Others
are cited by Cowan and Cowan (1964--see Section VII E).

2771. Anderson, R.A. Fighting the Mill Creeks. Chico Record
Press, Chico, California, 1909.
[Killing off the Yana and Yahi]

2772. Bailin, R. One of the last human hunts of civilization and
the basest and most brutal of them all. Image 3
Graphics. San Francisco, 1971.

2773. Bruff, J.G. Gold rush: the journals, drawings, and other
papers of J. Goldsborough Bruff. G.W. Read and R.
Gaines, (eds.). Columbia University Press, 1949.
[One of hundreds of accounts of gold rush partici-
pants which contains reference to Indians. Contains
numerous sketches of Indians seen--depicted are
houses, dress, tools, etc.]

2774. Bunnell, L.H. Discovery of the Yosemite and the Indian war
of 1851. Chicago, 1911.

2775. Cline, G.G. Exploring the Great Basin. University of Oklahoma
Press, 1963.
[While treating mainly with the Great Basin, many of the
accounts cited also deal with California]

2776. Cook, S.F. The conflict between the California Indian and
white civilization: III, The American Invasion 1848-
1870. Ibero-Americana 23, 1943. Berkeley. Reprinted
by University of California Press, 1976.

2777. Coy, O.C. The Humboldt Bay region, 1850-1875. California
State Historical Association, Los Angeles, 1929.
[Much of Indian-White relations in northwestern
California]

2778. Devereux, G. Mohave chieftainship in action: a narrative
of the first contacts of the Mohave Indian with the
United States. Plateau 23:33-43. Flagstaff, 1951.

2779. Fages, Pedro. A historical, political and natural descrip-
tion of California. Translated by H.I. Priestley.
University of California Press, 1937.
[Much on Indians in the area between San Diego and
San Francisco in the 1770's]

193

2780. Fassin, A.G. The Con-Cow Indians. Overland Monthly 4:
7-14, 1884.
[History of the Indians of Butte County as told by
Uh-le-ma, Concow chief]

2781. Garces, F. On the trail of a Spanish pioneer. Ed. by E.
Coues. F.P. Harper, New York, 1900.
[Diary of a Franciscan friar who describes Indians
from Colorado River to the southern San Joaquin Valley]

2782. Goetzmann, W.H. Exploration and empire. A. Knopf, New York,
1967.
[Detailed account of western exploration; numerous
references to Indians encountered and described;
fully documented; illustrated]

2783. Heizer, R.F. Walla Walla expeditions to the Sacramento Valley,
1846-1848. California Historical Society Quarterly
21:1-7, 1942.
[Record of Columbia River tribal expeditions to
California to secure horses and New Almaden cinnabar,
1800-1848]

2784. _____ Collected documents on the causes and events
in the Bloody Island massacre of 1850. UC-ARF, 1973.
[Reports by army officers, historians, and Indians
of this event which concerned the Pomo]

2785. _____ They were only Diggers. BP-PAEH 1, 1974.
[Collection of newspaper articles 1851-1866 on
Indian-White relations]

2786. Heizer, R.F. and A.J. Almquist. The other Californians.
University of California Press, 1971.
[Deals briefly with the first two decades of Indian-
American relations; treats with the Indian indenture
act of 1850]

2787. Kibbe, W.C. Report of the expedition against the Indians
in the northern part of this state. C.T. Botts,
State Printer, Sacramento, 1860.
[Republished in Reprints of various papers on
California archaeology, ethnology and Indian history.
R.G. Heizer, (ed.), UC-ARF 1973]

2788. Kotzebue, Otto von. A voyage of discovery into the South
Sea and Beering's Straits. London, 1821.
[Descriptions and drawings of Indians at San Francisco
mission]

2789. _____ A new voyage round the world, 1823-1826.
London, 1830.
[Kotzebue visited and described the Costanoans at
missions and Pomo Indians at Fort Ross, illustrated]

2790. La Perouse, J.F.G. A voyage round the world. London, 1807.
[Long account of Costanoan Indians and the living
regime at Carmel Mission]

2791. Latta, F.F. San Joaquin primeval: Uncle Jeff's story--a
tale of a San Joaquin Valley pioneer and his life
with the Yokuts Indians. Tulare, 1929.

2792. Leonard, Zenas. Narrative of the adventures of Zenas Leonard,
fur trader and trapper, 1831-1836. Ed. by W.F.
Wagner. Cleveland, 1904.
[Good accounts of Indians in the San Joaquin Valley,
and of some of the missions at the time they were
about to be secularized]

2793. Loeffelholz, K. von. Die Zoreisch-Indianer der Trinidad-Bai
(Californien). Mittheilungen der Anthropologischen
Gesellschaft Wien 23:101-123, 1893.
[Eyewitness account of the Yurok of Trinidad Bay in
1857. Translation in Heizer and Mills 1952, cited
in I A2]

2794. Longinos, Jose M. The expedition of Jose Longinos Martinez.
San Marino, 1938.
[Includes important information on Indians of southern
California in the late eighteenth century]

2795. Loud, L.L. Ethnogeography and archaeology of the Wiyot
territory. UC-PAAE 14:221-436, 1918.
[Pp. 305-336, Indian-White relations in northwestern
California 1850-1864]

2796. Lovell, C.C. Lovell's report on the Cahuilla Indians, 1854.
Ed. by R.W. Frazier. Journal of San Diego History
22:4-10, 1976.

2797. Marshall, M. The whites come to Hoopa Valley. Pacific
Historian 15:55-61, 1971.
[Compare with P.E. Goddard, Hupa texts. UC-PAAE
2:198-201, 1904]

2798. Massey, E. A Frenchman in the Gold Rush. Translated by
M.E. Wilbur. Special publication of the California
Historical Society, 1927.
[Deals mainly with the Indians of northwestern
California]

2799. Moak, S. The last of the Mill Creeks. Chico, 1923.
[Killing off the Yana and Yahi]

2800. Mitchell, A.R. Major James D. Savage and the Tularenos.
California Historical Society Quarterly 28:323-341,
1949.
[A Gold Rush period exploiter of Indians who got what
was coming to him]

2801. Rawls, J.R. Gold Diggers: Indian miners in the California gold rush. California Historical Quarterly 55:28-45, 1976.

2802. Rogers, F.B. Early military posts of Del Norte County. California Historical Society Quarterly 26:1-11, 1947. [American period]

2803. Royce, J. California: a study of American character. Peregrine Publishers. Santa Barbara and Salt Lake City, 1970. [Detailed and accurate study of the first ten years of American rule. Originally published 1886]

2804. Wheat, C.I. The maps of the California gold region, 1848-1857. Grabhorn Press. San Francisco, 1942. [Useful in showing former place names and locations]

2805. Vanley, N.R. Domestication versus extermination: treatment of the northwest California Indians, 1850-1860. Masters Abstracts 10 (1972):333. University Microfilms M-3623, 1972.

2806. Von Langsdorff, George H. Narrative of the Rezanov voyage to Nueva California in 1806. Translated by T.C. Russell. San Francisco, 1927. [Descriptions and pictures of Indians in the missions around San Francisco Bay]

2807. Work, J. Fur brigade to the Bonaventura. Edited by A.B. Maloney. California Historical Society Special Publication No. 19, 1945. [Journal of a Hudson Bay Company trapper in the Sacramento Valley in 1933. Records the effects of the 1833 pandemic of malaria among the Indians. See No. 2368]

2808. Wilkes, C. Narrative of the United States exploring expedition. 5 vols. Philadelphia, 1845. [Contains many observations on the Indians of northern California at the time]

2809. Yount, G.C. George C. Yount; his Chronicles of the West. Old West Publishing Co., Denver, 1966. Edited by Charles L. Camp. [Contains much on Indians, especially Yuma, Mohave and the Indians of the Napa Valley]

III C: PERIOD OF ANGLO CONQUEST 1846-1873): TREATY
MAKING; LAND TITLES

The Spanish made no treaties with California Indians.
On the northern frontier in the Mexican period (1821-1846)
M.G. Vallejo made two treaties between 1836-1838 with
Southern Pomo and Lake Miwok tribelets (Lathrop 1932).
Several unofficial "treaties" with California Indians are
printed in Heizer and Hester (1970). The eighteen unratified treaties of 1851-1852 are discussed by Ellison (1925)
and Heizer (1972) and the treaty-making expedition of one of
the commissioners, R. McKee, is detailed by George Gibbs
(Heizer 1972, Hoopes 1970). All land cessions up to the
date of publication are described in Royce (1899).

2810. California State Assembly. Committee report on Indian
reservations specified in the 1851-1852 treaties.
California Assembly Journal, 3rd Session, pp. 202-205.

2811. California State Senate. Majority and minority reports of the
special committee to inquire into the treaties made
by the United States Indian commissioners with the
Indians in California. California Senate Journal,
3rd Session. Appendix, pp. 597-604.

2812. Crouter, R.E. and A.F. Rolle. Edward Fitzgerald Beale and the
Indian peace commissioners in California 1851-1854.
Historical Society of Southern California Quarterly
42:107-131.
[Treaty-making, early reservation affairs]

2813. Dana, S.T. and M. Krueger. California lands: ownership,
use and management. American Forestry ASsociation.
Washington, 1958.
[Evolution and developing patterns of land ownership
and use. A useful companion to the volume by W.W.
Robinson, 1948]

2814. Ellison, W.H. Rejection of California Indian treaties: a
study in local influence on national policy. Grizzly
Bear 36, No. 217 (May pp. 4-5); No. 218 (June pp.
4,5,7); No. 219 (July pp. 6-7).

2815. Gibbs, G. Journal of the expedition of Colonel Redick
McKee, United States Indian agent, through northwestern California. Performed in the summer and fall
of 1851.
[Originally published in vol. 3 of H. Schoolcraft's
Indian Tribes, 1853. Reprinted in facsimile, 1972,
gy the UC-ARF]

2816. Hardie, Major J.A. Letter to Colonel R.B. Mason, Sonoma,
June, 1848. U.S. National Archives, War Department
RG98, Letters received, 10th Military Department 1848,

Nos. 366 and 366 No. 2.
[Treaty with Clear Lake Pomo]

2817. Heizer, R.F. The eighteen unratified treaties of 1851-1852
between the California Indians and the United States
Government. UC-ARF, 1972.
[Sample treaties are reprinted in full; others in part.
Discusses history of making and rejection of the
treaties by the U.S. Senate. The transcript of the
secret debate in the Senate leading to rejection of the
treaties has not been found. The Senate injunction
of secrecy in 1852 which kept the original government
copies hidden for fifty-three years seems to have
been a pointless act. One fully executed copy of each
treaty was given by the commissioners to a representative of each of the eighteen treaty groups. How
many of these have survived we do not know. The
copy of Treaty H is reported in the Redding Courier
Free Press, May 6, 1927, to be in Major P.B. Reading's
papers. In California during the time the treaties
were being negotiated in 1851-1852, full public
accounts of the proposed treaty reserves appeared in
newspapers (e.g., Daily Alta California, May 10,29,
21, 1851), the point here being that the cat was
already out of the bag before the Senate refused to
ratify the treaties and attempted its Watergate-style
coverup]

2818. _____ George Gibbs' journal of Redick McKee's
expedition through northwestern California in 1851.
UC-ARF, 1972.
[Reprinted from Schoolcraft 1853 with annotations.
This journal was written by Gibbs who was McKee's
interpreter on the treaty-making expedition]

2819. Heizer, R.F. and T.R. Hester. Names and locations of some
ethnographic Patwin and Maidu villages. UC-ARF-C
9:79-118, 1970.
[Document 2a-c, Some Early Treaties with California
Indians, pp. 107-111]

2820. Hoopes, A.W. The journal of George W. Barbour. Southwestern
Historical Quarterly 40:145-153; 247-261, 1936-1937.
[Diary of one of the Treaty Commissioners of 1851-
1852]

2821. Hoopes, C.L. Redick McKee and the Humboldt Bay region, 1851-
1852. California Historical Quarterly 49:195-220,
1970.
[Story of McKee's treaty-making expedition to northwestern California]

2822. Indian Historian. The rejected California treaties. The
Indian Historian 6 (1), 1973.
[Text from the California Senate Journal. Cf. Nos. 2801,
2802] 198

2823. Kelsey, H. The California Indian treaty myth. Southern
        California Quarterly 15 (3):225-235, 1973.

2824. Keyes, Capt. E.D. Report (to Capt. F. Steele of military
        guard escorting treaty commissioner Barbour). U.S.
        National Archives, Records War Department, RG98.
        Letters received, 10th Military Department, 1851, No. K11.

2825. Kroeber, A.L. The nature of land-holding groups in aboriginal
        California. UC-ARF 56:19-58, 1962.
        [Also published in Ethnohistory 2:303-314, 1955]

2826. Lathrop, M.L. The Indian campaigns of General M.G. Vallejo.
        Quarterly, Society of California Pioneers 9:161-205,
        1932.
        [Includes treaties made 1836-1838 with various groups
        of Southern Pomo and Lake Miwok]

2827. McKee, J. Minutes kept by John McKee, secretary, on the
        expedition from Sonoma through Northern California.
        U.S. Senate Documents, Special Session March 4, 1853.
        Document No. 4:134-187, 1953.
        [Journal of the treaty-making expedition of 1851.
        Compare with Biggs]

2828. Native American Training Associates. California Indian
        land - private property. Vol. 1 (1). June.
        Sacramento, 1976.

2829. Parker, H. The treaty of Temecula. In The historic valley
        of Temecula. Librito 2. Paisano Press, San Diego,
        1967.

2830. Robinson, W.W. Land in California. University of California
        Press, 1948.
        [The best study written on land titles, land grants,
        etc. from the Spanish mission period on]

2831. Royce, C.C. Indian land cessions in the United States.
        BAE-AR 18, Pt. 2, 1899.
        [Lists all land cessions; discusses a number of
        unratified treaties]

2832. U.S. Senate Executive Documents. Official reports by the
        treaty commissioners (McKee, Barbour and Wozencraft and
        sub-agent Adam Johnston) to the Commissioner of Indian
        Affairs on their treaty-making activities. GPO,
        Washington, 1851.

2833. Wessells, Capt. H.W. Report (to Col. J. Hooker of events
        under his command of a detachment of 36 privates, U.S.
        Dragoons as military escort to Redick McKee on the
        latter's treaty-making expedition to northwestern
        California). U.S. House of Representatives, 34th

Congress, 3d Session, Executive Document 76, Serial No. 906, pp. 59-68, 1853.

III D: PERIOD OF ANGLO CONQUEST (1846-1873): RESERVATIONS (RELATIONS OF MILITARY AND INDIANS; FEDERAL INDIAN POLICY)

The first 25 or 30 years of American control of California was a disastrous one for California Indians. After the 18 treaties of 1851-1852 were rejected by the Senate, military reservations were established (Beale 1854, Bonsal 1912, Dale 1949, Ellison 1922, Heizer 1973, Hoopes 1932) and there are annual reports from district agents to the Commissioner of Indian Affairs (Reports 1852-) which are usually more imaginary than truthful if we can believe J. Ross Browne's official (Heizer 1973) and un-official (Browne 1867) reports.

One Indian war deserving of that term involved the Modocs in the early eighteen-seventies (Dillon 1973, Murray 1959, Payne 1938, Riddle 1914).

2834. Anderson, G.E. The Hoopa Valley Indian reservation in northwestern California: a study of its origins. Unpublished M.A. thesis, University of California, Berkeley, 1956.

2835. Bancroft, H.H. History of California, 1860-1890. Vol. 7 The History Company, San Francisco, 1890. [Chap. XVIII, The extermination of the Indians]

2836. Beale, E.F. Reports of E.F. Beale, Superintendent of Indian Affairs for California, 1853. House of Representatives, 33d Congress, 1st Session, Doc. 1, pp. 464-481, 1854. [Earliest activities in establishing reservations in California, 1853]

2837. Bender, A.B. The march of empire. University of Kansas Press. Lawrence, 1952. [Indian affairs 1848-1860]

2838. Bledsoe, A.J. Indian wars in the northwest: a California sketch. Bacon and Co. San Francisco, 1885.

2839. Bonsal, S. Edward Fitzgerald Beale. New York, 1912. [Ch. X: Indian affairs; establishment of the first reservations in California]

2840. Browne, J.R. Crusoe's island. Harper and Brothers, New York, 1867. [Pg. 284-308 deal with the California Indian reservations]

2841. Bunker, W.M. In the Lava Beds. The Californian 1:161-166, 1880.
[Modoc War]

2842. California State Legislature. Majority and minority reports of the special joint committee on the Mendocino War. C.T. Botts, State Printer, Sacramento, 1860.
[Brief majority and minority reports followed by a large number of depositions taken from white ranchers and Indian Bureau personnel. Deals with conditions on Round Valley Reservation and Nome Cult Farm. Details of the infamous Jarboe's Indian hunting expeditions]

2843. Casebier, D.B. Carleton's Pah-Ute campaign. Norco, California, 1972.
[Major Carleton's hi-jinks against the Southern Paiute in the Mohave Desert in 1860]

2844. _____ The battle at Camp Cady. Norco, California, 1972.
[Fight between Southern Paiutes and U.S. Dragoons in 1866 in the Mohave Desert. The troops lost]

2845. Costo, R. and J. Henry. The American Indian in California history. Indian Historian 1:24-27,30, 1967-1968.

2846. Crampton, C.G. (ed.) The Mariposa Indian war, 1850-1851. Salt Lake City, 1957.

2847. Crevelli, J.P. Four hundred years of Indian affairs in the North Bay counties of California. Unpublished M.A. dissertation. University of California, Berkeley, 1959.

2848. Dale, E.E. The Indians of the Southwest. University of Oklahoma Press. Norman, 1949.
[Ch. 3, 6 deal with California. Excellent summary of the history of the California Indian reservations]

2849. Dillon, R. Burnt out fires: California's Indian Mococ war. Prentiss-Hall. Englewood Cliffs, New Jersey, 1973.
[The most recent and best, of a large number of books on the subject]

2850. Dunn, J.P. Massacres of the mountains: a history of the Indian wars of the Far West. Harper and Bros., 1886.
[Modoc War, pp. 543-583]

2851. Eccleston, R. The Mariposa Indian war, 1850-1851: Diaries of Robert Eccleston. Edited by C.G. Crampton. Salt Lake City, 1957.
[The California Gold Rush, Yosemite and the High Sierra]

2852. Ellison, W.H. The federal Indian policy in California, 1846-1860. Mississippi Valley Historical Review 9:37-67, 1922.
[Unratified treaties, reservations]

2853. Evans, W.E. The Garra uprising: conflict between San Diego Indians and settlers in 1851. California Historical Society Quarterly 45:339-349, 1966.
[Deals with the last Indian uprising in Southern California]

2854. Fry, J.B. Army sacrifices. Van Nostrand, New York, 1879.
[Pp. 185-254, Modoc "treachery"]

2855. Guinn, J.M. Yuma Indian depredations and the Glanton War. Publications of the Historical Society of Southern California 6:50-62, 1903-1905.

2856. Heizer, R.F. The destruction of California Indians. Peregrine Publishers. Salt Lake City, 1974.
[Collection of letters of military officers on Indian affairs, 1846-1865]

2857. Hoopes, A.W. Indian affairs and their administration with special reference to the Far West, 1849-1860. University of Pennsylvania Press, 1932.
[Ch. III: Indian policy in California 1847-1860; the origins and development of the reservation system]

2858. Hostler, P. History of the Hoopa tribe. Hoopa Valley Business Council, 1967.

2859. Howard, O.O. My life and experiences among our hostile Indians. A.D. Worthington, Hartford, 1907.
[Pg. 226-231, Modoc War]

2860. _____ Famous Indian chiefs I have known. Century Co., New York, 1908.
[Pg. 149-165, Captain Jack, Modoc]

2861. Kibby, L.P. California, the Civil War, and the Indian problem. Journal of the West 4:183-209, 377-410, 1965.

2862. King, L.E. Hugo Reid and his Indian wife. Publications of the Historical Society of Southern California 4:111-113, 1897-1899.
[Reid was author of the famous letters on the Indians of Los Angeles County. His wife was a Gabrielino Indian]

2863. Knoop, A.M. The federal Indian policy in the Sacramento Valley, 1846-1860. Unpublished M.A. dissertation. University of California, Berkeley, 1941.

2864. Kroeber, A.L. and C.B. A Mohave war reminiscence, 1854-1880.
       UC-PA 10, 1974.
       [Verbatim recording of what one man, Jo Nelson
       (Chooksa homar) remembered in 1901 of Mohave warfare.
       Some of this concerns intertribal battles, but most
       is about conflicts with whites and especially U.S.
       Army troops. Contains abundant ethnohistoric docu-
       mentation and evaluates the different opinions on
       themes and motives of Mohave warfare advanced by
       other ethnographers and ethnohistorians]

2865. Leonard, C.B. Federal Indian policy in the San Joaquin
       Valley, its application and results, 1846-1876.
       Unpublished Ph.D. dissertation, University of
       California, Berkeley, 1924.

2866. McCall, G.A. Camp Yuma - 1852. Southern California
       Quarterly 52:170-184, 1970.

2867. Mitchell, A.R. Major James D. Savage and the Tularenos.
       California Historical Quarterly 28:323-341, 1949.
       [Life and experiences with the Yokuts Indians of an
       early settler, trader and Indian fighter who was
       finally disposed of by the Indians]

2868. Murray, K.A. The Modocs and their war. University of
       Oklahoma Press, 1959.

2869. Parker, H. The Temecula massacre. The Westerners Brand
       Book. Los Angeles, Corral No. 10, 1963.

2870. Payne, D.P. Captain Jack, Modoc renegade. Binfords and
       Mort, Portland, Oregon, 1938.
       [The Modoc War]

2871. Polley, F. Renegade Indians of San Gabriel. Annual
       Publications of the Historical Society of Southern
       California 3:22-25, 1896.

2872. Reports of the Commissioner of Indian Affairs. U.S.
       Government Printing Office, 1852-
       [See the California sections for the annual reports
       of reservation agents]

2873. Riddle, J.C. The Indian history of the Modoc War.
       San Francisco, 1914.
       [Riddle was a Modoc Indian]

2874. Rogers, F.B. Early military posts of Mendocino County.
       California Historical Society Quarterly 27:215-228,
       1948.

2875. Rosborough, A.S. A.M. Rosborough, special Indian agent.
       California Historical Society Quarterly 26:201-207, 1947.

2876. Smith, K. Sergeant Ferlner's furlough;   perils and profits
        of a scientific journey into Modoc tribal lands in
        1860. Association for Northern California Records
        and Research. Research Paper No. 3. Chico, California,
        1975.

2877. Smith, G.A., R. Sexton and E.J. Koch. Juan Antonio,
        Cahuilla Indian chief, a friend of the whites.
        Quarterly of the San Bernardino County Museum
        Association 8 (1), 1960.
        [Interesting collection of information on this Indian
        leader]

2878. Stewart, G.W. The Indian war on Tule River. Overland
        Monthly 3:46-53, 1884.

2879. Stewart, K.M. A brief history of the Mohave Indians since
        1850. Kiva 34:218-236, 1968-1969.

2880. Tassin, A.G. The chronicles of Camp Wright. Overland
        Monthly (July-November issues), 1887.

2881. Thompson, W. Reminiscences of a pioneer. San Francisco,1912.
        [Pp. 75-131, Modoc War]

2882. Van Alstyne, P.W. Captain Jack, was he guilty? Pacific
        Historian 14:90-97, 1970.

2883. War of the Rebellion Records. A compilation of the
        official records of the Union and Confederate armies.
        Published under the direction of the Secretary of
        War. 70 volumes. Government Printing Office.
        Washington, D.C., 1880-1901.
        [Contains much on Indians affairs and the U.S.
        military during the Civil War period]

2884. Weber, F.J. Rumblings at Pala. Journal of San Diego
        History 21:38-42, 1975.
        [Report of C. Maltby, Supt. of Indian Affairs for
        California on conditions at Temecula and Pala Mission
        in 1866]

2885. Whipple, A.W., T. Ewbank and W.W. Turner. Report upon
        the Indian tribes. United States War Department
        Report of Explorations and Surveys...for a Railroad
        from the Mississippi River to the Pacific Ocean.
        Volume III, 1855.
        [Early observations on the Mohave and the Chemehuevi]

2886. Woodward, A. The Garra revolt of 1851. The Westerners
        Brand Book, Los Angeles, Corral, 1947.

2887. Wheeler-Voegelin, E. Letter from E.A. Stevenson to T.W.
Henley, Red Bluffs, September 30, 1857. Ethnohistory
4:66-95, 1957.
[Visit of Indian agent to the Achomawi, Atsugewi
and Modoc]

2888. Wilke, P.J. and H.W. Lawton. The expedition of Capt. J.W.
Davidson from Fort Tejon to the Owens Valley in 1859.
BP-PAEH No. 4, 1976.

III E: PERIOD OF ANGLO CONQUEST (1846-1873): SOCIAL
CONDITIONS

Indian-White relations in the first twenty years of
American rule are discussed in Cook (1943), the best
survey of what happened during this period. A collection
of newspaper reports dating from 1851-1866 (Heizer 1973)
can be read as historical documentation. Conditions on
reservations (Browne 1944) or in Southern California
(Caughey 1952) or on one of the Mexican land grants awarded
to Americans (Currie 1957) all sound pretty much the same.
Cook (1943) traces the course of changing marriage-family
patterns after 1850.

Here again we lack any thorough treatment of what
life as an Indian was like from the eighteen-fifties on.

2889. Browne, J.R. The Indians of California. Colt Press.
San Francisco, 1944.
[Reservations and how little they helped the
Indians]

2890. Caughey, J.W. (ed.) The Indians of Southern California
in 1852: the B.D. Wilson report and a selection of
contemporary comment. Huntington LIbrary, San Marino,
1952.

2891. Cook, S.F. The conflict between the California Indian
and white civilization: III, the American invasion,
1848-1870. Ibero-Americana 23, 1943. Reprinted, 1976,
by University of California Press.
[Much on living conditions in this period]

2892. _____ The conflict between the California Indian, and
white civilization: IV, trends in marriage and
divorce since 1850. Ibero-Americana 24, 1943.
[Survey of marriage data]

2893. Currie, A.H. Bidwell rancheria. California Historical
Society Quarterly 36:313-325, 1957.
[Study of a Maidu Indian village "belonging" to
one of the Americans who held Mexican land grants
before 1846]

2894. Heizer, R.F. They were only Diggers. Ballena Press. Ramona,
        California, 1973.
        [Collection of 188 newspaper articles on California
        Indian-White relations, 1851-1866]

2895. Jackson, Helen Hunt. Glimpses of California and the missions.
        Little, Brown, and Company. Boston, 1902.
        [Pp. 103-161, "The Present Conditions of the Mission
        Indians in Southern California"]

2896. Painter, C.C. A visit to the Mission Indians of Southern
        California, and other western tribes. Office of
        Indian Rights Association, Philadelphia, 1886.

2897. Phillips, G.H. Chiefs and challengers: Indian resistance
        and cooperation in Southern California. University
        of California Press, 1975.

2898. Robinson, W.W. The Indians of Los Angeles: a story of the
        liquidation of a people. G. Dawson, Los Angeles,
        1952.

2899. Smith, G., R. Sexton and E. Koch. Juan Antonio, Cahuilla
        Indian Chief: a friend of the whites. Quarterly
        of the San Bernardino County Museum Association
        Vol. 8, No. 1, 1960.

        IV A: THE AFTERMATH OF CONQUEST (1873-1977): RESERVATION
               AFFAIRS; CONDITION OF INDIANS; ACCULTURATION

        In the eighteen-seventies the public conscience was
aroused by reports such as those by Ames (1874) and Wetmore
(Bureau of Indian Affairs 1875) pointing up the shameful
neglect of California Indians by the federal government.
Helen Hunt Jackson (Jackson and Kinney 1883) made her
voice heard, both officially and publicly through the
book A Century of Dishonor. Certain published works
dealing only with the Mission Indians may be found below
in Section IV B.

        The references cited here cover the last century of
relations between the federal government and California
Indians.

        A special aspect of acculturation, namely loan words
from Spanish or Russian adopted by the Indians, or names
for introduced domestic animals is discussed in Section I B
(Bright 1959, 1960; Oswalt 1958; Sawyer 1964).

        Included under the heading of "Condition of Indians"
are the subjects of health care, housing, employment, etc.
Education of Indians is treated separately in IV B.

2900. Ablon, J. Relocated American Indians in the San Francisco Bay area: concepts of acculturation, success and identity in the city. Unpublished Ph.D. dissertation. University of Chicago, 1963.
[Important study of Indians in an urban area]

2901. _____ Relocated American Indians in the San Francisco Bay area: social interaction and Indian identity. Human Organization 23:296-304, 1964.

2902. _____ American Indian relocation: problems of dependency and management in the city. Phylon 26:362-371, 1965.

2903. Aginsky, B.W. The interaction of ethnic groups: a case study of Indians and Whites. American Sociological Review 14:288-293, 1949.
[Observed changes in Pomo and white relations 1934 to 1948]

2904. American Friends Service Committee. Indians of California: past and present. American Friends Service Committee. San Francisco, n.d.
[A useful survey prepared by Frank Quinn]

2905. Angulo,J. de. Indians in overalls. Hudson Review III:327-377, 1950.

2906. Anonymous. Indian Agent H.N. Rust--conflict of interest. San Francisco Chronicle, August 27, 1892.
[Account of a venal Mission Indian agent's activites; reprinted in Reprints of various papers on California archaeology, ethnology and Indian history. R.F. Heizer, ed. Archaeological Research Facility, Berkeley, 1973]

2907. _____ Agua Caliente allotments. SM-M 23:91, 1949.

2908. _____ Use of public health and medical resources by American Indians in ten California counties. California's Health 20:73-76, 1962.

2909. Armsby, E.R. and J.G. Rockwell. New directions among Northern California Indians. The American Indian 4 (3):12-23, 1948.

2910. Bean, L.J. and C. Wood. The crisis in Indian health: a California sample. The Indian Historian 2 (3), 1969.

2911. Board of Indian Commissioners. Annual report of the Commissioner of Indian Affairs to the Secretary of the Interior. Government Printing Office, 1867-1932.
[Despite the fact that these are written by Indian Bureau officials they are of basic importance]

2912. Bourne, A.R. Some major aspects of the historical development of Palm Springs between 1880 and 1938, and in
addition a continuation of the historical changes
in the Indian land problems and four cultural
institutions until 1948. Unpublished M.A. thesis
in History, Occidental College, California, 1953.

2913. Bureau of Indian Affiars. Annual report of the Commissioner
of Indian Affairs to the Department of the Interior.
Government Printing Office, 1873-1934.

2914. _____ California Rancheria Task Force
report. Bureau of Indian Affairs, Sacramento Area
Office, 1972.

2915. Burrows, J. The vanished Miwoks of California. Montana
Magazine, Montana Historical Society 21:28-39, 1971.
[Recollections of the surviving Miwok at Murphys in the
1930's]

2916. Bushnell, J.H. From American Indian to Indian American:
the changing identity of the Hupa. AA 70:1108-1116,
1968.

2917. California Indian Legal Services, Inc. An explanation of
termination. California Indian Legal Services.
Berkeley, 1968.

2918. California State Department of Public Health. Use of
public health and medical resources by American
Indians in ten California counties. California Health
20 (10), 1962.

2919. Clarke, E.P. The decline of the Mission Indians: is the
Gringo to blame? Overland Monthly 25:89-92, 1895.
[Compare with J.M. Scanland, 1894]

2920. Commonwealth Club of California. Indians in California.
Transactions of the Commonwealth Club 21 (3), 1926.
San Francisco.
[Includes information on contemporary conditions]

2921. Cook. S.F. The mechanism and extent of dietary adaptation
among certain groups of California and Nevada
Indians. Ibero-Americana 18, 1941.
[Records persistence of old dietary preferences]

2922. _____ Migration and urbanization of the Indians of
California. Human Biology 15:33-45, 1943.
[Movement from rural to urban settings]

2923. _____ Racial fusion among the California and Nevada
Indians. Human Biology 15:153-165, 1943.

2924. Cook, S.F. The conflict between the California Indian and White civilization, IV: Trends in Marriage and Divorce Since 1850. Ibero-Americana 24, 1943.

2925. Culin, S. A summer trip among the Western Indians. Bulletin of the Free Museum of Science and Art of the University of Pennsylvania 3:1-21, 88-122, 143-175, 1901.
[Pp. 108-117, conditions and way of life of residents of Hoopa Reservation in 1900 as reported by a sympathetic and unofficial anthropological observer]

2926. Department of Industrial Relations, Division of Fair Employment Practices. American Indians in California. State of California, Department of Industrial Relations, Division of Fair Employment Practices. San Francisco, 1965.
[Statistics on residence in urban and reservation areas, educational attainment, employment, income, family size 1959-1960]

2927. Davis, A.R. The Indians of California today. Out West 33:337-344, 1911.
[History, education, relations with federal government]

2928. Davis, C.C. "Ramona"" the ideal and the real. Out West 19:575-596, 1903.
[Identifies the persons in Helen Hunt Jackson's book]

2929. Devereux, G. The function of alcohol in Mohave society. Quarterly Journal of Studies on Alcohol 9: 207-251, 1948.

2930. Devereux, G. and E.M. Loeb. Antagonistic acculturation. American Sociological Review 8:133-147, 1943.
[Mainly on the Mohave]

2931. Downs, J.F. The two worlds of the Washo. Holt, Rinehart, and Winston. New York, 1966.
[Summary of aboriginal Washo culture and survey of the Washo people in post-contact times]

2932. Drown, D.B. Indian grape pickers in California. Overland Monthly 65:554-558, 1915.

2933. Dyer, R.C. The Indians' land title in California: a case in federal equity, 1851-1942. R. and E. Research Associates, San Francisco, 1975.

2934. Ewers, R. Fig Tree John. Desert Magazine 30:6-7, 1953.
[True story of "Juanite Razon" colorful Cahuilla character upon which Edwin Coyale based his fictional account]

2935. Faye, P.L. Christmas fiestas of the Cupeno. AA 30: 651-
658, 1928.
[Observations in 1919 of changing customs]

2936. Fee, H.T. The Indians of Yosemite Valley. Overland Monthly
59:469-471, 1912.
[The Yosemite Miwok at this time]

2937. Fisher, A. Cathedral in the sun. New York: Carlyle House,
1940.
[Acculturation of Costanoan Indians]

2938. Forbes, A.S.C. Lace making by Indian women. Out West
16:613-616, 1902.

2939. Force, L. Letter to J.V. Farwell concerning health conditions
on the Hoopa Valley Reservation, July 20, 1871.
Serial No. 1505, House Executive Documents No. 1,
Part 5. 42nd Congress, 2nd Session, 1871.

2940. Foster, G.M. A summary of Yuki culture. UC-AR 5 (3), 1944.
[Pp. 219-222, recent religious movements, Ghost Dance,
Pentacostal Church]

2941. Freed, S.A. Changing Washo kinship. UC-AR 14 (6), 1960.
[Study of changes in Washo social organization in
the historic period]

2942. Freed, S.A. and R.S. The persistence of aboriginal ceremonies
among the Washo Indians. UU-AP No. 67:25-40, 1963.

2943. Fry, W.S. Humboldt Indians. Out West 21:503-514, 1904.
[Description of contemporary conditions among Hupa,
Yurok, and Wiyot. Changes in basketmaking in
response to collectors' preferences]

2944. Goldschmidt, W.R. and H.E. Driver. The Hupa White Deerskin
dance. UC-PAAE 35:103-142, 1940.
[The Deerskin Dance in 1935 and 1937 is described.
Particular attention is paid to changes then going
on and to differences developed since 1901]

2945. Gontz, T. Indians of the Hoopa reservation. Overland
Monthly 37:630-637, 1901.
[Contemporary conditions]

2946. Grinnell, G.B. The Indians of today. H.S. Stone, Chicago,
1900.
[Pp. 75-140, survey of various California reservations]

2947. Guidotti, T.L. Health care for a minority: lessons from
the Modoc Indian country in California. California
Medicine 118:98-104, 1973.

2948. Handelman, D. Transcultural shamanic healing: a Washo
example. Ethnos 32:149-166, 1967.

2949. Harvey, H.R. The Luiseno: an analysis of change in patterns
of land tenure and social structure. In American
Indian Ethnohistory, California Indians, Vol. 2:
97-206. Garland Publishing, New York, 1974.

2950. Heizer, R.F. and T.R. Hester. Names and locations of some
ethnographic Patwin and Maidu villages. UC-ARF-C 9:
79-118, 1970.
[Five ethnohistoric documents on numbers, village
names and locations]

2951. Hirshen, Gammill, Trumbo and Cook et al. A study of
existing physical and social conditions and the economic
potential of selected Indian rancherias and reservations
in California. Sacramento, 1976.
[Detailed study, 169 pp., of 19 rancherias in northern
California, 6 rancherias in Central California and
6 reservations in southern California. Physical,
historical, cultural, social and economic conditions
in 31 rancherias and reservations each with less than
640 acres. Each site report contains a map. Report
prepared with funds from U.S. Department of Housing
and Urban Development through Office of Planning and
Research, State of California, Sacramento. Report
prepared in part by Native American Training Associates,
Sacramento; State Department of Housing and Community
Development, Sacramento; California Indian Assistance
Programs; State of California Office of Planning and
Research]

2952. Hill, J.J. History of Warner's Ranch and its environs.
Privately printed. Los Angeles, 1927.

2953. Holmes, W.H. Anthropological studies in California.
USNM-AR 1900, pp. 155-188, 1902.
[Observations on living conditions of California
Indians at the turn of the century. The Pomo, Miwok,
and Mission Indians are discussed]

2954. House of Representatives. Indian tribes of California.
Hearings before the Subcommittee of the Committee on
Indian Affairs, House of Representatives, 66th
Congress, 2nd Session. March 23, 1920.
[Concerns HR 12788, The Raker Bill. On pp. 112-114
are responses to a questionnaire sent to County
health officers and physicians in California about
health care for non-reservation Indians]

2955. Indian Assistance Program: State of California: Dept. of
Housing and Community Development. Governmental
organization and legislative history. Sacramento, 1974.

2956. Indian Assistance Program: State of California: Dept. of Housing and Community Development. Report on implementation of recommendations contained in document entitled: Governmental organization and legislative history. Sacramento, 1975.

2957. Johnston, B.E. California's Gabrielino Indians. Southwest Museum, Hodge Anniversary Publication Fund, Vol. 8, 1962.
[Pp. 128-189, Gabrielino history during the mission, Mexican and American periods]

2958. Kasch, C. The Yokayo rancheria. California Historical Society Quarterly 26:209-216, 1947.
[A historical sketch]

2959. Kelsey, C.E. Memorial of the Northern California Indian Association. U.S. Senate, 58th Congress, 2d Session, Doc. No. 131, 1904.
[Asking for relief for landless Indians in northern California. Kelsey was Secretary of the Northern California Indian Association]

2960. _____ Report of the Special Agent for California Indians to the Commissioner of Indian Affairs. Carlisle Indian School Print, 1906.
[Kelsey was appointed as Special Agent by the Secretary of Interior through an Act of Congress approved June 30, 1905 "to investigate...existing conditions of the California Indians and to report to Congress"]

2961. _____ Census of non-reservation California Indians, 1905-1906. UC-ARF, 1971. Berkeley.
[Detailed census giving names of persons and location of landless Indians, mainly in northern California]

2962. Kennedy, M.J. Culture contact and acculturation of the Southwestern Pomo. Ph.D. dissertation. University of California, Berkeley, 1955.

2963. Klein, B.T. Reference encyclopedia of the American Indian. 2 vols. Todd Publication, Rye, New York, 1973.
[Vol. 1:165-170. List of California reservations, P.O. address, number of persons and tribes on each]

2964. Kroeber, A.L. The elusive Mill Creeks. Travel Magazine, August, 1911.
[The last remnant of the Yahi tribe]

2965. _____ California Indian population about 1910. UC-PAAE 47:218-225, 1957.
[Concludes there were 20,000]

2966. Kroeber, T. Ishi in two worlds. University of California Press. Berkeley, 1961.
[The definitive study of this interesting person]

2967. Kroeber, T.K. and R.F. Heizer (eds). Ishi: a documentary history. To be published by University of California Press, 1977.

2968. Lawton, H. Willie Boy: a desert manhunt. Paisano Press. Balboa Island, California, 1960.

2969. Lee, D.D. The linguistic aspect of Wintu acculturation. AA 45:435-440, 1940.

2970. Lee, R.L. Changes in Yuma social organization. Ethnology 2:207-277, 1963.

2971. Lee, S.W. A survey of acculturation in the intermontane area of the United States. Idaho State University Museum Occasional Papers No. 19, 1967.
[Treats briefly with what is known about this subject for western Great Basin and eastern California tribes]

2972. Lloyd, N. The Chumash: a study of the assimilation of a California Indian tribe. M.A. dissertation, University of Arizona, 1955.
[Chumash in the mid-twentieth century]

2973. Lummis, C.F. Reviving an ancient craft. Out West 23: 539-543, 1905.
[Revival of basket-making among the Mission Indians]

2974. MacGregor, G. The social and economic adjustment of the Indians of the Sacramento Jurisdiction of California. Proceedings of the (Fifth) Pacific Science Congress VI (iv):53-58, 1939.

2975. McLendon, S. Spanish words in Eastern Pomo. Romance Philology 23:39-53, 1969-1970.

2976. Martin, D.D. Indian-White relations on the Pacific slope, 1850-1890. Dissertation Abstracts (1969/70) pp. 4897A-4898A. UM 70-8423, 1970.

2977. Martin, L.J. A history of the Modoc Indians: an acculturation study. Chronicles of Oklahoma 47:398-446, 1969-1970.

2978. Mayall, D.H. Directed social change in a California Indian group (Pomo). Unpublished M.A. dissertation. University of California, Berkeley, 1958.

2979. Miller, J. Life amongst the Modocs. London, 1873.

213

2980. Miller, V.P. The 1870 Ghost Dance and the Methodists: an unexpected turn of events in Round Valley. JCA 3:66-74, 1976.

2981. Moriarty, J.R. Federal Indian reservations in San Diego county. American Indian Cultural Center Journal 4 (2): 13-25, 1973.

2982. _____ Accommodation and conflict resolution techniques among Southern California Indian groups. Southern California Quarterly 56 (2):109-121, 1974.

2983. Neuman, H.R. Implications of federal withdrawal from Indian affairs in California. Unpublished M.A. dissertation. University of California, Berkeley, 1953.

2984. Noble, W.B. A day with the Mono Indians. Out West 21: 413-421, 1904.
[Contemporary conditions among the Western Mono or Monache]

2985. Pilling, A.R. and P. Pilling. Cloth, clothes, hose and bows: nonsedentary merchants among the Indians of Northwestern California. In Migration and Anthropology, pp. 97-119. Proceedings of the 1970 Annual Spring Meeting of the American Ethnological Society. University of Washington Press, 1970.
[Interesting study of "cultural brokers", both white and Indian, among the Native Californians of Northwestern California]

2986. Price, J.A. Washo culture change. In 1962 Great Basin Anthropological Conference. Nevada State Museum Anthropological Papers, No. 9:40-54, 1963.

2987. _____ The migration and adaptation of American Indians to Los Angeles. Human Organization 27:168-175, 1968.

2988. _____ Cultural divergence related to urban proximity on American Indian reservations. University of Minnesota Training Center for Community Programs, 1971.

2989. Sabin, E.L. The Mission Indians: as they were and are. Touring Topics, July, pp. 12-19, 37, 1931.
[Some good pictures; information on extreme age reached by some Native Californians]

2990. Sargent, L. Indian dances in Northern California. The Californian 1:464-479, 1880.
[Excellent description of McCloud River Wintu camp and dances]

2991. Senate of the State of California. Senate Interim Committee on California Indian Affairs. Sacramento, California,

1955.
[Statistical report on land, education, etc]

2992. Senate of the State of California. Progress Report to the Legislature. Senate Interim Committee on California Indian Affairs, 1957. Sacramento.

2993. _____ Progress Report to the Legislature. Senate Interim Committee on California Indian Affairs, 1959. Sacramento.

2994. Seymour, C.F. Relations between the United States Government and the Mission Indians of Southern California. Unpublished M.A. thesis in History, University of California, Berkeley, 1924.

2995. Simirenko, A. Socio-economic variables in the acculturation process--a pilot study of two Washo communities. Educational Resources Information Center (HEW), ED No. 01834, 1966.

2996. Simoons, F.J. Changes in Indian life in the Clear Lake area, along the northern fringe of Mexican influence in early California. Americana Indigena XIII (2):103-108, 1953.
[An historical survey]

2997. Smith, W.H. In re California Indians to date. Out West 30: 130-147, 1909.
[Statement from Leupp, Indian Commissioner on Indian affairs in California; statement by C.E. Kelsey and others]

2998. Southern California Indian Congress. Proceedings of the conference for the Indians of Southern California. Held at Riverside, California, March 17, 18, 1934, to discuss the Wheeler-Howard Indian Bill. Mimeographed, no place given, 1934.
[66 pp.]

2999. State Advisory Commission on Indian Affairs. Progress report to the Governor and the Legislature on Indians in rural and reservation areas. California Office of State Printing. Sacramento, 1966.
[Detailed report on social and economic conditions of California Indians based on investigations made in 1964. Includes data on distribution of Indian population, patterns of migration, analyzes the California Roll of 1950, surveys conditions of Indians on reservations and in rural areas as regards employment, education, health, welfare, law and justice. Contains a map showing location and number of Indians in each county. An important body of data which cannot be

found in any other source]

3000. State Advisory Commission on Indian Affairs. Final report to the Governor and Legislature. Sacramento, California, 1969.

3001. Stewart, K.M. Chemehuevi (Southern Paiute) culture changes. Plateau 40:14-21, 1967.

3002. Susman, A. The Round Valley Indians of California. UC-ARF-C 31, 1976. Berkeley.
[Historical survey of the Round Valley reservation and abundant observations on culture change in 1937]

3003. Sutton, I. Private property in land among reservation Indians in Southern California. Yearbook of the Association of Pacific Coast Geographers 29:69-89, 1967.

3004. _____ Indian land tenure: bibliographical essays and a guide to the literature. Clearwater Publ. Co., New York and Paris, 1975.
[The fullest and best treatment of this subject yet done]

3005. Taber, C. California and her Indian children. Northern California Indian Association. San Jose, 1911.

3006. Theodoratus, D.J. Identity crises: changes in life style of the Manchester band of Pomo Indians. Unpublished Ph.D. dissertation, Syracuse University, 1971.
[Acculturation of Central Coast Pomo]

3007. _____ Cultural and social change among the Central Coast Pomo. Journal of California Anthropology 1 (2): 206-219, 1974.
[Acculturation of Central Coast Pomo or Bokeya]

3008. Thomas, R.M. The Mission Indians: a study of leadership and cultural change. Unpublished Ph.D. dissertation in Anthropology, UCLA, 1964.

3009. Treganza, A.E., E.S. Taylor and W.W. Wallace. The Hindil, a Pomo Indian dance in 1946. SM-M 21:119-125, 1947.

3010. Trennert, R.A. The far western Indian frontier and the beginnings of the reservation system, 1846-1851. Unpublished Ph.D. dissertation in History, University of California, Santa Barbara.

3011. True, C.D. Experiences of a woman Indian agent. Outlook 92:331-336, 1909.

3012. Wood, C.S. A multiphase health screening of three Southern California Indian reservations. Social Science and

Medicine 4:579-587, 1970.

3013. U.S. Department of Interior. Memorandum from Commission of
Indian Affairs to all employees. Bureau of Indian
Affairs. Washington, 1963.
[Tabulates California Indian Reservations, land areas
in acres and population in 1962-1963]

3014. U.S. Senate Committee on Indian Affairs. Senate Report
No. 1522, 48th Congress, 2d Session. Mr. Davies,
Committee on Indian Affairs, Report on the Round
Valley reservation investigation. Washington, 1885.

3015. U.S. Senate Subcommittee on the Committee on Indian Affairs.
A survey of the conditions of the Indians in the
United States, Part II. Government Printing Office, 1929.
[Includes hearings at San Francisco and Riverside
in November, 1928, with verbatim transcript of
testimony given by Indians and Indian welfare workers]

3016. _____ A survey of the conditions of Indians in
the United States, Vol. II. Government Printing Office,
1932.
[California is included]

3017. Waterman, T.T. The Yana Indians. UC-PAAE 13 (2), 1918.
[History of the destruction of the Yahi Indian tribe]

3018. Walker, F.A. The Indian question. J.R. Osgood. Boston,
1874.
[California Indians, pp. 263-268]

3019. White, R.C. Two surviving Luiseno ceremonies. AA 55:
569-578, 1953.

3020. Wilson, B. Ukiah Valley Pomo religious life, supernatural
doctoring, and beliefs: observations of 1939-1941.
UC-AS-R 72, 1968.
[Recorded memories of pre-contact religious cults;
detailed record of the Maru Cult and transition to
Christianity]

3021. Woodward, J.A. The anniversary: a contemporary Diegueno
complex. Ethnology 7:86-94, 1968.

IV B: THE AFTERMATH OF CONQUEST (1873-1977): CONDITION
OF MISSION INDIANS OF SOUTHERN CALIFORNIA (1874-1973)

Published accounts of the neglect by federal
authorities of the so-called Mission Indians, who com-
prised the survivors of tribes south of Los Angeles, are
numerous. Some of these are cited in this section, and
more will be found in IV A.

3022. Ames, J.G. Mission Indians of Southern California. House of
      Representatives, 43d Congress, 1st Session, Executive
      Document No. 91. Washington, 1874.
      [Report on conditions of the neglected and abused
      Mission Indian tribes]

3023. _____ Report of Special Agent John G. Ames in regard
      to the condition of the Mission Indians of California,
      with recommendations. Report of the Commissioner of
      Indian Affairs for 1873, Appendix A, pp. 29-40, 1874.
      [Reprinted in Reprints of various papers on California
      archaeology, ethnology and Indian history. R.F.
      Heizer, Ed. UC-ARF 1973]

3024. Bureau of Indian Affairs. A report of Charles A. Wetmore,
      Special United States Commissioner to the Mission
      Indians. GPO, Washington, 1875, D.C.

3025. DuBois, C.G. The condition of the Mission Indians of
      Southern California. Indian Rights Association.
      Philadelphia, 1901.

3026. _____ Our American "Reconcentrados" (Mission Indians)
      Indian Rights Association, 18th Annual report 1901:
      29-30, 1901.
      [Conditions and needs of Mission Indians]

3027. Foote, K. Mission Indians taxed and untaxed. United States
      Department of the Interior Census Office, 11th Census.
      (Pp. 207-216). Government Printing Office, 1890.

3028. Forbes, J.D. Indians of Southern California in 1888. SM-M
      33:71-76, 1959.
      [Summarizes data from C.F. Holder's All about Pasadena
      and its vicinity, 1889]

3029. H.H. (Helen Hunt Jackson). The present condition of the
      Mission Indians in Southern California. The Century
      Magazine, August, 1883:511-529, 1883.

3030. Hill, J. History of Warner's Ranch and its environs.
      Los Angeles: privately published, 1927.

3031. House of Representatives. Indian reservation in San Diego
      County, California. House of Representatives, 41st
      Congress, 2d Session, Ex. Doc. No. 296. Washington,
      1870.
      [Establishment of reservation on San Pasqual and Pala
      Valleys, 1870]

3032. _____ Relief of certain Mission Indians in California.
      House of Representatives, 57th Congress, 1st Session.
      Doc. No. 319. Washington, 1902.
      [Federal action to aid Indians]

218

3033. Humphrey, S.K. The Indian dispossessed. Little, Brown and Co. Boston, 1906.
[Pp. 202-245, Mission Indians and their treatment by the Government]

3034. Indian Rights Association. The case of the Mission Indians in Southern California and the actions of the Indian Rights Association in supporting the defense of their legal rights. Indian Rights Association, Philadelphia, 1886.

3035. _____ The pressing needs of the Warner Ranch and other Mission Indians in Southern California. Indians Rights Association, Philadelphia, 1901.

3036. _____ Annual report of the executive committee of the IRA. Philadelphia, 1897-1913.
[Known to the compilers of this bibliography and dealing with California Indians, mostly Mission Indians, is Annual Report No. 14 for 1896 (1897) through Annual Report No. 31 for 1913 (1914)]

3037. Jackson, H. and A. Kinney. Report on the condition and needs of the Mission Indians of California, made by special agents Helen Jackson and Abbot Kinney, to the Commissioner of Indian Affairs. Appendix XV, Report of the Commissioner of Indian Affairs for 1883.

3038. Lewis, F.D. The Warner Ranch Indians and why they were moved to Pala. Overland Monthly 42:171-173, 1903.

3039. Lummis, C.F. A new Indian policy. Land of Sunshine 15: 457-464, 1901.
[A proposal for fair treatment of the Mission Indians]

3040. _____ The exiles of Cupa. Out West 16:465-479, 1902.
[Present conditons of Warners Ranch or Cupeno Indians]

3041. _____ The Mission Indians. Outlook 74:738-742, 1903.
[Relations with and treatment by federal agencies]

3042. _____ Condition of the Mission Indians in 1905. Sequoya League Bulletin II, 1905.

3043. Painter, C.C. A visit to the Mission Indians. Indian Rights Association, Philadelphia, 1886.

3044. _____ The present condition of the Mission Indians of California. Indian Rights Association, Philadelphia, 1887.

3045. _____ Conditions of Indian affairs in Indian Territory and California. Indian Rights Association, Philadelphia, 1888.

3046. Parker, H. The Temecula massacre. Paisano Press, Balboa, 1971.

3047. Polley, F. Life today in the Pala Mission station. Annual Publication of the Historical Society of Southern California 3 (1):41-46, 1893.

3048. Rust, H.N. Rogerio's theological school. Out West 21: 243-248, 1904.
[Story of Rogerio Rocha, a Fernandeno Indian]

3049. Scanland, J.M. The decline of the Mission Indians: was it the fault of the Padres? Overland Monthly 24:634-639, 1894.
[Compare with E.P. Clarke, 1895, cited in IV A]

3050. Smith, W.H. The scattered sheep of Mission flocks. Out West 27:332-342, 1907.
[Present condition of Indian affairs in Southern California]

3051. Wallace, G. The exiles of Cupa. Out West 19:25-41, 1903.
[Account of the removal of 98 Warners Ranch Indians to Pala]

3052. Warner's Ranch Indian Commission. Turning a new leaf. Out West 18:445, 589-602, 1903.
[Full report by the Commission on treatment of Warner Ranch Indians]

3053. Williams, E.L. The old Mission Indians. Overland Monthly 15: 461-466, 1890.
[Habits of Mission Indians and examination of the old age they are reputed to attain]

3054. Williamson, M.B. Saboba Indians of Southern California. Out West 30:148-158, 1909.
[Present social conditions and way of life on Saboba Reservation]

3055. Women's National Indian Association. The Ramona Mission and the Mission Indians. Place of publication not given, 1889.
[Ramona is a Cahuilla reservation of 560 acres of Indian Trust land. Today no Indians live there]

IV C: THE AFTERMATH OF CONQUEST (1873-1977): EDUCATION

Articles treating recent and current trends in Indian education are also cited here. An important source is Berry (1968). See also State Advisory Commission on Indian Affairs (1966) cited above in IV A.

Beginning in 1969 several major Universities and colleges in the state of California instituted Ethnic Studies Departments. Many of these included Native American Studies programs in response to the need to develop a Native American perspective. Unfortunately no comprehensive survey of these programs exists, and a valuable service would be to conduct such an assessment.

3056. Ad Hoc Committee on California Indian Education. California Indian education: report on the first all-Indian statewide conference on California Indian education. Modesto, California, 1967.

3057. Anonymous. Lame dancing-masters: an Indian viewpoint of government schools. Land of Sunshine 12:356-358, 1900.
[Critical review of Indian education written by an unnamed Native Californian]

3058. Barcus, W.F. A controlled study of Indian and White children in the Sierra Joint Union High School District, Tollhouse, Fresno County, California. Unpublished M.A. thesis, Fresno State College, 1956.

3059. Barth, P.J. Franciscan education and the social order in Spanish North America, 1501-1821. Unpublished Ph.D. thesis, University of Chicago, 1945.

3060. Berry, B. The education of American Indians: a survey of the literature. Research Foundation, Ohio State University. Final Report of Project No. 7-0813; Contract No. OEC-3-7-070813-3032, United States Department of Health, Education and Welfare, Office of Education, Bureau of Research. Typescript, 176 pp., 1968.
[An important survey; extensive bibliography]

3061. Cooper, G., K. Martin and R. Cook. California Indian Education Association, Fifth Annual State Conference and American Indian Education Workshops. California Indian Education Association. Modesto, 1973.

3062. House of Representatives. Hearings before a Subcommittee of the Committee on Indian Affairs. 66th Congress, 2d Session, 1920.
[Pp. 109-112, responses to a questionnaire sent to County Superintendents of Schools in California on grade school education of Indian children]

3063. _____ Hearing before the Subcommittee on Indian Affairs of the Committee on Interior and Insular Affairs. House of Representatives, United States Congress, 1st Session, 1963.
[California relocation centers and vocational training authorized by Public Law 959 of 1956]

3064. Lund, B.F. A Survey of comparative achievement and scholar-
ship records of California Indian children in the
Auburn Public Schools. Unpublished M.A. thesis,
Sacramento State College, 1963.
[Although limited in the coverage this is one of the
few studies made]

3065. McHugh, J.J. Educational aspects of the Mission systems
in Upper California. Unpublished M.A. dissertation,
Catholic University of America, 1922.

3066. Porter, M.L. Indian education in the United States, with
special reference to the California Indians. Unpublished M.A. thesis, San Francisco State College,
1956.

3067. Rosenfelt, D.M. Indian schools and community control.
Stanford Law Review 25 (4):492-550, 1973.

3068. Walker, H.P. Teacher to the Mohaves: the experiences of
George W. Nock, 1887-1889. Arizona and the West
9:143-166, 1967.

3069. Vassar, R. The Fort Bidwell, California, Indian school:
a study of the federal Indian education policy,
1898-1930. Unpublished M.A. thesis, University of
California, Berkeley, 1953.

3070. Wallace, W.J. Hupa education: a study in primitive
socialization and personality. Unpublished Ph.D.
dissertation. University of California, Berkeley,
1946.

IV D: THE AFTERMATH OF CONQUEST (1873-1973):
RELIGIOUS MOVEMENTS

The Ghost Dance of 1870 (DuBois 1939, Gayton 1930)
seemed to offer some hope of a return to the old pre-
White way of life through the revivalistic cult practices,
but this soon subsided. In Central California some
tribes fused the Ghost Dance beliefs with the older
Kuksu Cult(Meighan and Riddell 1972; Wilson 1968).

3071. DuBois, C. The 1870 Ghost Dance, UC-AR 3(1), 1939.

3072. Gayton, A.H. The Ghost Dance of 1870 in South-central
California. UC-PAAE 28:57-82, 1930.

3073. Gilmour, J.H. An Indian prophet: a Banning witch doctor's forebodings. San Francisco Chronicle (newspaper), June 17, 1892.
[Reprinted in UC-AR 15, No. 2, pp. 155-156, 1955]
[Possible evidence of the Ghost Dance]

3074. Meighan, C. and F. Riddell. The Maru Cult of the Pomo Indians: a California Ghost Dance survival. SM-P 23, 1972.
[The Maru Cult is partly an outgrowth of the historic Ghost Dance Religion of the last century]

3075. Nash, P. The place of religious revivalism in the formation of the intercultural community on Klamath Reservation. In Social Anthropology of North American Tribes, F. Eggan, ed., pp. 375-442. University of Chicago Press, 1955.

3076. Valory, D. The focus of Indian Shaker healing. KAS-P 35: 69-111, 1966.

3077. White, R.C. Luiseno social organization. UC-PAAE 48:91-194, 1963.
[Traces changes through the historic period]

3078. Wilson, B. Ukiah Valley Pomo religious life, supernatural doctoring, and beliefs: observations of 1939-1941. UC-AS-R 72. Berkeley, 1968.

IV E: THE AFTERMATH OF CONQUEST (1873-1973): LEGAL STATUS OF INDIANS

The best study of Indians and the law is by Goodrich (1926). Certain important state laws and Court decisions affecting Indians are cited here.

Legal prohibitions such as those concerning voting, buying liquor, possessing firearms and going to school are briefly referred to in Heizer and Almquist (1971--cited in III B).

An excellent survey of discriminatory legislation aimed at California Indians is the article by Fernandez (1968).

Compare the listing here in IV E with that for the period 1846-1873 in Section III A.

3079. Aschenbrenner, P.J. State power and the Indian treaty right to fish. California Law Review 59 (2): 485-524, 1971.

3080. Bussellen, H.J., Jr. A study of the federal termination of a California rancheria and its effects upon the social and economic integration of the Indian population involved. Unpublished M.A. thesis in History, California State University, Sacramento, 1962.

3081. California Statutes 1869-1870, Chap. 556, par. 56.
[Education of Indian children must be in separate schools]

3082. California Statutes 1880, Chap. 44, par. 62.
[Separate school requirement for Indian children eliminated]

3083. California Statutes 1887.
[California Indians who moved away from their tribe and adopted the habits of "civilized life" became U.S. citizens. Cal. 24, Stat. 390, 1887]

3084. California Statutes 1893, Chap. 193, par. 33.
[Reinstatement of requirement that Indian children attend separate schools at the discretion of Boards of Trustees]

3085. California Statutes 1921, Chap. 685, par. 1.
[Indians living within 3 miles of a school established by the U.S. Government for Indians were not permitted to enter California public schools]

3086. California Supreme Court, 1924, Piper vs. Big Pine School District, 193 Cal. 664, 226 P.
[Held that separate schooling for Indian children as specified in Cal Stat. 1921, Chap. 658, par. 1 was unconstitutional]

3087. Court of Claims of the United States. No. K-344, decided October 5, 1942. The Indians of California, Claimants, by U.S. Webb, Attorney General of the State of California v. the United States. GPO, Washington, 1943.

3088. District Court of Appeals. Acosta v. San Diego County, et. al. 92 Cal., 272 Pac., 1954.
[Welfare rights of reservation Indians]

3089. Ericson, R. and D.R. Snow. The Indian battle for self-determination. California Law Review 58 (2):445-490, 1970.

3090. Fay, G.E. Charters, constitutions and by-laws of the Indian tribes of North America. Part VIII, The Indian tribes of California (cont'd). University of Northern Colorado. Occasional Publications in Anthropology Ethnology Series, No. 9. Greeley, Colorado, 1970.

3091. Fernandez, F.F. Except a California Indian: a study in legal discrimination. Southern California Quarterly 50:161-176, 1968.
[Excellent survey of discriminatory legislation aimed at denying California Indians certain citizens' rights]

3092. Goodrich, C.S. The legal status of the California Indian. California Law Review 14:83-100, 157-187, 1926.

3093. House of Representatives, Committee on Indian Affairs. Reservation courts of Indian offenses. Hearings before the Committee on Indian Affairs, House of Representatives, Sixty-Ninth Congress, First Session on H.R. 7826. Government Printing Office, 1926.
[Contains a number of statements by Indians given in hearings of the Committee]

3094. Indian Rights Association. The case of the Mission Indians in Southern California and the action of the Indian Rights Association in supporting the defense of their legal rights. Indian Rights Association. Philadelphia, 1886.

3095. People v. Bray. 105 Cal. 344, 1894.
[Selling liquor to Indians. See also California Penal Code, Sec. 397, amended Stats. of 1893, p. 98]

3096. Sondheim, H.B. and J.R. Alexander. Federal Indian water rights: a retrogression to quasi-riparianism. Southern California Law Review 34 (1):1-61, 1960.

3097. Supreme Court of the State of California. Thompson v. Doaksum. 68 Cal. 593; 10 Pac. 199 (1886).
[Land title]

3098. _____ Byrne v. Alas. 74 Cal. 628 (1888).
[Rancherias on Mexican land grants]

3099. _____ Anderson v. Mathews. 174 Cal. 537, 163 Pac. 902 (1917).
[Citizenship of non-reservation Indians]

3100. U.S. Supreme Court. Botiller v. Dominguez. 130 U.S. 238 (1889).
[Land title]

3101. _____ Barker v. Harvey. 181 U.S. 481 (1901).
[Cupa expulsion order]

IV F: THE AFTERMATH OF CONQUEST (1873-1973): CLAIMS
CASES

A most important court case of the
California Indians as plaintiffs and the federal
government as defendants, was K344 (Johnson 1966)
in 1928 which resulted in 1944 in an award of
$5,024,842. The Indian Claims Commission Act of
August 13, 1946, enabled California Indians to sue
for all remaining claims (Stewart 1961), and in 1965
a settlement of $29,100,000 was secured (Forbes 1969--
cited in I D1).

3102. Bailey, L. The Indian problem in California, 1848-1860.
        Unpublished M.A. dissertation, Stanford University,
        1933.

3103. Barker, R.W. The Indian Claims Commission--the conscience
        of the nation in its dealings with the original
        American. Federal Bar Journal 20:240-247, 1960.

3104. Barney, R.A. Legal problems peculiar to Indian Claims
        litigation. Ethnohistory 2:315-325, 1955.

3105. _____ Some legal problems under the Indian Claims
        Commission Act. Federal Bar Journal 20:235-239,
        1960.

3106. Bureau of Indian Affairs. List of enrolled California
        Indians entitled to per capita payment when addresses
        are reported. B.I.A., Sacramento Area Office, 1954.
        Mimeographed, 196 pp.
        [Contains names of persons on 1933 Roll, on Part II
        of 1933 Roll, Supplemental; and the Roll approved
        November 23, 1951]

3107. Cutter, D.C. Clio and the California claims case.
        Journal of the West 13:35-38, 1975.
        [Author was an expert witness for the Indian plaintiffs]

3108. Heizer, R.F. and A.L. Kroeber. For sale: California at 47
        cents per acre. JCA 3:38-65, 1976.
        [Courtroom testimony of 1955 in California Claims
        Case on the federal government's "ecological theory"
        on California Indian land use]

3109. Horr, D.A. (ed.) American Indian ethnohistory. Garland
        Publishing Company. New York, 1974.
        [An encyclopaedic, 118 volume, coverage of the Indian
        Claims Commission Act of 1946. Includes 6 volumes on
        California, the data being overweighted in terms of the
        Defendant's reports. Since the Plaintiffs, the
        California Indians, won the suit, it is curious that
        so much space is given to providing information which

the Indian Claims Commissioners judged to be inadequate]

3110. House of Representatives, Subcommittee on Indian Affairs.
Indian Tribes of California. Hearings before a
Subcommittee of the Committee on Indian Affairs.
Sixty-sixth Congress, Second Session (March 23, 1920).
[This hearing concerned the Raker Bill. Included are
statements by E.B. Meritt, Assistant Commissioner of
Indian Affairs; F.G. Collett, Executive Representative
of the Indian Board of Cooperation; M. McDowell, Board
of Indian Commissioners; responses, pp. 109-112, to a
questionnaire sent to County Superintendents of Schools]

3111. _____ Hearing before the Subcommittee of the Committee
on Indian Affairs. House of Representatives, 67th
Congress, 2d Session. Part II. Government Printing
Office, 1922.
[Information gathering re K344]

3112. _____ Indian Tribes of California. House of
Representatives, Hearing before a Subcommittee of the
Committee on Indian Affairs, 69th Congress, 1st Session
on H.R. 8036 and H.R. 9497. Washington, 1926.
[Re K344]

3113. _____ A review of California Indian affairs. Washington,
1963.

3114. _____ To provide for the disposition of funds appropri-
ated to pay a judgment in favor of certain Indians in
California. Washington, 1966.
[Case K344--see Johnson 1966]

3115. House of Representatives. S. 1651. Report No. 1736.
Union Calendar No. 631. House of Representatives,
75th Congress, 3d Session. Washington, 1938.

3116. Johnson, K.M. K344, or the Indians of California vs. the
United States. Dawson Book Shop. Los Angeles,
1966.

3117. Kenny, R.W. History and proposed settlement, claims of
California Indians. California State Library, Docu-
ments Section. California State Printing Office,
Sacramento, 1944.
[Re K344]

3118. LeDuc, T. The work of the Indian Claims Commission under
the Act of 1946. Pacific Historical Review 26 (1):
1-16, 1957.

3119. Mission Indian Federation, Inc. California Indians charge
violation of Indian Claims Act of 1946. Place of

publication not given, 1966.
[40 pp. reproduces many documents, letters, newspaper articles]

3120. Robinson, W.W. Land in California. University of California Press, 1948.
[Pp. 19-20 claims cases]

3121. Rogers, W. California Indians--Jurisdictional Act. House of Representatives, 75th Congress, 3d Session, Report No. 1736. Washington, 1938.

3122. Ross, N.A. Index to the decisions of the Indian Claims Commission. New York: Clearwater Publishing Company, 1973.

3123. _____ Index to the expert testimony before the Indian Claims Commission: the written reports. New York: Clearwater Publishing Company, 1973.

3124. Stewart, O.C. Kroeber and the Indian Claims Commission cases. KAS-P 25:181-190, 1961.

3125. _____ Anthropologists as expert witnesses for Indians: claims and peyote cases. The Indian Historian Press, San Francisco, 1973.

3126. U.S. Commission on Civil Rights. Report No. 5, Justice Department. Washington, 1961.
[Includes data from California. Notes segregated schools in Round Valley until 1958; avoidance of providing welfare services, etc]

V A: PERIOD OF INDIAN NATIONALISM (1920-1973): INDIAN WELFARE ORGANIZATIONS

Organizations devoted to Indian welfare usually operate on a rather informal basis, at least as regards their newsletters. We have not found any complete files of these, and suggest that a useful project for some student would be to draw up a complete list of such orgnizations, the years of their operation, repository of the records of these associations, and a listing of libraries which hold complete or partial files of newsletters.

3127. American Friends Service Committee. (Full citation in section IV A), n.d.
[P. 36, partial list of state and national Indian welfare organizations]

3128. American Indian Defense Associaton. Bulletin.
[The AIDA was established February 27, 1923. It was

228

preceded by the Indian Defense Association of Santa
Barbara. John Collier was the moving spirit in AIDA
until he became Commissioner of Indian Affairs. Duration
of the Association's active life not known - to 1933?]

3129. Bureau of Catholic Missions. The Indian Sentinel. Washington,
1910.

3130. Indian Board of Cooperation. California Indian Herald.
Vol. 1, No. 1, January, 1923.
[Duration of publication not known for certain. G.W.
James was editor 1920-1923; the latter year marking
his death. He was succeeded by F.W. Collett, Executive
Director, who died in 1955]

3131. Indian Rights Association. Annual report of the Executive
Committee. Indian Rights Association Press.
Philadelphia, 1888-1904.

3132. Indian Rights Association, Inc. Indian Truth. (ed. by
M.K. Sniffen), 1924-?

3133. Jordan, D.S. Helping the Indians: what the Riverside
Indian conference accomplished--demand for homes,
physicians, educators, and protection. Sunset
Magazine 22:57-61, 1909.
[See also C.F. Lummis, 1908]

3134. Kelsey, C.E. The rights and wrongs of the California
Indians. Transactions of the Commonwealth Club of
California 4:417-429, 1909-1910.
[See other writings of Kelsey cited in the present
bibliography]

3135. Lummis, C. (ed.) The Sequoyah League Bulletin. Los Angeles,
1901-1911 (?).

3136. _____ Getting together. Out West 27:504-508,
1908.
[Report on the Indian Conference at Riverside held
April 27-29, 1908. See also Jordan 1909]

3137. Northern California Indian Association. Newsletter. Mount
Hermon, California, 1906-?

3138. _____ Memorial of the Northern California Indian
Association. (Full reference in section IV A).
[Report on numbers and condition of California Indians
in 1904 and memorial to Congress signed by officers
of the Association]

3139. "Spectator". Account of an Indian conference held in California
for the purpose of giving the California Indians an
opportunity of telling their needs. Outlook 89:104-
106, 1908.

3140. State Senate Interim Committee on California Indian Affairs.
Progress report to the Legislature. Sacramento, 1955.
[Pp. 56-86, list of Indian welfare organizations and
political organizations of Indians]

3141. Watkins, F.E. Charles F. Lummis and the Sequoyah League.
Quarterly of the Historical Society of Southern
California, Vol. 26:99-114, 1944.

V B: PERIOD OF INDIAN NATIONALISM (1920-1973):
POLITICAL ORGANIZATIONS OF INDIANS

As in the just-mentioned list of Indian welfare
organizations, there is a real need for an information
survey to be made.

3142. American Indian Historical Society, J. Henry, ed. The
Indian Historian. San Francisco, 1964-____.

3143. California Indian Education Association, K. Black, ed.
The Early American. (Bimonthly newsletter). Modesto,
California, 1969-____.

3144. California League for American Indians. San Francisco,
(Newsletter).

3145. California Rural Indian Health Board. C.R.I.H.B. Project
News. (Quarterly newsletter). Berkeley, 1970-1973.

3146. Colorado River Tribal Council Smoke Signals (newsletter),
1955-____.

3147. Council of California Indians, Inc. San Francisco, California.
(Newsletter).

3148. Human Rights Commission. California Indian directory.
Human Rights Commission, Native American Advisory
Committee. San Francisco, 1971.

3149. Inter-Tribal Council of California. The Tribal Spokesman.
Sacramento, California, 1964-____.

3150. Indians of All Tribes. Alcatraz is not an island. Wingbow
Press. Berkeley, 1972.

3151. Mission Indian Federation. Collection of newspaper clippings
from period 1920-1930 in Bancroft Library. University
of California. Berkeley.

3152. Northern California Brotherhood of Indians. File in C. Hart
Merriam Collection. Department of Anthropology.
University of California. Berkeley, 1920-1930.

3153. State of California Department of Housing and Urban
Development. California Indian assistance program
field directory. Sacramento, 1976.
[Part I (pp. 1-76), important assessment of trust
lands, tribal information and location maps of
rancherias and reservations; Part II (unnumbered)
gives directory of California Indian organizations,
addresses and names of Chairmen and Executive Directors]

3154. State of California Indian Assistance Program. Field
directory of the California Indian community.
California Department of Housing and Community
Development. Sacramento, 1976.
[Detailed maps of Trust Lands and Directory of
California Indian Organizations, State and Federal
Services]

V C: PERIOD OF INDIAN NATIONALISM (1920-1973): RECENT
INDIAN NATIONALISM

The occupation of Alcatraz Island and the Pit
River Struggle are discussed in the references listed here
(see also VII C). San Francisco daily papers (Chronicle,
Examiner) followed these events closely and it would be
useful to have a list of these, as well as of court cases
and official government communications. This has not yet
been done to our knowledge.

3155. Akwesasne Notes. Vol. I 1961 to date. All volumes are
available in microfilm from 3M International Microfilm Press, 3M Center, St. Paul, Minnesota.
[This material contains articles and essays regarding
contemporary political, social and economic conditions among California Indians]

3156. Barton, C.W. Riverside's new Indian school. Sunset Magazine 7:153-156, 1901.
[Report on the recently established Sherman Insitute]

3157. Castillo, E. Twentieth century secular movements. Manuscript to appear in Vol. VIII, Handbook of North
American Indians. Smithsonian Institution, 1977.

3158. Costo, R. Alcatraz. Indian Historian, n.s., 3:4-12,
64, 1970.

3159. Glazier, H. Bridgeport Paiutes meet Catch-22. In Personal
reflections of the Shoshone, Paiute, Washo; pp. 6-9.
Intertribal Council of Nevada. University of Utah
Printing Service, 1974.

3160. Hyatt, E. The Indian and our public schools. Out West 39:
110-112, 1914.

3161. Indians of All Tribes. The Clear Lake statement. Clear Creek,
No. 5, August, 1971.
[Newspaper. Pomo occupation of Rattlesnake Island,
Clear Lake, California Spring, 1970]

3162. _____ Alcatraz, more than an island. Clear Creek, No. 6,
September, 1971.
[Newspaper]

3163. March, Ray. On the 40th day of the Indian occupation of
Alcatraz Island. San Francisco Business, February,
1970: 34-40.
[Magazine]

3164. Oaks, R. Alcatraz is not an island. Ramparts Magazine,
December, 1972:35-40; 67.

3165. Wassaja. Published by the American Indian Historical
Society. San Francisco, 1973.
[Newspaper. Bi-monthly national and local Indian
newspaper; contains contemporary news concerning
Native Americans. Wide-ranging in topics; thorough;
balanced]

VI. WORKS WRITTEN BY INDIANS

Listed here are a series of works by Indian authors.
In one sense all of the ethnographic and ethno-historic
record can be considered to be technically of Indian
authorship with the ethnographer acting as the recorder.

The earliest Indian-authored writing from California
is Captain Salvador Palma's letter of 1776 (Palma 1967).
Two dictated personal narratives by former mission neophytes
(Cesar 1879; Lorenzo Asisara 1892) are unique documents.
Indian-dictated or Indian-written versions of the Bloody
Island massacre of 1850 by Augustine (1881) and Benson
(1932) do not altogether agree with the official account by
Captain Nathaniel Lyon (Heizer 1973--cited in IIIB).

3166. Adams, Jane. Autobiography of Jane Adams. In E. Colson,
Autobiographies of three Pomo women:215-216. UC-ARF,
1974.
[Life history of Jane Adams, fictional name for the
person involved]

3167. Aginsky, B.W. An Indian's soliloquy. American Journal of
Sociology 46:43-44, 1940.
[Concerns the Pomo; a remarkable document]

3168. Allen, E. Pomo basket making, a supreme art for the weaver.
Naturegraph Publications. Healdsburg, California, 1972.
[Life story of a Pomo woman born in 1899; her experi-
ences in Indian schools]

3169. Allen, J. Chief of the Pomos: life story of Allen James. A. Connor, ed. Santa Rosa, 1972.
[A remarkable personal document of a Kashia Pomo born in 1904; covers period up to about 1933]

3170. Angulo, J. de and W.R. Benson. The creation myth of the Pomo Indians. Anthropos 28:261-274; 779-796, 1932.
[Benson is a Pomo]

3171. Asisaro, Lorenzo. The death of Padre Andres Quintana. Story of the rebellion at Santa Cruz Mission and the murder of Quintana. Told to Lorenzo by his father Venancio Azar, gardener of the Mission of Santa Cruz. In J.M. Amador, Memorias sobre la Historia de California, manuscript in Bancroft Library, 1877.

3172. Augustine, Chief. Indian versions of the Bloody Island massacre of 1850. In L.L. Palmer, History of Napa and Lake Counties, California. Slocum, Bowen and Co. San Francisco, 1881.
[An Indian's account of the massacre]
[Reprinted in Heizer 1973--cited in III]

3173. Azbill, H. Native dances. Indian Historian, Vol. I, No. 1, 1968.

3174. _____ Maidu Indians of California. Indian Historian, 4(2):21-27, 1971.

3175. Bean, L.J. and K.S. Saubel. Temalpakh. Malki Museum Press. Banning, California, 1968.
[Ms. Saubel is a Cahuilla Indian]

3176. Benson, W.R. The Stone and Kelsey "massacre" on the shores of Clear Lake in 1849: the Indian viewpoint. California Historical Society Quarterly 11:266-273, 1932.
[Reprinted in Heizer 1973--cited in IIIB]

3177. Brown, Mable. Autobiography of Mable Brown. In E. Colson, Autobiographies of three Pomo women:99-107. UC-ARF, 1974.
[Life history of Mable Brown, a fictional name, born c. 1850, the mother of Sophie Martinez]

3178. Castillo, E. History of the impact of Euro-American exploration and settlement on the Indians of California. Manuscript to be published in Vol. VIII of the Handbook of North American Indians, Smithsonian Institution, 1977.

3179. _____ Twentieth century secular movements. Manuscript to appear in Vol. VIII, Handbook of North American Indians, Smithsonian Institution, 1977.

233

3180. Cesar, J. Cosas de Indios de California. Ms. in Bancroft
      Library, University of California, Berkeley, 1879.
      [Verbatim life history of Luiseno born at Mission
      San Luis Rey in 1824]

3181. Charles, Nels. Autobiography. In C. DuBois, Wintu
      Ethnography. UC-PAAE 36(1):95-97, 1935.
      [Life history of Nels Charles, a Wintu born c. 1890
      and the story of how he became a shaman]

3182. Colson, E. Autobiographies of three Pomo women. UC-ARF,
      1974.
      [Extended life histories recorded 1939-1941 in short-
      hand. All names of persons and places have been
      changed so that identification of individuals is im-
      possible. Dr. Colson's original field notes and work-
      ing papers have been destroyed]

3183. Coo-vai-en-yu. The children's war. With A.B. Adams. Out
      West 30:83-87, 1909.
      [Account of war between the Yuma and the Maricopa
      written by Adams and Coo-vai-en-yu, a Yuma Indian]

3184. Costo, R. The American Indian today. Indian Historian, 1(5),
      1968.

3185. _____ How they stole the State of California: a case
      in history. American Indian Historical Society. San
      Francisco, 1973.

3186. Cuero, D. The autobiography of Delfina Cuero. Edited by
      F. Shipek. Malki Press. Banning, California, 1970.
      [Life history of a Southern Diegueno woman born about
      1900; pressures of white culture on Native Californians]

3187. Dominguez, C. Cahuilla texts. H. Seiler, (ed.). Indiana
      University Press, 1970.
      [Partial life history of Chona Dominguez, a Desert
      Cahuilla, born about 1850 near Thermal. She died
      in 1960]

3188. Galvan, P.M. The Ohlone story. Indian Historian 1(2), 1968.

3189. Hiparopai. The Words of Hiparopai: a leaf from a traveler's
      diary, showing the Indian's outlook upon the transition
      period. The Craftsman 13:293-297, 1907.
      [A story of the life of Hiparopai, a Yuma woman, and
      the problems facing Indians following the Dawes Act
      which attempted to assimilate the Indians into white
      culture by force]

3190. Isidora ("Princess Solano"). My years with Chief Solano.
      Touring Topics 22:39,52, 1930.
      [From the original in Bancroft Library. Story of the

widow of Chief Solano. She was born ca. 1784 and
her life history was recorded in 1874 for H.H. Bancroft]

3191. Jones, Jeff. Autobiography of Jeff Jones. In Nomlaki
ethnography. Walter Goldschmidt. UC-PAAE 42 (4),
1951. University of California Press, Berkeley.
[Pp. 433-434, life history of a Nomlaki man born
near Paskenta ca. 1865. This record was made in 1936]

3192. Kroeber, A.L. A Yurok war reminiscence: the use of autobiographical evidence. SWJA 1:318-322, 1945.
[Autobiography of Sregon Jim, a Yurok, born ca. 1835]

3193. _____ A Mohave historical epic. UC-AR 11 (2), 1951.
University of California Press, Berkeley.
[A long dream myth recorded at intervals from 1902-
1908]

3194. Kroeber, A.L. and C.B. Kroeber. A Mohave war reminiscence,
1854-1880. UC-PA 10, 1973.
[Verbatim accounts by Chooksa homar recorded in 1901]

3195. Lorenzo. Personal narrative of a former neophyte born at
Santa Cruz Mission in 1819. In E.S. Harrison,
History of Santa Cruz County, California. Pp. 45-48,
Pacific Press Publishing Co. San Francisco, 1892.

3196. Martinez, Elaine. Autobiography of Elaine Martinez. In
E. Colson, Autobiographies of Three Pomo Women: 98-99.
UC-ARF, 1974.
[Life story of Elaine Martinez, a fictional name,
the granddaughter of Sophie Martinez]

3197. Martinez, Sophie. Life history of Sophie Martinez. In
E. Colson, Autobiographies of Three Pomo Women:
35-97. UC-ARF, 1974.
[Autobiography of Sophie Martinez, a fictional name,
a Pomo woman born ca. 1880 on the Round Valley Reser-
vation]

3198. Miranda, Mike (Yukaya) Autobiography. In C.F. Voegelin,
Tubatulabal texts. UC-PAAE 34 (3):222-241, 1935.
[Life history of Mike Miranda, a Tubatulabal, born
ca. 1888, the son of Steban Miranda, the Tubatulabal
chief]

3199. Nolasquez, C. Mulu'wetam: the first people. Edited by
J.H. Hill. Malki Press. Banning, California, 1973.
[Cupeno linguistic text: includes personal history
and descriptions of the culture]

3200. Oswalt, R.L. Kashaya texts. UC-PL 36, 1964.
[Folk histories told by Herman James and Essie Parrish]

3201. Pablo, W. The story of the Indians of the Pacific Southwest. In Romero John Bruno. Vantage Press. New York, 1954.
[Pp. 1-15. Narrative of Cahuilla life in the late 19th century by a traditional Cahuilla captain]

3202. Pahmit. Personal narrative. In Handbook of Yokut Indians. F.F. Latta. Kern County Museum. Bakersfield, California, 1949.
[Pp. 217-223. Autobiography of a Yokuts man born ca. 1830. Recorded in 1928 by F. Latta]

3203. Palma, Salvador. Letter addressed to Bucareli dictated to and written by J. Bautista de Anza, Nov. 11, 1776. In Anza and the Northwest frontier of New Spain. J.N. Bowman and R.F. Heizer. SM-P 20, 1967. (Pp. 148-155).
[Palma was the Yuma tribal chief]

3204. Patencio, F. Stories and legends of the Palm Springs Indians as told to Margaret Boynton. Times-Mirror Press. Los Angeles, 1943.

3205. _____ Desert hours with Chief Patencio. Palm Springs Desert Museum, 1971.

3206. Phillips, Frances. Autobiography of Frances Philips. In E.W. Voegelin, Tubatulabal ethnography, UC-PAAE 2 (1): 72-80, 1938.
[Life history of a Tubatulabal born c. 1865]

3207. Pico, E. Translation into Chumash of the glorious events of the 4th of July, 1776. UC-AR 15:188-193, 1955. Berkeley.
[A linguistic text prepared at the request of H.W. Henshaw in 1890]

3208. Riddle, J.C. The Indian history of the Modoc War. Urion Press. Eugene, Oregon, 1974.
[Reprint of earlier edition of 1914. Riddle was a Modoc]

3209. Spott, R. and A.L. Kroeber. Yurok narratives. UC-PAAE 35 (9), 1942.
[Spott was a Yurok]

3210. Sregon Jim. Sregon Jim's reminiscence. In A.L. Kroeber, A Yurok war reminiscence: the use of autobiographical evidence. SWJA 1 (3): 318-332, 1945.
[Partial life history of Sregon Jim (Sra'-mau), born c. 1830-1840.. Recollections of feuds with other villages]

3211. Steward, J. and S. Newland. Two Paiute autobiographies.
UC-PAAE 33 (5), 1934. Berkeley.
[Verbatim autobiographical records made by J.H.
Steward. Life histories of J. Steward born ca.
1837, and S. Newland, born ca. 1840]

3212. Tak (or Tac), P. Conversion de los San Luisenos de Alta
California. XXIII ICA New York, 1928:635-648,
1930.
[Account of customs of the Luisenos written about
1834 by an Indian convert]

3213. _____ Indian life and customs at Mission San Luis Rey:
a record of California Indian life written by Pablo
Tac, an Indian neophyte (Rome, 1835). The Americas
9:87-106, 1952.

3214. Thompson, L. To the American Indian. Eureka, California,
1916.
[An account of Yurok culture written by a Yurok
woman]

3215. Wood, Ellen. Life history of Ellen Wood. In E. Colson, Autobiographies of Three Pomo Women: 109-213. UC-ARF, 1974.
[Life story of Ellen Wood, a fictional name, born 1882]

3216. Yoimut. Yoimut's story: the last Chunut. In F.F. Latta,
Handbook of the Yokut Indians, pp. 223-276. Kern
County Museum. Bakersfield, California, 1949.
[Autobiography of a Chunut Yokuts woman born near
Visalia ca. 1854; died in Hanford in 1933]

3217. Young, L. Out of the past: a true Indian story. California
Historical Society Quarterly 20:349-369, 1941.
[Recollections of a Wailaki woman born ca. 1848.
Includes her memories of life on Round Valley
Reservation in the early eighteen-sixties]

VII A: SOURCE MATERIALS: MUSEUM COLLECTIONS

No effort is made to provide a list of all museums
which hold California Indian materials in their collections.
Bean and Vane (entry No. 3230) have an extensive listing
of museums and California Indian material in the collections.

A useful project would be to determine the number and
nature of such objects in all existing collections. The
British Museum (London), for example, holds the Vancouver
collection of California Indian objects secured at Trinidad
Bay, San Francisco, Monterey and Santa Barbara; the Musee
de l'Homme (Paris) has a substantial collection of archaeological and ethnographic Chumash material, and some German
and Russian museums have such collections.

3218. Chicago Natural History Museum, Chicago.
[Especially good Pomo material]

3219. Lowie Museum of Anthropology, University of California,
Berkeley.
[Collections from all California tribes]

3220. Malki Museum, Banning, California.

3221. Oakland Public Museum, Oakland, California.

3222. San Diego Museum of Man, San Diego, California.

3223. Southwest Museum, Highland Park, Los Angeles.

3224. State Indian Museum (Sutter's Fort), Sacramento, California.

3225. United States National Museum of Natural History,
Smithsonian Institution, Washington, D.C.
[Includes material from early American exploring and
military expeditions as well as objects collected by
ethnographers]

3226. University of California at Davis, Department of
Anthropology.
[Merriam Collection of California basketry]

VII B: SOURCE MATERIALS: DOCUMENTARY ARCHIVES

The list given here is only a sampling on California
Indians. Mission archives still in the possession of the
Catholic church are numerous. The American Philosophical
Society (Philadelphia) has quantities of linguistic records
on California. Local historical societies, some with museums,
also contain such records. County archives have a wealth
of stored materials dealing with local Indian affairs,
some of this dating back to the Spanish-Mexican pre-statehood
period (Coy 1919).

3227. Allen, J. and D. Moristo. An introduction to the Bureau
of Indian Affairs: Agency Records and Bureau of
Indian Affairs Archive Records housed in the San
Francisco and Bell Federal Records Centers. American
Indian Culture Center, University of California,
Los Angeles, 1971.

3228. American Indian Historical Society, San Francisco.

3229. Bancroft Library, University of California, Berkeley.

3230. Bean, L.J. and S.B. Vane. California Indians: primary
resources: a guide to manuscripts, artifacts,
documents, serials, music and illustrations. BP-AP 7,

1977. Ramona, California.
[Research materials inventoried by county in California, states other than California, and foreign countries]

3231. Bell Federal Records Center, Bell, California. S.F. Cook Collection. Manuscript notes (copies and abstracts) of book, journal, archival and newspaper accounts of California Indians and Indian-White relations in the Spanish, Mexican and American periods. 8 file boxes of 5 x 8 cards, 8 boxes of field notes, abstracts of ethnohistoric and demographic data. UC-ARF Manuscript No. 456.

3232. Coy, O.C. Guide to the county archives of California. California Historical Commission, Sacramento, 1919. [Detailed catalogue of archives of all California counties]

3233. Federal Records Center, San Bruno, California.

3234. Geiger, M.J. Calendar of documents in the Santa Barbara Mission archives. Publications of the Academy of American Franciscan History, Bibliographical Series, Vol. 1, 1947.

3235. Huntington Library, San Marino, California.

3236. C. Hart Merriam Collection, Department of Anthropology, University of California, Berkeley.
[See Catalogue of the C. Hart Merriam Collection of Data Concerning California Tribes and Other American Indians. UC-ARF, 1969]

3237. National anthropological archives, Smithsonian Instituion, Washington, D.C.

3238. Special collections, University of California at Los Angeles Library.

3239. Tutorow, N.E. Source materials for historical research in the Los Angeles Federal Records Center. Southern California Quarterly 53:333-344, 1971.

3240. Valory, D. Guide to ethnological documents (1-203) of the Department and Museum of Anthropology, University of California, Berkeley, now in the University Archives. UC-ARF, 1971.

3241. Wadlow, T.W. and A.R. Abel (compilers). Preliminary inventory of the records of the Bureau of Indian Affairs: Northern California and Nevada Agencies (Record Group 75). Archives Branch of the Federal Records Center. SAn Francisco, 1966.
[Classified list of federal records of California BIA

jurisdictions, 1864-1920 in Federal Records Center,
San Bruno, California]

VII C: SOURCE MATERIALS: FILMS; PHONOGRAPH RECORDS

Most films made purporting to show the lifeway,
materials culture, and economic pursuits of California Indians
are so inaccurate as to be downright misleading if they are
represented as ethnographically correct. Despite the admission
by Barrett (1961) of "concessions to modernism" and pro-
testations that the "true record of the habitual, ancient
procedure" was usually secured in his American Indian Films
project, it is unfortunately the plain fact that none of
the films purporting to show aboriginal California Indian
manufacturing and food processing practices are ethnologically
accurate. This correction is considered justifiable when we
consider the alternative of these films being taken in future
as the photographic documentation of what California Indians
did in the days before Portola crossed the Colorado River
in 1769. The American Indian Films made under S.A. Barrett's
direction and dispensed by the University of California
Extension Center to the extent that they are alleged to
depict aboriginal techniques of making Yurok bows, cooking
acorn mush or gathering pinenuts, and many more subjects,
are misleading and incorrect in many details.

The Lowie Museum of Anthropology has a very large
collection of California Indian music on tapes. These
were originally recorded on wax cylinders.

3242. Building a Yurok Canoe. Shenandoah Productions, 538 G.
        Street, Arcata, California 95521.
        [Sound filmstrip, 50 frames, with sound track]

3243. California Indian Songs. Barr Films, P.O. Box 7-c,
        Pasadena, California 91104.
        [8 Yokuts songs on a record]

3244. Chitu--Most Beautiful Basket. Shenandoah Productions, 538
        G. Street, Arcata, California, 95521.
        [Elsie Allen, a Pomo basketmaker, demonstrates kinds,
        uses and decorations of baskets. Sound filmstrip,
        50 frames, with sound track]

3245. The Dispossessed. A 16mm Documentary film on the Pit
        River Indians Struggle to regain their lands.
        June, 1970. 33 minutes.
        [G. Ballis, a Discussion Manual for The Dispossessed.
        1970. Piedmont, California]

3246. The Earth is our Mother. A 16 mm film by Robert Mendoza.
        1969. 22 Minutes.
        [Concerns June 6, 1970 occupation of Pacific Gas
        and Electric campground by Native Californians]

3247. European Influences on Northern California Indians.
Shenandoah Productions, 538 G Street, Arcata, CA., 95531.
[A Native American version of history since arrival
of the whites. Sound filmstrip, 50 frames, with sound
track]

3248. Forty-seven Cents. A 16mm film. 1972. 30 minutes.
[Concerns Pit River Struggle objecting to claims case
settlement]

3249. Hupa White Deerskin Dance - Arthur Barr Films. P.O. Box 7c,
Pasadena, CA, 91104.
[Filmed in 1958]

3250. Hupa Net Making. Shenandoah Productions, 538 G Street, Arcata,
CA 95531.
[Sound film strip, 50 frames]

3251. Indian Mainstream. Shenandoah Productions, 538 G Street,
Arcata, CA, 95531.
[Hupa, Karok, Yurok and Tolowa elders doing oldtime
traditional things--basketmaking, netmaking, canoe
making, social dancing, etc]

3252. Indians of California (Parts I, II). Available from
National Educational Television, Indiana University,
Bloomington, Indiana 47405; also from Barr Films,
P.O. Box 7c, Pasadena, CA 91104.
[Mainly Yokuts - covers a wide range of activities.
Filmed 1964]

3253. Ishi in Two Worlds. (movie) Contemporary Films/McGraw Hill,
New York.

3254. Karuk (Salmon) Dip-netting. Shenandoah Productions, 538
G Street, Arcata, CA, 95531.
[Sound film strip, 50 frames]

3255. MacDougall, J. and D. Indians and Chiefs. A 16mm film.
40 minutes. 1972.
[A film on the Second Annual Los Angeles Indian Fair
by Native Americans]

3256. Nature and the Northern California Indians. Shenandoah
Productions, 538 G Street, Arcata, CA, 95531.
[Parts 1, 2, each 50 frames on film strip with sound
track]

3257. Northern California Indian Gambling Games. Shenandoah
Productions, 538 G S-reet, Arcata, CA, 95531.
[Card game, gambling songs. Film Strip, 50 frames,
with sound track]

3258. Our Songs Will Never Die. Shenandoah Productions, 538 G Street, Arcata, CA, 95531.
[Tolowa and Karuk summer camps for reconstructing old village dance sites. Other cultural activities displayed]

3259. Pomo Feather Dancers. Shenandoah Productions, 538 G Street, Arcata, CA, 95531.
[Sound film strip, 50 frames]

3260. Tolowa Surf-fishing and Sand Break Making. Shenandoah Productions, 538 G Street, Arcata, CA, 95531.
[Sound film strip, 50 frames]

3261. Washoe. Contemporary/McGraw Hill Films, 1221 Avenue of the Americas, N.Y. 10020.
[Washo settlements, Pine Nut and Girls' Puberty dances]

3262. Washo Peyote Songs. Folkways Records, 701 Seventh Avenue, N.Y., 10036.
[Recorded by W. d'Azevedo, a foremost student of the Washo]

3263. Wintun Culture. Shenandoah Productions, 538 G Street, Arcata, CA, 95531.
[Sound film strip, 50 frames]

3264. Wright, B. The Way of Our Fathers. A 16mm film by various northern California Indians. 33 minutes. 1972.
[Covers attempts by Northern California Indians to retain and revive aspects of native culture]

VII D: SOURCE MATERIALS: PICTORIAL ARCHIVES

In addition to the archival collections listed, there are other kinds of pictorial documents which show Indians. Many of the early explorers (e.g., Malaspina, Vancouver, La Perouse, Langsdorff, von Kotzebue) had artists with them who drew pictures of Indians. Many of the original sketches or wash drawings survive, and numbers of these are engraved and published.

There exist, also, large numbers of photographs of Indians which are filled in out-of-the-way repositories. Some of these are listed by Bean and Vane (entry No. 3230).

A useful work could be done by compiling a catalogue of illustration of all kinds which show California Indians, their cultures, and their activities.

3265. American Museum of Natural History, New York.

3266. Baird, J.A., Jr. Grace Carpenter Hudson (1865-1937).
California Historical Society. San Francisco, 1962.
[Catalogue of Grace C. Huston's paintings of Ukiah
Pomo Indians 1892-1927]

3267. _____ Catalogue of original paintings, drawings,
and watercolors in the Robert B. Honeyman, Jr. Collection.
Friends of the Bancroft Library, Berkeley, 1968.
[Contains much on California Indians. Most of the
Indian pictorial material is reproduced in Kroeber,
Elsasser and Heizer, 1977]

3268. California Historical Society, San Francisco.

3269. California History Center, De Anza College. Six sets of
35mm color slides depicting native territories,
persons, artifacts, and activities. Number of slides
varies according to area: Central, 60; Northwestern,
34: Colorado River, 28: Southern, 29: Desert, 13.
Available from CHS, DeAnza College, Cupertino,
California.

3270. California State Library, Sacramento, California.

3271. Hudson, D.T. A photographic anthology of the Chumash
people. Pacific Coast Archaeological Society Quarterly
11:1-12, 1975.

3272. Huntington Library (Grace Nicholson Collection), San Marino,
California.

3273. Jackson, W.H. Descriptive catalogue of photographs of
North American Indians by W.H. Jackson, Photographer
of the Survey. U.S. Geological and Geographical
Survey of the Territories, Misc. Publication No. 9,
1877.
[Pp. 88-90, Modocs]

3274. Kroeber, T. and R.F. Heizer. Almost ancestors: The first
Californians. Sierra Club. San Francisco, 1968.
[Text and numerous photographs of Indians]

3275. Kroeber, T., A.B. Elsasser and R.F. Heizer. Drawn from
life: California Indians in pen and brush. Ballena
Press, Socorro, N.M., 1977.
[Collection of over 300 drawings, engravings, sketches
and paintings showing California Indians from 1599
to 1870]

3276. Lowie Museum of Anthropology, University of California, Berkeley.

3277. Malki Museum, Banning, California.

3278. C. Hart Merriam Collection. Department of Anthropology, University of California, Berkeley. [For listing of photos see Heizer et.al., 1969--cited in Section VII B]

3279. Museum of the American Indian, Heye Foundation, New York.

3280. National Anthropological Archives, Smithsonian Institution, Washington, D.C. [Especially good photographic collection]

3281. Oakland Public Museum, Oakland, California.

3282. San Diego Museum of Man, San Diego, California.

3283. Southwest Museum, Highland Park, Los Angeles.

3284. Taft, R. Artists and illustrators of the Old West, 1850-1900, 1953. Scribner's Sons, New York. [Notes on early artists who depicted the scenery and people]

VII E: SOURCE MATERIALS: BIBLIOGRAPHIES

The compiling of bibliographies is laborious, and since such works are rarely cited, scholars tend to avoid doing this kind of work because the product is usually utilized without being acknowledged. Few efforts which contribute to the communication of information (or in this case its sources) are more useful and bring smaller return to the person who does the work.

3285. Almstedt, R.F. Bibliography of the Diegueno Indians. Ballena Press. Ramona, California, 1974.

3286. American Indian Historical Society. Index to literature on the American Indian. Indian Historian Press. San Francisco, 1971. [pp. 191-230, "Native American Publications". Includes California]

3287. Anderson, E.N., Jr. A Bibliography of the Chumash and their predecessors. UC-AS-R 61:24-74, 1964.

3288. Anonymous. Author and title index to University of California Publications in American Archaeology and Ethnology (UC-PAAE). UC-ARF-C 32, 1976.

3289. Bean, L.J. and H. Lawton. A bibliography of the Cahuilla Indians. Malki Museum Press. Banning, California, 1967

3290. Bright, W. A bibliography of the Hokan-Coahuiltecan Languages. IJAL 21:276-285, 1954. [Hokan is one of the largest linguistic stocks of native California]

3291. Callaghan, C. California Penutian: history and bibliography,
       IJAL 97-107, 1958.
       [Penutian is the main language family of Central
       California]

3292. Cowan, R.E. and R.G. A bibliography of the history of
       California, 1510-1930. Los Angeles, 1964.
       [This prestigious and authoritative bibliography on
       California almost entirely neglects Indians;
       California history to Cowan and Cowan was White
       history]

3293. Heizer, R.F. The Indians of California: a critical biblio-
       graphy. Center for the Study of American Indian
       History. Newberry Library. Chicago, 1976.
       [Covers much the same ground as the present biblio-
       graphy]

3294. Heizer, R.F. and A. B. Elsasser. A bibliography of California
       archaeology. UC-ARF-C 6, 1970.
       [Includes archaeology and physical anthropology]

3295. Heizer, R.F. and K.M. Nissen. The human sources of California
       ethnography. UC-ARF, 1973.
       [List of over 2,000 native ethnographic informants
       with reference bibliography. Includes tribal affilia-
       tion and birthdate]

3296. Henry, J. (ed.) Textbooks and the American Indians. Indian
       Historian Press. San Francisco, 1972.
       [Includes a section on California]

3297. Hodge, W.H. A bibliography of contemporary North American
       Indians. Interland Publishing Co., New York, 1975.
       [Includes California]

3298. Kroeber, A.L. Handbook of the Indians of California.
       Bureau of American Ethnology, Bulletin 78, 1925.
       [Pp. 943-966, annotated bibliography of Californian
       anthropological works]

3299. Lummis, C.F. A reading list on Indians. Out West 18:357-
       365, 1903.
       [Old but still useful]

3300. McConnell, W. California Indians: annotated list of
       material in the California State Library. California
       State Library, News Notes of California Libraries
       10: 484-523. Sacramento, 1915.
       [Useful listing, but compiled by a person with
       limited knowledge of California Indians. Classified
       and annotated]

3301. Murdock, G.P. and T.J. O'Leary. Ethnographic bibliography
          of North America, 4th ed. 5 Vols. Human Relations
          Area Files, New Haven, Conn., 1975.
          [Vol. 1 contains a general ethnographic bibliography
          of California; Vol. 3 has a detailed tribe-by-tribe
          listing of published materials. Of basic importance]

3202. Pitkin, H. A bibliography of the Wintun family of languages.
          IJAL 28:43-54, 1962.

3303. Wuertele, E. Bibliographical history of California anthro-
          pological research, 1850-1917. UC-C-ARF 26, 1975.

VIII. OBITUARIES OF ANTHROPOLOGISTS

The researcher often wishes to know something about the person whose published work he is reading. Provided here is a list of anthropologists who interviewed California Indians as a part of their professional work and a reference to their obituary or biography.

Angulo, Jaime de (1887-1950). In D.L. Olmsted, Achumawi Dictionary. University of California Publications in Linguistics 45: 1-7, 1966.

Barrett, Samuel A. (1879-1965). Kroeber Anthropological Society Papers No. 33, 1965.

Bancroft, Hubert H. (1832-1918) In H. Clark, A venture into history: the production, publication and sale of the Works of Hubert Howe Bancroft. University of California Press, 1973.

Cessac, Leon de (1842?-1891). H. Reichlen and R.F. Heizer, La Mission de Leon de Cessac en Californie, 1877-1879. Objets et Mondes 3:17-34, 1963.

Cook, Sherburne F. (1896-1974). Hispanic American Historical Review 55:749-759, 1975.

Curtis, Edward S. (1868-1953). Southwest Museum Masterkey 26: 196-197, 1952.

Dixon, Roland B. (1875-1934). American Anthropologist 38:297-300, 1936.

Gibbs, George (1815-1873). S.D. Beckham, George Gibbs, 1815-1873, Historian and Ethnologist. Unpublished Ph.D. dissertation in History, University of California at Los Angeles (University Microfilms 70-14, 258).

Gifford, Edward W. (1887-1959). American Antiquity 25:257-259, 1959. American Anthropologist 62:327-330, 1960.

Goddard, Pliny E. (1869-1928). American Anthropologist 31:6-8, 1929.

Harrington, John P. (1884-1961). American Anthropologist 65:370-381, 1963.

Henshaw, Henry W. (1859-1930). Anthropological Linguistics 2:1-5, 1960.

Kroeber, Alfred L. (1876-1960). National Academy of Sciences, Biographical Memoirs 36:192-253, 1962. J. Steward, Alfred Kroeber. Columbia University Press, 1973.

Loeb, Edwin M. (1894-1966). American Anthropologist 69:200-204, 1967.

Loud, Llewellyn L. (1879-1946). American Antiquity 12;180, 1947.

Lowie, Robert H. (1883-1957). National Academy of Sciences, Biographical Memoirs 44:175-212, 1974.

Mason, J. Alden (1885-1967). American Anthropologist 71:871-880, 1969.

Merriam, C. Hart (1855-1942). National Academy of Sciences, Biographical Memoirs 24:1-57, 1945.

O'Neale, Lila (1886-1948). American Anthropologist 50:657-665, 1948.

Pinart, Alphonse (1852-1911). R. Parmenter, Explorer, linguist and technologist: a descriptive bibliography of the published works of Alphonse Louis Pinart, with notes on his life. Southwest Museum, Los Angeles, 1966.

Powers, Stephen (1840-1904). S. Park, Contributions of the Archaeological Research Facility 28, 1975. Also, American Anthropologist 6:367, 1904.

Radin, Paul (1883-1959). American Anthropologist 61:839-844, 1959.

Reid, Hugo (1808-1852). S.D. Dakin, A Scotch paisano: Hugo Reid's life in California, 1832-1852. University of California Press, 1939.

Sapir, Edward (1884-1939). American Anthropologist 41:465-477, 1939.

Spier, Leslie (1893-1961). American Anthropologist 67:1258-1278, 1965.

Steward, Julian H. (1902-1972). American Anthropologist 75:886-897, 1973.

Strong, William D. (1899-1962). American Anthropologist 65:1102-1111, 1963.

Waterman, T.T. (1885-1936). American Anthropologist 39:528-529, 1937.

Yates, Lorenzo G. (1837-1909). Charles L. Camp, Old Doctor Yates, Journal of the West 2:377-400, 1963.

Bean, L.J., 79, 80, 1843, 2402, 2499, 2572, 2573, 2597, 2659, 2910, 3175, 3220, 3289.
Beardsley, R.K., 275, 956, 1214, 1390, 1391, 2290.
Beaton, J., 2154.
Beattie, G.W., 81, 82, 2684.
Beattie, H.P., 82, 2403.
Beatty, M.E., 522.
Beck, J.L., 1215, 1297.
Becker, G.F., 733, 1298.
Beckwith, E.G., 157.
Beechey, F.W., 2660, 2685.
Beeler, M.S., 2686.
Beers, C.D., 1518.
Begole, R.S., 383, 1743.
Belcher, E., 158.
Belden, L.B., 384, 553, 734, 957, 958, 1744-1747.
Belding, L., 1257.
Bell, L., 523, 1748.
Bell, W.H., 2574.
Belous, R.E., 678, 1216.
Benedict, R., 2404.
Bender, A.B., 2837.
Bennet, W., 1299.
Bennyhoff, J.A., 225, 959, 1030, 1031, 1217, 1519, 1749, 2301, 2687.
Benson, W.R., 3170, 3176.
Berger, R., 689, 703, 1655.
Berkholz, M.F., 554, 581.
Berry, B., 3060.
Berryman, L., 1302.
Bettinger, R.L., 1750-1752.
Bierman, A., 926, 2157.
Bingaman, J.W., 2405.
Birdsell, J.B., 2197, 2198.
Bixby, L.B., 159, 160.
Blackburn, T.C., 79, 292, 1520, 2069, 2726, 2499, 2549.
Blackwelder, E., 7, 8.
Blake, J., 357, 1032.
Blake, W.P., 385, 735, 736.
Blanc, R.P., 9.
Bledsoe, A.J., 2838.
Bleeker, S., 2406, 2688.
Block, G., 2634.
Bloomquist, R.A., 386.
Board of Indian Commissioners, 2911.
Boas, F., 2199-2202, 2863.
Bock, A.J., 388, 1753.
Bode, F.D., 737.

Boloyan, D.S., 474, 1362.
Bolton, H.E., 2661-2664.
Bonin, G.V., 2203.
Bonnot, P., 10.
Bonsal, S., 2839.
Borah, W., 2689.
Borden, F.W., 679.
Boule, M., 738.
Bourke, J.G., 2522.
Bourne, A.R., 2912.
Boutwell, J.M., 739.
Bowden, A.O., 740, 1980, 1981.
Bowers, S., 226, 524, 1521-1527, 1982.
Bowman, H.R., 161.
Bowman, J.N., 2690-2692.
Brabender, I., 2204, 2205.
Brainerd, G.W., 680, 741, 1754, 1983.
Branco, W., 742.
Brand, D.D., 582, 583.
Brandt, J.C., 390.
Breede, W., 2275.
Breschini, G.S., 1470, 1471.
Brewer, W.H., 743.
Brewster, E.T., 744.
Bright, E., 2320.
Bright, M., 681.
Bright, W., 2317-2320, 2364, 2318, 3290.
Brindamour, B.G., 1984.
Broadbent, N.D., 965.
Broadbent, S.M., 960, 2326, 2665, 2727, 2728.
Broms, R.S.D., 1755.
Brooks, S.T., 1985, 2206, 2207, 2223.
Brott, C.W., 162, 1035.
Brown, A.K., 1392, 1393, 1528, 2365, 2666, 2667, 2680.
Brown, M., 3177.
Brown, R.O., 1559, 1560, 2036.
Brown, V., 2391.
Browne, J.R., 85, 2840, 2889.
Bryan, A.L., 745.
Bryan, B., 163, 254, 1529, 1530, 1986-1991.
Bryan, K., 11.
Bruff, J.G., 2773.
Brunker, L., 2376.
Bunker, W.M., 2841.
Bunnell, L.H., 2774.
Bureau of Catholic Missions, 3129.

252

Kelsey, H., 2823.
Kemnitzer, L., 1421.
Kennard, T.G., 190.
Kennedy, K.A.R., 652, 2232.
Kennedy, M.J., 2962.
Kennedy, M.M., 390.
Kenny, R.W., 3117.
Kessler, D.E., 2311.
Kettl, J.W., 446.
Keyes, Capt. E.D., 2824.
Kibbe, W.C., 2787.
Kibby, L.P., 2861.
King, A.R., 2606.
King, C.D., 237, 238, 1422,
    1607, 2066-2069.
King, L., 1422, 2070.
King, L.E., 2862.
King, T.F., 280, 984, 1066-1068,
    1183-1189, 1264, 1333-1337,
    1423, 1424, 1752, 1833, 1834.
King, T.J., 1835, 1836.
Kingman, G., 1837.
Kinney, A., 3037.
Kirk, R.E., 329.
Klein, B.T., 2963.
Klette, W., 447.
Klimek, S., 110, 1069, 2233,
    2433.
Kniffen, F.B., 2448.
Knight, L.C., 281, 283.
Knoop, A.M., 2863.
Knudtson, P.M., 2532.
Koch, E.J., 1927, 2877, 2899.
Koch, F.J., 831.
Koloseike, A., 239, 653-656.
Kowalski, B.R., 188.
Kowta, M., 1608, 1838, 2071.
Krause, F., 111, 1070.
Krieger, A.D., 1071.
Kritzman, G., 482, 1017, 2136,
    2169, 2285.
Kroeber, A.L., 112-120, 240,
    282, 330-335, 832, 833, 1072-
    1079, 1137, 1241, 1265, 1425,
    2324, 2334-2336, 2378-2380,
    2434, 2449-2457, 2510, 2511,
    2533-2536, 2558-2560, 2569,
    2581, 2582, 2608-2610, 2642-
    2645, 2654, 2711, 2742, 2864,
    2964, 2965, 3108, 3192-3194,
    3209, 3298.
Kroeber, C.B., 2511, 2607, 2864,
    3194.
Kroeber, T.K., 2381, 2966, 2967,
    3274, 3275.

Krueger, M., 2813.
Kunkel, P.H., 2512.

LaFave, J., 1693.
Laidlaw, G.E., 1426.
Lamb, S.M., 2337.
LaMonk, C.S., 448, 1492.
Landberg, L., 2458, 2583.
Langdon, M., 2338.
Lanning, E.P., 1839.
LaPerouse, J.F.G., 2790.
Lathrap, D.W., 449, 1338, 1463,
    1464, 1840.
Lathrop, M.L., 2826.
Latta, F.F., 189, 363, 601, 1266,
    2459, 2791.
Laudermilk, J.D., 190.
Lawbaugh, A.L.V., 450, 566, 1841,
    1842.
Lawton, H., 1843, 1844, 2402,
    2572, 2888, 2968, 3289.
Leadabrand, R., 451-455, 1845.
Leakey, L.S.B., 834, 835.
LeConte, J.L., 2234.
LeDuc, T., 3118.
Lee, D.D., 2611, 2612, 2969.
Lee, R.L., 2970.
Lee, S.W., 2971.
Lee, T.E., 836.
Leigh, R.W., 2235.
Lemert, E.M., 812, 2050.
Leonard, C.B., 2865.
Leonard, N.N., 1609, 2072-2074.
Leonard, Z., 2792.
Leonhardy, F.C., 1138.
Leroi-Gourhan, A., 1610.
Levy, R.L., 2339.
Lewis, F.D., 3038.
Lewis, H.T., 2584.
Lewis, W.S., 532.
Lillard, J.B., 1242, 1243.
Lindgren, W., 837.
Linsdale, J.M., 28.
Lissitzyn, O.S., 2673.
Lister, R.H., 1080.
Littlejohn, H.W., 1339.
Littlewood, R.A., 2236.
Lloyd, N., 2972.
Loeb, E.M., 2461, 2537, 2538,
    2646, 2930.
Loew, O., 456.
Loeffelholz (or von Loeffelholz),
    K., 191, 2793.
Long, P.V., 2045, 2075.

Longinos, J.M., 2794.
Lopatin, I., 740, 838, 1846, 1980, 1981.
Lorenzo, 3195.
Loud, L.L., 657, 1139, 1427, 2460, 2795.
Lounsberry, N., 2076.
Lovell, C.C., 2796.
Lowie, R.H., 2462, 2647.
Lucas, B.J., 839, 1847.
Lummis, C.E., 2973, 3039-3042, 3135, 3136, 3299.
Lund, B.F., 3064.
Luomala, K., 2614.
Lyhne, B.(R.), 985, 1428.
Lyman, F., 457.
Lyon, C., 192.
Lytton, A.C., 1848, 2077.

MacCurdy, G.G., 840, 1140.
MacGregor, G., 2974.
MacDougall, D.T., 458.
MacLean, J.J., 1141, 1190.
MacLeod, W.C., 1081.
Maguire, B., 364.
Mahaffey, J., 1849.
Malamud, C.G., 927, 2158.
Mallery, G., 460, 461.
Maloney, A.B., 2674.
Mann, F.J., 2673.
Mannion, L., 1191, 1430.
Mannion, M.C., 986, 1191, 1340.
March, R., 3163.
Marcou, J., 841.
Marcus, L.F., 703.
Marshall, G.C., 462.
Marshall, M., 2797.
Marshall, N.F., 2279.
Martin, D.D., 2976.
Martin, K., 3061.
Martin, L.J., 2977.
Martin, P.S., 658, 708, 1082.
Martinez, Elaine, 3196.
Martinez, Sophie, 3197.
Martz, P., 2079.
Mason, J.A., 121, 2464.
Mason, J.D., 1611.
Mason, O.T., 122, 136, 1083, 1142, 2562.
Mason, W.M., 2659, 2712.
Massey, E., 2798.
Massey, W.C., 2554.
Matiega, H., 2237.
Matson, R.G., 45, 209, 716, 1341, 1342.

May, R.V., 955, 987, 988, 2075.
Mayall, D.H., 2978.
Mayer, D., 463.
Mayer, P.J., 2585.
McAdie, A.G., 44.
McAlexander, M., 1267.
McCall, G.A., 2866.
McChesney, , 1429.
McConnell, W., 3300.
McCown, B.E., 1850-1857, 2081-2083.
McCown, T.D., 813, 842, 1415, 2221, 2238.
McDonald, P.M., 459.
McGee, W.J., 843, 844.
McGeein, D.J., 1102, 1431.
McGinty, B., 989.
McGuire, J.D., 567.
McHenry, H., 2239.
McHugh, J.J., 3065.
McKee, J., 2827.
McKenney, J.W., 1858.
McKern, T.W., 2240, 2382.
McKern, W.C., 2463, 2561.
McKinney, A., 283, 365, 2009, 2084-2087.
McKusick, M.B., 1287, 1612-1614, 2088.
McLellan, P.M., 1343.
McLendon, S., 2975.
McLeod, N., 2652.
Mead, G.R., 464, 1859, 1860, 2009, 2090, 2587.
Mead, J.R., 2091.
Mehringer, P.J., 708.
Meighan, C.W., 533, 534, 568, 569, 709, 845-847, 990, 1084-1086, 1192-1197, 1275, 1364, 1432, 1493, 1840, 1861-1865, 2092-2097, 2161, 2297, 2312, 3074.
Meister, C.W., 284.
Meredith, H.C., 193, 1087, 1244.
Merriam, A., 2648.
Merriam, C.H., 46, 124-129, 337, 848, 1344-1346, 2383, 2465-2469, 2539, 2586, 2713-2715.
Merriam, J.C., 849-858, 1088, 1347.
Merrill, R.E., 338, 2563.
Michels, J.W., 710, 711, 1866.
Miles, C., 1143.
Miller, A.H., 825.
Miller, D.S., 194, 1660.

262

2595, 2622, 2624, 2699, 2784,
2789, 2816, 2826, 2903, 2953,
2958, 2962, 2975, 2978, 2996,
3006, 3007, 3009, 3020, 3074,
3078, 3161, 3166-3170, 3172,
3176, 3177, 3182, 3196, 3197,
3200, 3215, 3244, 3259, 3266.

Salinan 2344, 2407, 2464.

Serrano 2404, 2487.

Shasta 2413, 2443.

Shoshone (Panamint, Koso) 2408.

Sierra Miwok 2326, 2405, 2505,
2527, 2529, 2548, 2585, 2623,
2774, 2800, 2846, 2851, 2915,
2936, 2953.

Sinkyone 2471.

Southern Paiute: see Chemehuevi

Tolowa 2419, 2508, 3251, 3258,
3260.

Tübatulabal 2359, 2493, 3198,
3206.

Tulareños: see Yokuts

Wailaki 2637, 3217.

Wappo 2349, 2350, 2415, 2809.

Washo 2398, 2411, 2462, 2523,
2647, 2648, 2931, 2941, 2942,
2948, 2986, 2995, 3261, 3262.

Western Mono (Monache) 2429,
2503, 2553, 2633.

Wintu 2420, 2532, 2611, 2612,
2627, 2630, 2969, 2990, 3181.

Wintun 2521, 2626, 3263, 3302.

Wiyot 2355, 2460, 2650, 2753,
2795, 2943.

Yahi 2565, 2649, 2771, 2799,
2964, 2966, 2967.

Yana 2348, 2433, 2480, 2495,
2626, 2653, 2771, 2799, 3017,
3253.

Yokuts 2340, 2429, 2430, 2459,
2503, 2553, 2616, 2633, 2640,
2671, 2686, 2700, 2791, 2800,
2846, 2851, 2867, 2878, 3202,
3203, 3216, 3243, 3253.

Yuki 2389, 2423, 2427, 2432,
2575, 2576, 2842, 2940, 2980,
3002.

Yuma 2426, 2528, 2638, 2855,
2866, 2970, 3183, 3189, 3203.

Yurok 2308, 2347, 2496, 2564,
2569, 2602, 2604, 2609, 2610,
2615, 2620, 2645, 2652, 2654,
2753, 2793, 2943, 2985, 3192,
3209, 3210, 3214, 3242, 3251.

DATE DUE